Programming Entity Framework: DbContext

Julia Lerman and Rowan Miller

O'REILLY®

Beijing · Cambridge · Farnham · Köln · Sebastopol · Tokyo

Programming Entity Framework: DbContext

by Julia Lerman and Rowan Miller

Copyright © 2012 Julia Lerman and Rowan Miller. All rights reserved.
Printed in the United States of America.

Published by O'Reilly Media, Inc., 1005 Gravenstein Highway North, Sebastopol, CA 95472.

O'Reilly books may be purchased for educational, business, or sales promotional use. Online editions are also available for most titles (*http://my.safaribooksonline.com*). For more information, contact our corporate/institutional sales department: (800) 998-9938 or *corporate@oreilly.com*.

Editors: Meghan Blanchette and Rachel Roumeliotis	**Cover Designer:** Karen Montgomery
Production Editor: Teresa Elsey	**Interior Designer:** David Futato
	Illustrators: Robert Romano and Rebecca Demarest

Revision History for the First Edition:
    2012-02-23   First release

See *http://oreilly.com/catalog/errata.csp?isbn=9781449312961* for release details.

ISBN: 978-1-449-31296-1

[LSI]

1330008586

Table of Contents

Preface

Microsoft's principal data access technology, ADO.NET Entity Framework, has had two major releases as part of the .NET Framework. .NET 3.5 brought us the first version of Entity Framework, which is covered in the first edition of *Programming Entity Framework* (O'Reilly). In 2010, Microsoft .NET 4 was released, containing the next version of Entity Framework, referred to as Entity Framework 4. The completely revised second edition of *Programming Entity Framework* (O'Reilly) was dedicated to teaching readers how to use this version of Entity Framework in Visual Studio 2010.

When .NET 4 was released, the Entity Framework team was already hard at work on a new addition, called Code First, to provide an alternative way of building the Entity Data Model that is core to Entity Framework. Rather than using a visual designer, Code First allows you to create the model from your existing classes. At the same time, the team devoted resources to making Entity Framework easier to use. They focused on the most commonly used features and tasks in Entity Framework and built a new API called the DbContext API.

This book is dedicated to teaching readers how to use the features of the DbContext API. In addition to the `DbContext` class, you'll find the `DbSet` class for performing set operations, improved APIs for change tracking and handling concurrency conflicts, and a Validation API that integrates with validation features already present in .NET.

In this book, you will learn how to query and update data using the new API, whether you are working with individual objects or graphs of objects and their related data. You'll learn how to take advantage of the change tracking features and Validation. You'll find myriad samples and delve into taking advantage of advanced features presented by the API.

Audience

This book is designed for .NET developers who have experience with Visual Studio and database management basics. Prior experience with Entity Framework is beneficial but not required. The code samples in the book are written in C#, with some of these samples also expressed in Visual Basic. There are a number of online tools you can use to convert snippets of C# into Visual Basic.

Contents of This Book

This book contains nine chapters.

Chapter 1, Introducing the DbContext API
    This chapter provides a high-level, end-to-end overview of the DbContext API. You'll learn why the Entity Framework team decided to create the DbContext API and how it makes the Entity Framework easier to use. You'll find example code, but there are no walkthroughs in this first chapter.

Chapter 2, Querying with DbContext
    In this chapter you'll learn about retrieving data from the database using Entity Framework's query capabilities. You'll learn how to find an entity based on its key and how to load all entities of a given type. You'll learn how to use Language Integrated Query (LINQ) to sort and filter data. This chapter also explores the various strategies for loading related data.

Chapter 3, Adding, Changing, and Deleting Entities
    Once you've learned how to query for data, this chapter will cover how to make changes to that data and save those changes to the database. You'll see how to add new data as well as change and delete existing data. You'll learn how Entity Framework keeps track of changes as you make them and how it saves them using the SaveChanges method.

Chapter 4, Working with Disconnected Entities Including N-Tier Applications
    In this chapter, you'll learn about using Entity Framework to persist changes that were made to entities while they were not being managed by a context. This challenge is most common in N-Tier applications where a server component is responsible for retrieving data and returning it to a client application. The client application then modifies this data and sends it back to the server to be saved. You'll learn about various approaches to solving this challenge and how the Change Tracker API can be used to implement them.

Chapter 5, Change Tracker API
    The Change Tracker API is first introduced in Chapter 4 and this chapter is dedicated to exploring the remaining functionality of the change tracker. You'll learn how to access the information that Entity Framework keeps about the state of your entity instances. You'll also learn about the operations that can be performed from the Change Tracker API, including refreshing an entity from the database. This chapter wraps up with some examples of how the Change Tracker API can be used to solve some common application requirements.

Chapter 6, Validating with the Validation API

Chapter 6 introduces the new Validation API that integrates with the DbContext and how it can be used to validate changes to your data before they are sent to the database. This chapter covers how the Validation API makes use of the existing validation functionality included in the .NET Framework. You'll learn how validation is integrated into the SaveChanges pipeline and how you can also trigger validation manually. You'll learn how to set up validation rules and how to inspect validation errors when your data violates these rules.

Chapter 7, Customizing Validations

This chapter explores some more advanced features of the Validation API, which was introduced in Chapter 6. You'll learn how to customize the logic used to validate entities, including customizing the logic that determines which entities need to be validated. These advanced techniques will allow you to write validation that interacts with the context, which opens up more validation possibilities, such as validating the uniqueness of a column. This chapter will also provide guidance regarding the dangers of using the Validation API for tasks other than validation.

Chapter 8, Using DbContext in Advanced Scenarios

Chapter 8 is devoted to covering some advanced functionality that's available in the DbContext API. You'll learn about techniques for unit testing and how to write tests that don't hit a database. You'll also see how to bypass Entity Framework's query pipeline and interact directly with the database when the need arises. Should your requirements exceed what is possible from the DbContext API, you'll see how to drop down to the underlying ObjectContext API. The chapter wraps up with a look at creating smaller bounded contexts that allow you to interact with a subset of your complete model.

Chapter 9, What's Coming Next for Entity Framework

This book was written based on the features of the DbContext API available in the Entity Framework 4.3 release. At the time of writing, there are a number of previews available that demonstrate some of the features that the DbContext API will gain in upcoming releases. This chapter shares available information about these future releases.

Conventions Used in This Book

The following typographical conventions are used in this book:

Italic

Indicates new terms, URLs, email addresses, filenames, and file extensions.

`Constant width`

Used for program listings, as well as within paragraphs to refer to program elements such as variable or function names, databases, data types, environment variables, statements, and keywords.

Constant width bold
> Shows commands or other text that should be typed literally by the user.

Constant width italic
> Shows text that should be replaced with user-supplied values or by values determined by context.

> This icon signifies a tip, suggestion, or general note.

> This icon indicates a warning or caution.

Using Code Examples

This book is here to help you get your job done. In general, you may use the code in this book in your programs and documentation. You do not need to contact us for permission unless you're reproducing a significant portion of the code. For example, writing a program that uses several chunks of code from this book does not require permission. Selling or distributing a CD-ROM of examples from O'Reilly books does require permission. Answering a question by citing this book and quoting example code does not require permission. Incorporating a significant amount of example code from this book into your product's documentation does require permission.

We appreciate, but do not require, attribution. An attribution usually includes the title, author, publisher, and ISBN. For example: "*Programming Entity Framework: DbContext* by Julia Lerman and Rowan Miller (O'Reilly). Copyright 2012 Julia Lerman and Rowan Miller, 978-1-449-31296-1."

If you feel your use of code examples falls outside fair use or the permission given above, feel free to contact us at *permissions@oreilly.com*.

Safari® Books Online

Safari Books Online (*www.safaribooksonline.com*) is an on-demand digital library that delivers expert content in both book and video form from the world's leading authors in technology and business. Technology professionals, software developers, web designers, and business and creative professionals use Safari Books Online as their primary resource for research, problem solving, learning, and certification training.

Safari Books Online offers a range of product mixes and pricing programs for organizations, government agencies, and individuals. Subscribers have access to thousands of books, training videos, and prepublication manuscripts in one fully searchable database from publishers like O'Reilly Media, Prentice Hall Professional, Addison-Wesley Professional, Microsoft Press, Sams, Que, Peachpit Press, Focal Press, Cisco Press, John Wiley & Sons, Syngress, Morgan Kaufmann, IBM Redbooks, Packt, Adobe Press, FT Press, Apress, Manning, New Riders, McGraw-Hill, Jones & Bartlett, Course Technology, and dozens more. For more information about Safari Books Online, please visit us online.

How to Contact Us

Please address comments and questions concerning this book to the publisher:

O'Reilly Media, Inc.
1005 Gravenstein Highway North
Sebastopol, CA 95472
800-998-9938 (in the United States or Canada)
707-829-0515 (international or local)
707-829-0104 (fax)

We have a web page for this book, where we list errata, examples, and any additional information. You can access this page at:

http://shop.oreilly.com/product/0636920022237.do

To comment or ask technical questions about this book, send email to:

bookquestions@oreilly.com

For more information about our books, courses, conferences, and news, see our website at *http://www.oreilly.com*.

Find us on Facebook: *http://facebook.com/oreilly*

Follow us on Twitter: *http://twitter.com/oreillymedia*

Watch us on YouTube: *http://www.youtube.com/oreillymedia*

Acknowledgments

We are grateful for the people who spent their precious free time reading through and even trying the walkthroughs in this book and providing feedback. Thanks to Rowan's teammates, Arthur Vickers, Pawel Kadluczka, and Diego Vega, for their help in ensuring our accuracy throughout this book. Roland Civet, Mikael Eliasson, and Daniel Wertheim also provided invaluable feedback that helped us fine-tune our explanations and our code.

Thanks to Microsoft for making it possible for Rowan to participate in this project.

Thanks once again to O'Reilly Media, especially our editors, Meghan Blanchette and Rachel Roumeliotis, for their support, their copyediting, and their extreme patience as many schedule conflicts delayed our promised deadlines.

CHAPTER 1

Introducing the DbContext API

Since its first release, the most critical element in Entity Framework has been the ObjectContext. It is this class that allows us to interact with a database using a conceptual model. The context lets us express and execute queries, track changes to objects and persist those changes back to the database. The ObjectContext class interacts with other important Entity Framework classes such as the ObjectSet, which enables set operations on our entities in memory, and ObjectQuery, which is the brains behind executing queries. All of these classes are replete with features and functionality—some of it complex and much of it only necessary for special cases. After two iterations of Entity Framework (in .NET 3.5 SP1 and .NET 4) it was clear that developers were most commonly using a subset of the features, and unfortunately, some of the tasks we needed to do most frequently were difficult to discover and code.

Recognizing this, the Entity Framework team set out to make it easier for developers to access the most frequently used patterns for working with objects within Entity Framework. Their solution was a new set of classes that encapsulate this subset of ObjectContext features. These new classes use the ObjectContext behind the scenes, but developers can work with them without having to tangle with the ObjectContext unless they need to specifically use some of the more advanced features. The new set of classes was originally released as part of Entity Framework 4.1 (EF 4.1).

The prominent classes in this simplified API surface are the DbContext, DbSet, and DbQuery. This entire package of new logic is referred to as the DbContext API. The new API contains more than just the DbContext class, but it is the DbContext that orchestrates all of the new features.

The DbContext API is available in the *EntityFramework.dll* assembly, which also contains the logic that drives Entity Framework Code First. This assembly is separate from .NET and is even deployed separately as the EntityFramework NuGet package. A major portion of the Entity Framework is part of the .NET Framework (primarily *System.Data.Entity.dll*). The components that are included in .NET are considered the "core components" of Entity Framework. The DbContext API is completely dependent on these core components of Entity Framework. The Entity Framework team has indicated that they are working to move more of these core components out of .NET and into the *EntityFramework.dll* assembly. This will allow them to deliver more features between releases of the .NET Framework.

In Table 1-1, you can see a list of the high-level features and classes in the DbContext API, how they relate to the API surface from Entity Framework 4 (EF4), their general purpose, and their benefits.

Table 1-1. Overview of DbContext API features

DbContext API feature	Relevant EF4 feature/class	General purpose	Benefit of DbContext API
DbContext	ObjectContext	Represent a session with the database. Provide query, change tracking and save capabilities.	Exposes and simplifies most commonly used features of ObjectContext.
DbSet	ObjectSet	Provide set operations for entity types, such as Add, Attach and Remove. Inherits from DbQuery to expose query capabilities.	Exposes and simplifies most commonly used features of ObjectSet.
DbQuery	ObjectQuery	Provide querying capabilities.	The query functionality of DbQuery is exposed on DbSet, so you don't have to interact with DbQuery directly.
Change Tracker API	ObjectContext.ObjectStateManager	Get access to change tracking information and operations (e.g., original values, current values) managed by the context.	Simpler and more intuitive API surface.
Validation API	n/a	Provide automatic validation of data at the data layer. This API takes advantage of validation features already existing in .NET 4.	New to DbContext API.
Code First Model Building	n/a	Reads classes and code-based configurations to build in-memory model, metadata and relevant database.	New to DbContext API.

Getting the DbContext API into Your Project

The DbContext API is not released as part of the .NET Framework. In order to be more flexible (and frequent) with releasing new features to Code First and the DbContext API, the Entity Framework team distributes *EntityFramework.dll* through Microsoft's NuGet distribution feature. NuGet allows you to add references to your .NET projects by pulling the relevant DLLs directly into your project from the Web. A Visual Studio extension called the Library Package Manager provides an easy way to pull the appropriate assembly from the Web into your projects. Figure 1-1 displays a screenshot of the Library Package Manager being used to download and add the EntityFramework NuGet package into a project.

Figure 1-1. Getting EntityFramework.dll from the Library Package Manager

You can learn more about using NuGet and the Library Package Manager at nuget.org (*http://nuget.org*).

At the time of this book's publication (early 2012), the current version of EntityFramework package is 4.3. Chapter 9 provides an overview of what to expect in future versions.

Looking at Some Highlights of the DbContext API

DbContext API is mostly targeted at simplifying your interaction with Entity Framework, both by reducing the number of methods and properties you need to wade through and by providing simpler ways to access commonly used tasks. In previous versions of Entity Framework, these tasks were often complicated to discover and code. We have a few favorites that act as great ambassadors to the new API, which we'll share with you here. You'll learn more about these as you work your way through the book.

The samples used in this chapter are for explanation purposes only and not intended for you to perform in Visual Studio. Beginning with the next chapter, you'll find walkthroughs that you can follow in Visual Studio.

Let's start by looking at how the DbContext API simplifies the context that we define and work with. We'll compare the ObjectContext and DbContext based context classes from the model we'll be using in this book, based on BreakAway Geek Adventure's business applications. We'll expose queryable sets of People, Destinations, and Trips based on a Person class, a Destination class, and a Trip class.

Example 1-1 shows a subset of the BreakAwayContext class used in Entity Framework 4, based on an ObjectContext. It wraps up some known types into ObjectSets, which you can query against.

Example 1-1. BreakAwayContext that inherits from ObjectContext

```
public class BreakAwayContext : ObjectContext
{
  private ObjectSet<Person> _people;
  private ObjectSet<Destination> _destinations;
  private ObjectSet<Trip> _trips;

  public ObjectSet<Person> People
  {
    get { return _people ?? (_people = CreateObjectSet<Person>("People")); }
  }

  public ObjectSet< Destination > Contacts
  {
    get { return _destinations?? (_destinations =
            CreateObjectSet< Destination >("Destinations")); }
  }

  public ObjectSet<Trip> Trips
  {
    get { return _trips?? (_trips = CreateObjectSet<Trip>("Trips")); }
  }
}
```

Example 1-2 shows the same context and sets using a DbContext and DbSets instead. Already you can see a big improvement. You can use automatic properties with DbSet (that's the simplified get;set; pattern), something you can't do with ObjectSet. This makes for much cleaner code right out of the gate. There is a CreateDbSet method that's relative to CreateObjectSet, but you aren't required to use it for the purpose of creating a DbSet when you have no other logic to apply.

Example 1-2. BreakAwayContext inheriting from DbContext

```
public class BreakAwayContext : DbContext
  {
    public DbSet<Person> People { get; set; }
    public DbSet<Destination> Destinations { get; set; }
    public DbSet<Trip> Trips { get; set; }
}
```

Reducing and Simplifying Ways to Work with a Set

In Entity Framework 4, there are a number of tasks that you can achieve from both ObjectContext and ObjectSet. For example, when adding an object instance to a set, you can use ObjectContext.AddObject or ObjectSet.AddObject. When adding an object into the context, the context needs to know which set it belongs to. With ObjectContext.AddObject, you must specify the set using a string, for example:

```
context.AddObject("Trips", newTrip);
```

When ObjectSet was introduced in Entity Framework 4, it came with its own AddObject method. This path already provides knowledge of the set so you can simply pass in the object:

```
context.Trips.AddObject(newTrip);
```

With this new method available, the only reason ObjectContext.AddObject continued to exist in Entity Framework 4 was for backward compatibility with earlier versions. But developers who were not aware of this reason were confused by the fact that there were two options.

Because the DbContext API is new, we don't have to worry about backward compatibility, so the DbContext does not have a direct method for adding an object. Additionally, rather than providing the clunky AddObject method in DbSet, the method name is now simply Add:

```
context.Trips.Add(newTrip);
```

ObjectContext also has AttachObject and DeleteObject. DbContext does not have these methods either. DbSet has Attach and Remove, which are equivalent to ObjectSet's Attach and Delete Object. You'll learn more about interacting with DbSet beginning in Chapter 2.

Retrieving an Entity Using ID with DbSet.Find

One task that developers perform frequently is retrieving an entity by providing its key value. For example, you may have access to the PersonId value of a Person in a variable named _personId and would like to retrieve the relevant person data.

Typically you would construct and execute a LINQ to Entities query. Here's a query that uses the SingleOrDefault LINQ method to filter on PersonId when executing a query on context.People:

```
context.People.SingleOrDefault(p => p.PersonId == _personId)
```

Have you written that code so often that you finally wrote a wrapper method so you could pass the key value in and it would execute the LINQ query for you? Yeah, us too. Now DbSet has that shortcut built in with the Find method, which will return an entity whose key property matches the value passed into the method:

```
context.People.Find(_personId)
```

`Find` has another benefit. While the `SingleOrDefault` query above will always query the database, `Find` will first check to see if that particular person is already in memory, being tracked by the context. If so, that's what will be returned. If not, it will make the trip to the database. Under the covers, `DbContext` is executing logic on `ObjectContext` to perform the necessary tasks. You'll learn more about `DbSet.Find` in Chapter 2.

Avoiding Trolling Around the Guts of Entity Framework

These are just a few examples of how much more natural it is to work with the DbContext API than the `ObjectContext` API. If you read *Programming Entity Framework, 2e*, you might be familiar with the many extension methods that Julie created and combined to simplify retrieving instances of objects that are being tracked by the context from the `ObjectStateManager`. One simple property, `DbSet.Local`, now performs that same task. In fact, thanks to the new Change Tracker API, there's no need to dig into the `ObjectStateManager`. It's not even part of the `DbContext` API. Instead you can use `DbContext.Entry` or `DbContext.Entries` to find and even change the information being tracked by the context. You'll learn more about these methods in Chapter 5.

Working with the BreakAway Model

This book follows the model built around the BreakAway Geek Adventures company in the book *Programming Entity Framework: Code First* (O'Reilly). Even though the examples in this book use a model defined with Code First, the concepts apply just as well to a model built using the designer.

Getting the Sample Solution

If you want to follow along the book's examples, you'll need to download the starting solution from the download page of the book's website at *http://learnentityframework .com/downloads*. In the solution you'll find three projects:

1. The *Model* project contains the domain classes, which are configured using Data Annotations.
2. The *DataAccess* project contains the `BreakAwayContext` class that derives from `DbContext`.
3. The *BreakAwayConsole* project is a console application where you can add and execute methods as we explore the many capabilities of the DbContext API.

When using Code First you begin with your classes. Code First uses convention to infer what the schema of the relevant database looks like and how Entity Framework can translate from your classes to that database. Code First's conventions do not always align with your reality, however, so you can tweak how Code First maps your classes to the database by performing additional configuration. There are two ways to apply this additional configuration. One is by adding attributes to your classes and their properties (called Data Annotations) and the other is by using Code First's Fluent API. In the Code First book, we showed you how to use both features and built up two versions of the BreakAway model—one that uses Data Annotations to configure the mappings and the other using the Fluent API.

The examples in this book and the sample download are based on the version of the model that uses Data Annotations. For example, the first class you'll encounter in Chapter 2 is the Destination class, which is displayed here in Example 1-3.

Example 1-3. A class using Data Annotations to specify Code First configuration

```
[Table("Locations", Schema = "baga")]
public class Destination
{
  public Destination()
  {
    this.Lodgings = new List<Lodging>();
  }

  [Column("LocationID")]
  public int DestinationId { get; set; }
  [Required, Column("LocationName")]
  [MaxLength(200)]
  public string Name { get; set; }
  public string Country { get; set; }
  [MaxLength(500)]
  public string Description { get; set; }
  [Column(TypeName = "image")]
  public byte[] Photo { get; set; }
  public string TravelWarnings { get; set; }
  public string ClimateInfo { get; set; }

  public List<Lodging> Lodgings { get; set; }
}
```

The Destination class has a number of Data Annotations. It begins with a Table attribute indicating that the Destination class will map to a database table named Locations which has the schema baga. Without this annotation, Code First would presume the table name is the plural of Destination (Destinations), in the default dbo schema. The DestinationId property is configured to map to a column in the table named LocationId and the Name column to one called LocationName, with a max length of 200. The System.Data.SqlClient provider will default to specifying that the LocationName column is an nvarchar(200). Another annotation ensures that Code First understands that the Photo property maps to a column whose type is image.

The BreakAway context class inherits from System.Data.Entity.DbContext, the central class of the DbContext API. It contains properties that reflect sets of the various model classes contained in the solutions. For example a property named Destinations returns a queryable set of Destination types. The queryable set comes in the form of a DbSet class—another piece of the DbContext API. Example 1-4 gives you a sampling of properties in the `BreakAwayContext` class, which you'll see more of beginning with the next chapter.

Example 1-4. A context class exposing three DbSets that wrap domain classes

```
public class BreakAwayContext : DbContext
{
  public DbSet<Destination> Destinations { get; set; }
  public DbSet<Lodging> Lodgings { get; set; }
  public DbSet<Trip> Trips { get; set; }
}
```

Code First can either create a database for you or be used to map to an existing database. By default, Code First will create a database for you on your local SQL Express instance, using the namespace-qualified context name as the name for the database. For the sake of simplicity, the examples in this book will let Code First create a database automatically. After running some of the sample code, you will find a `DataAccess.BreakAway Context` database on your local SQL Express instance.

 You can learn much more about Code First, its configurations, and its database interactions in *Programming Entity Framework: Code First*.

Getting DbContext from an EDMX Model

Although the book samples use Code First, you may not be using Code First to describe the model in your applications. If, instead, you are using the Entity Data Model Designer and want to take advantage of the DbContext API, there's an easy way to do that. Visual Studio uses the Text Template Transformation Toolkit (T4) generator to generate the default `ObjectContext` and classes from an EDMX file. The generator uses a default template, which is designed to create class fields in a particular way. With the default template, each entity in the model becomes a class that inherits from `EntityOb ject` and a separate class is generated to manage the entities that inherits from `Object Context`.

Microsoft provides alternative templates that you can use to generate POCO classes and a `DbContext`-based context from the EDMX. These are available online and can easily be selected from within the Entity Data Model Designer:

1. Open your EDMX file in the Entity Data Model designer.

2. Right-click on the model background and select "Add Code Generation Item..." as shown in Figure 1-2.

3. In the Add New Item window, select "Online Templates" from the left menu and then search for "DbContext." Select the DbContext Generator template from the search results, enter a name, and click "Add" (Figure 1-3).

As a result, two templates will be added to your project. One is a context template (*Model.Context.tt* in the sample shown in Figure 1-4), which generates a class that inherits from DbContext, shown in Example 1-5.

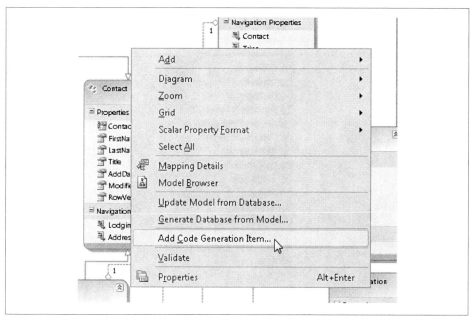

Figure 1-2. Adding a new T4 template code generation item from the model's context menu

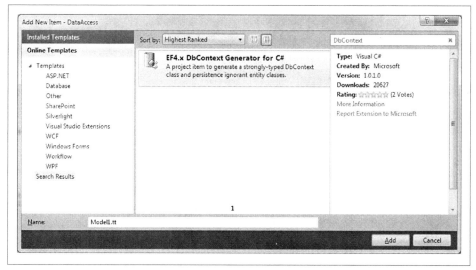

Figure 1-3. Selecting the DbContext Generator template

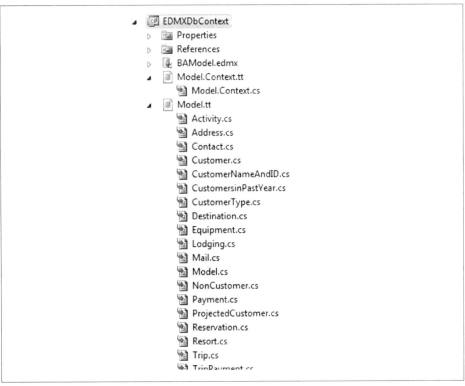

Figure 1-4. Project with .tt template files and their code-generated .cs files

Example 1-5. Generated BAEntities class inheriting from DbContext

```
public partial class BAEntities : DbContext
{
    public BAEntities()
        : base("name=BAEntities")
    {
        this.Configuration.LazyLoadingEnabled = false;
    }

    protected override void OnModelCreating(DbModelBuilder modelBuilder)
    {
        throw new UnintentionalCodeFirstException();
    }

    public DbSet<Activity> Activities { get; set; }
    public DbSet<Contact> Contacts { get; set; }
    public DbSet<CustomerType> CustomerTypes { get; set; }
    public DbSet<Equipment> EquipmentSet { get; set; }
    public DbSet<Trip> Trips { get; set; }
    public DbSet<Destination> Destinations { get; set; }
    public DbSet<Lodging> Lodgings { get; set; }
```

```
  public DbSet<Payment> Payments { get; set; }
}
```

The second template (also shown in Figure 1-4), here called *Model.tt*, is the one that generates POCO classes for each of the entities in your EDMX model. As you saw above, the context class exposes each of these POCO types in a DbSet.

Using this template, you can take advantage of an existing visual model and still benefit from the DbContext API, which you'll be learning about in this book.

Ensuring DbContext Instances Get Disposed

A DbContext (and its underlying ObjectContext) are responsible for managing and tracking changes to instances of the classes in its model. These classes are also responsible for managing a connection to the database. It's important to ensure that any resources used to perform these operations are cleaned up when the DbContext instance is no longer needed. DbContext implements the standard .NET IDisposable interface, which includes a Dispose method that will release any such resources.

The examples in this book will make use of the using pattern, which will take care of disposing the context when the using block completes (Example 1-6). If your application doesn't make use of the using pattern, ensure that the Dispose method is called on any DbContext instances when they are no longer needed.

Example 1-6. Instantiating and disposing a context with the using pattern

```
public static List<Destination> GetDestinations()
{
  using (var context = new BreakAwayContext())
  {
    var query= from d in context.Destinations
               orderby d.Name
               select d;
    return query.ToList();
  }
}
```

CHAPTER 2

Querying with DbContext

There are two things that almost every application that accesses a database has in common: the need to retrieve data from the database and to save changes to that data back into the database. Over the next two chapters you will see how the DbContext API makes it easy to achieve these tasks using the Entity Framework. The focus of this chapter will be on retrieving data from the database.

One of the great benefits of using an Object Relational Mapper (ORM), such as Entity Framework, is that once we have set up the mapping, we can interact with our data in terms of the objects and properties that make up our model, rather than tables and columns. When querying for objects, this means we no longer need to know how to write queries using the SQL syntax of our database.

Writing Queries with LINQ to Entities

Entity Framework queries are written using a .NET Framework feature known as Language Integrated Query, or LINQ for short. As the name suggests, LINQ is tightly integrated with the .NET programming experience and provides a strongly typed query language over your model. *Strongly typed* simply means that the query is defined using the classes and properties that make up your model. This provides a number of benefits such as compile-time checks to ensure your queries are valid and the ability to provide IntelliSense as you write your queries.

LINQ is a general query framework and isn't specific to Entity Framework, or even databases for that matter. A LINQ Provider is responsible for taking your LINQ query, translating it into a query against the data, and then returning results. For Entity Framework this provider is known as LINQ to Entities and is responsible for taking your LINQ query and translating it into a SQL query against the database you are targeting. The information you supplied to Entity Framework about the shape of your model and how it maps to the database is used to perform this translation. Once the query returns, Entity Framework is responsible for copying the data into instances of the classes that make up your model.

The capabilities of LINQ and its use within Entity Framework are beyond the scope of this book. This chapter will provide an overview to help you get up and running with queries using DbContext, but is not an exhaustive query guide. *Programming Entity Framework, 2e (http://shop.oreilly.com/product/9780596807252.do)*, provides a much more in-depth look at the query capabilities of Entity Framework, not only in Chapter 3 and Chapter 4, which are dedicated to querying, but throughout the book.

 In addition to LINQ, Entity Framework also supports a text-based query language known as Entity SQL, or ESQL for short. ESQL is typically used in more advanced scenarios where queries need to be dynamically constructed at runtime. Because ESQL is text-based, it is also useful in scenarios where the application needs to build a query against a model that isn't known until runtime. Given that ESQL is less commonly used, it is not exposed directly on the DbContext API. If your application requires the use of ESQL, you will need to access the ObjectContext API using the IObjectContextAdapter interface.

To follow along with the examples in this book you will need a Visual Studio solution containing a console application that references the BAGA model built in *Programming Entity Framework: Code First*. You can download a prebuilt solution from *http://learnentityframework.com/downloads*. This prebuilt solution also includes a database initializer that will reset the database and insert some seed data into the database each time you run the application. The seed data is used in the examples throughout this book.

Code First Migrations

Entity Framework 4.3 includes a new Code First Migrations feature that allows you to incrementally evolve the database schema as your model changes over time. For most developers, this is a big improvement over the database initializer options from the 4.1 and 4.2 releases that required you to manually update the database or drop and recreate it when your model changed.

The prebuilt solution still makes use of the DropCreateDatabaseAlways initializer rather than using Code First Migrations. This allows us to ensure the database is reset to a well-known state before you run each example in this book.

You can learn more about Code First Migrations at *http://blogs.msdn.com/b/adonet/archive/2012/02/09/ef-4-3-released.aspx*.

The Model project of the prebuilt solution contains classes that make up the BAGA domain model. The BAGA model includes a Destination class (Example 2-1) that represents all the wonderful places that our intrepid travelers can venture to.

Example 2-1. Destination class as listed in download solution

```
[Table("Locations", Schema = "baga")]
public class Destination
{
  public Destination()
  {
    this.Lodgings = new List<Lodging>();
  }

  [Column("LocationID")]
  public int DestinationId { get; set; }
  [Required, Column("LocationName")]
  [MaxLength(200)]
  public string Name { get; set; }
  public string Country { get; set; }
  [MaxLength(500)]
  public string Description { get; set; }
  [Column(TypeName = "image")]
  public byte[] Photo { get; set; }
  public string TravelWarnings { get; set; }
  public string ClimateInfo { get; set; }

  public List<Lodging> Lodgings { get; set; }
}
```

The BAGA model also includes a `Lodging` class (Example 2-2) that represents the accommodation that is available at the various `Destinations`.

Example 2-2. Lodging class as listed in download solution

```
public class Lodging
{
  public int LodgingId { get; set; }
  [Required]
  [MaxLength(200)]
  [MinLength(10)]
  public string Name { get; set; }
  public string Owner { get; set; }
  public decimal MilesFromNearestAirport { get; set; }

  [Column("destination_id")]
  public int DestinationId { get; set; }
  public Destination Destination { get; set; }
  public List<InternetSpecial> InternetSpecials { get; set; }
  public Nullable<int> PrimaryContactId { get; set; }
  [InverseProperty("PrimaryContactFor")]
  [ForeignKey("PrimaryContactId")]
  public Person PrimaryContact { get; set; }
  public Nullable<int> SecondaryContactId { get; set; }
  [InverseProperty("SecondaryContactFor")]
  [ForeignKey("SecondaryContactId")]
  public Person SecondaryContact { get; set; }
}
```

The Destination and Lodging classes will be used extensively for the examples throughout this book. To perform data access using these classes you will be using the BreakA wayContext from the DataAccess project. The project contains additional classes that are represented in BreakAwayContext as well as the Lodgings and Destinations. We'll be using Code First for the examples in this book, but the techniques you will learn apply to any context that derives from DbContext. This includes contexts created using the Model First or Database First workflows.

Example 2-3. BreakAwayContext class as listed in download solution

```
public class BreakAwayContext : DbContext
{
  public DbSet<Destination> Destinations { get; set; }
  public DbSet<Lodging> Lodgings { get; set; }
  public DbSet<Trip> Trips { get; set; }
  public DbSet<Person> People { get; set; }
  public DbSet<Reservation> Reservations { get; set; }
  public DbSet<Payment> Payments { get; set; }
  public DbSet<Activity> Activities { get; set; }
}
```

Querying All the Data from a Set

Arguably the simplest query you can write is one that fetches all the data for a given entity type. This is the equivalent of a SELECT * FROM mytable query in SQL. Fortunately you don't need to know SQL, because Entity Framework will take care of translating LINQ queries into SQL for you.

Getting all the data from a set doesn't require you to really write a query. You can simply iterate over the contents of any given DbSet and Entity Framework will send a query to the database to find all the data in that set. Let's add a PrintAllDestinations method to our console application that iterates over the Destinations set defined in our Break AwayContext and prints out the name of each Destination (Example 2-4).

Example 2-4. Query for all destinations

```
private static void PrintAllDestinations()
{
  using (var context = new BreakAwayContext())
  {
    foreach (var destination in context.Destinations)
    {
      Console.WriteLine(destination.Name);
    }
  }
}
```

When you debug the application, the console window will close when the application has finished executing, which may prevent you from inspecting the output. You can put a breakpoint at the end of the method for debugging. Alternatively, you can run without debugging (CTRL + F5), in which case Visual Studio will ensure that the console window remains open after the program has finished executing.

If you update the `Main` method to call this new `PrintAllDestinations` method and run the application, you will see that the name of each `Destination` in the database is printed to the console:

```
Grand Canyon
Hawaii
Wine Glass Bay
Great Barrier Reef
```

As the code began iterating over the contents of the `Destinations` set, Entity Framework issued a SQL query against the database to load the required data:

```
SELECT
[Extent1].[LocationID] AS [LocationID],
[Extent1].[LocationName] AS [LocationName],
[Extent1].[Country] AS [Country],
[Extent1].[Description] AS [Description],
[Extent1].[Photo] AS [Photo]
FROM [baga].[Locations] AS [Extent1]
```

The SQL may not look like the SQL you would have written. This is because Entity Framework has a generic query building algorithm that not only caters to this very simple query, but also for much more complex scenarios.

The query is sent to the database when the first result is requested by the application: that's during the first iteration of the `foreach` loop. Entity Framework doesn't pull back all the data at once, though. The query remains active and the results are read from the database as they are needed. By the time the `foreach` loop is completed, all the results have been read from the database.

One important thing to note is that Entity Framework will query the database every time you trigger an iteration over the contents of a `DbSet`. This has performance implications if you are continually querying the database for the same data. To avoid this, you can use a LINQ operator such as `ToList` to copy the results into a list. You can then iterate over the contents of this list multiple times without causing multiple trips to the database. Example 2-5 introduces a `PrintAllDestinationsTwice` method that demonstrates this approach.

Example 2-5. Iterating all Destinations twice with one database query

```
private static void PrintAllDestinationsTwice()
{
  using (var context = new BreakAwayContext())
  {
```

```
      var allDestinations = context.Destinations.ToList();

      foreach (var destination in allDestinations)
      {
        Console.WriteLine(destination.Name);
      }

      foreach (var destination in allDestinations)
      {
        Console.WriteLine(destination.Name);
      }
    }
  }
}
```

Because a query is sent to the database to find the items in a DbSet, iterating a DbSet will only contain items that exist in the database. Any objects that are sitting in memory waiting to be saved to the database will not be returned. To ensure added objects are included you can use the techniques described in "Querying Local Data" on page 24.

Using LINQ for Sorting, Filtering, and More

While this chapter will not be an exhaustive list of everything you can do with LINQ and Entity Framework, let's take a look at the patterns used to achieve some common query tasks. Let's say you want to print out the names of Destinations again, but this time you want them ordered alphabetically by Name. Add a new PrintAllDestinations Sorted method that uses a LINQ query to perform this sort (Example 2-6).

Example 2-6. Query for destinations sorted by name

```
private static void PrintAllDestinationsSorted()
{
  using (var context = new BreakAwayContext())
  {
    var query = from d in context.Destinations
                orderby d.Name
                select d;

    foreach (var destination in query)
    {
      Console.WriteLine(destination.Name);
    }
  }
}
```

The above code uses LINQ to create a query and then iterates the results of the query and displays the name of each destination. The query is expressed using a syntax that looks a little bit like SQL. You start by telling it what you want to select from (in our case, the Destinations set on our context). You give the set a name so that you can refer to it throughout the rest of the query (in our case that name is d). Following this, you use operators such as orderby, groupby, and where to define the query. Finally you specify what you want returned using the select operator. In our case we want the actual Destination objects returned, so we specify the name that we gave the set in the first line.

Remember that Entity Framework won't execute the query against the database until it needs the first result. During the first iteration of the foreach loop, the query is sent to the database. The query remains active and each result is read from the database as it is needed by the application. LINQ also includes methods that will copy the results of a query into a collection. For example, ToList can be called on a query to copy the results into a new List<T>. Calling a method such as this will cause all the results to be retrieved from the database and be copied into the new List<T>.

The code shown in Example 2-6 uses the LINQ *query syntax* to express the query. While most people find this the easiest to understand, there is an alternate *method syntax* that can be used if you prefer. Example 2-7 shows the same query expressed using method syntax.

Example 2-7. LINQ method syntax in C#

```
var query = context.Destinations
  .OrderBy(d => d.Name);
```

The method syntax makes use of lambda expressions to define the query. The LINQ methods are strongly typed, which gives you IntelliSense and compile-time checking for the lambda expressions you write. For example, in the OrderBy method we are using a lambda expression to specify that we want to order by the Name property. You start a lambda expression by giving a name to the thing you are operating on; this forms the left side of the expression. In our case we are operating on a Destination and we have chosen to call it d. Then, on the right side of the expression, you specify the body of the expression. In our case we just want to identify the Name property.

C# uses the lambda sign (=>) to separate the left and right sides of the expression. VB.NET uses the Function keyword followed by brackets to identify the left side of the expression. Example 2-8 shows the same query written in VB.NET using the method syntax.

Example 2-8. LINQ method syntax in VB.NET

```
context.Destinations.OrderBy(Function(d) d.Name)
```

Another common task is to filter the results of a query. For example, we may only want Destinations from Australia. Add the PrintAustralianDestinations method shown in Example 2-9.

Example 2-9. Query for Australian destinations

```
private static void PrintAustralianDestinations()
{
  using (var context = new BreakAwayContext())
  {
```

```
    var query = from d in context.Destinations
                where d.Country == "Australia"
                select d;

    foreach (var destination in query)
    {
      Console.WriteLine(destination.Name);
    }
  }
}
```

This code looks very similar to the `PrintAllDestinationsSorted` we saw in Example 2-6, except we are using the **where** operator instead of orderby. You can also combine these operators. Example 2-10 shows how to query for Australian `Destinations` sorted by name.

Example 2-10. Query combining filter and sort

```
var query = from d in context.Destinations
            where d.Country == "Australia"
            orderby d.Name
            select d;
```

Operators can also be combined in the method syntax. The same query from Example 2-10 is shown using method syntax in Example 2-11.

Example 2-11. Method syntax for combining filter and sort

```
var query = context.Destinations
  .Where(d => d.Country == "Australia")
  .OrderBy(d => d.Name);
```

So far our queries have returned collections of entities from our model, but this may not always be the case. In fact, we have been returning complete `Destination` objects when we really only need the name. You can use *projection* to create a query that selects from a set of entities in your model but returns results that are of a different type. For example, you can use projection to create a query that selects from a set of entities type but only returns a subset of the properties of that entity. It's called projection because you are projecting data from the shape of the source that you are selecting from onto the shape of the result set you want.

In our case we want to project a query about `Destinations` into a result set that just has a string representing the destination's name. Example 2-12 adds a `PrintDestination NameOnly` method that shows how we use the **select** section of our query to specify what we want the result set to contain.

Example 2-12. Querying for just the Destination name

```
private static void PrintDestinationNameOnly()
{
  using (var context = new BreakAwayContext())
  {
```

```
        var query = from d in context.Destinations
                    where d.Country == "Australia"
                    orderby d.Name
                    select d.Name;

        foreach (var name in query)
        {
          Console.WriteLine(name);
        }
      }
}
```

Example 2-13 shows how this same query can be written using method syntax by making use of the Select method.

Example 2-13. Method syntax for projection

```
var query = context.Destinations
  .Where(d => d.Country == "Australia")
  .OrderBy(d => d.Name)
  .Select(d => d.Name);
```

LINQ is a powerful query language and this section has just grazed the surface of its capabilities. *Programming Entity Framework, 2e,* contains a much deeper look into using LINQ with the Entity Framework. There are also more example queries available in the Entity Framework MSDN documentation: *http://msdn.microsoft.com/en-us/library/bb399367.aspx*.

Finding a Single Object

So far you've seen queries that return a collection of entities, but sometimes you will want to run a query that just returns a single object. The most common scenario for querying for a single object is to find the object with a given key. The DbContext API makes this very simple by exposing a Find method on DbSet. Find accepts the value to be searched for and will return the corresponding object if it is found. If there is no entity with the provided key, Find will return null.

One of the great things about Find is that it doesn't unnecessarily query the database. It's also capable of finding newly added objects that haven't yet been saved to the database. Find uses a simple set of rules to locate the object (in order of precedence):

1. Look in memory for an existing entity that has been loaded from the database or attached to the context (you'll learn more about attaching objects in Chapter 4).
2. Look at added objects that have not yet been saved to the database.
3. Look in the database for entities that have not yet been loaded into memory.

To see this behavior, add the FindDestination method shown in Example 2-14. This method accepts an ID from the user and then attempts to locate the Destination with the specified ID.

Example 2-14. Using Find to locate a Destination

```
private static void FindDestination()
{
  Console.Write("Enter id of Destination to find: ");
  var id = int.Parse(Console.ReadLine());
  using (var context = new BreakAwayContext())
  {
    var destination = context.Destinations.Find(id);
    if (destination == null)
    {
      Console.WriteLine("Destination not found!");
    }
    else
    {
      Console.WriteLine(destination.Name);
    }
  }
}
```

The code above uses the Find method to look up the Destination with the specified ID. If one is found, it prints out the name of the destination. If Find returns null, indicating there is no Destination with the specified ID, an error message is displayed to the user.

Find with Composite Keys

Entity Framework supports entities that have *composite keys*, that is, entities where the key is made up of two or more properties. For example, you may have a Passport entity that uses a combination of IssuingCountry and PassportNumber as its key. To locate entities with a composite key you supply each of the key values to Find:

```
context.Passports.Find("USA", "123456789")
```

The key values must be supplied in the same order that they appear in the model. If you are using Model First or Database First, this is the order that they appear in the designer. When composite keys are used, Code First requires you to specify an order for them. You can use the Column annotation with the Order parameter to specify the order. If you are using the Fluent API, a HasKey call is required; the order of the key properties is the order they appear in the body of the HasKey call.

There may be times when you want to query for a single object but are not able to use Find. These could include wanting to query by something other than the key or wanting to include related data in the query (as described in "Eager Loading" on page 33). To do this, you will need to create a standard LINQ query and then use the Single method to get a single object as the result.

Let's say we want to locate the Destination that has the name Great Barrier Reef. Name isn't the key of Destination but we know there is, and only ever will be, one Great Barrier Reef. Example 2-10 introduces a FindGreatBarrierReef method that will locate this single Destination.

Example 2-15. Query for single entity based on name

```
private static void FindGreatBarrierReef()
{
  using (var context = new BreakAwayContext())
  {
    var query = from d in context.Destinations
                where d.Name == "Great Barrier Reef"
                select d;

    var reef = query.Single();

    Console.WriteLine(reef.Description);
  }
}
```

The LINQ query looks the same as any other query that filters based on name. We then use the `Single` method to let Entity Framework know that we expect a single result. If the query returns no results, or more than one result, an exception will be thrown. If there are potentially no matches, you can use the `SingleOrDefault` method, which will return `null` if no results are found. Example 2-16 shows the `FindGreatBarrierReef` method updated to account for the fact it may not exist in the database.

Example 2-16. Query for single entity that may not exist

```
private static void FindGreatBarrierReef()
{
  using (var context = new BreakAwayContext())
  {
    var query = from d in context.Destinations
                where d.Name == "Great Barrier Reef"
                select d;

    var reef = query.SingleOrDefault();

    if (reef == null)
    {
      Console.WriteLine("Can't find the reef!");
    }
    else
    {
      Console.WriteLine(reef.Description);
    }
  }
}
```

`SingleOrDefault` uses the same database query that `Find` uses when it looks for entities in the database. The SQL selects the TOP two results so that it can ensure there is only one match:

```
SELECT TOP (2)
  [Extent1].[LocationID] AS [LocationID],
  [Extent1].[LocationName] AS [LocationName],
  [Extent1].[Country] AS [Country],
```

```
        [Extent1].[Description] AS [Description],
        [Extent1].[Photo] AS [Photo],
        [Extent1].[TravelWarnings] AS [TravelWarnings],
        [Extent1].[ClimateInfo] AS [ClimateInfo]
    FROM [baga].[Locations] AS [Extent1]
    WHERE N'Great Barrier Reef' = [Extent1].[LocationName]
```

If two rows are found, `Single` and `SingleOrDefault` will throw because there is not a single result. If you just want the first result, and aren't concerned if there is more than one result, you can use `First` or `FirstOrDefault`.

One important thing to remember is that LINQ queries against a `DbSet` always send a query to the database to find the data. So, if the Great Barrier Reef was a newly added `Destination` that hadn't been saved to the database yet, the queries in Example 2-15 and Example 2-16 won't be able to locate it. To look for newly added entities, you would also need to query the in-memory data using the techniques shown in "Querying Local Data" on page 24.

Querying Local Data

So far you've used LINQ to query a `DbSet` directly, which always results in a SQL query being sent to the database to load the data. You've also used the `Find` method, which will look for in-memory data before querying that database. `Find` will only query based on the key property though, and there may be times when you want to use a more complex query against data that is already in memory and being tracked by your `DbContext`.

One of the reasons you may want to do this is to avoid sending multiple queries to the database when you know that all the data you need is already loaded into memory. Back in Example 2-5, we saw one way to do this was to use `ToList` to copy the results of a query into a list. While this works well if we are using the data within the same block of code, things get a little messy if we need to start passing that list around our application. For example, we might want to load all `Destinations` from the database when our application loads. Different areas of our application are then going to want to run different queries against that data. In some places we might want to display all `Destinations`, in others we might want to sort by Name, and in others we might want to filter by `Country`. Rather than passing around a list of `Destination` objects, we can take advantage of the fact that our context is tracking all the instances and query its local data.

Another reason may be that you want the results to include newly added data, which doesn't yet exist in the database. Using `ToList` on a LINQ query against a `DbSet` will always send a query to the database. This means that any new objects that don't yet exist in the database won't be included in the results. Local queries, however, will include newly created objects in the results.

The in-memory data for a `DbSet` is available via the `Local` property. `Local` will return all the data that has been loaded from the database plus any newly added data. Any data that has been marked as deleted but hasn't been deleted from the database yet will be filtered out for you. More information on how entities get into these different states is available in Chapter 3.

Let's start with the very simple task of finding out how many `Destination`s are in memory and available to be queried. Go ahead and add the `GetLocalDestinationCount` method, as shown in Example 2-17.

Example 2-17. Checking how many Destinations are in-memory

```
private static void GetLocalDestinationCount()
{
  using (var context = new BreakAwayContext())
  {
    var count = context.Destinations.Local.Count;
    Console.WriteLine("Destinations in memory: {0}", count);
  }
}
```

The code accesses the `Local` property of the `Destinations` set that we created on our `BreakAwayContext`. Rather than running a query, we simply store the count in a variable and then print it to the console. If you run the application you will see that the count is zero:

```
Destinations in memory: 0
```

We're getting a zero count because we haven't run any queries to load `Destinations` from the database, and we haven't added any new `Destination` objects either. Let's update the `GetLocalDestinationCount` method to query some data from the database before getting the local count (Example 2-18).

Example 2-18. Checking in-memory data after a query

```
private static void GetLocalDestinationCount()
{
  using (var context = new BreakAwayContext())
  {
    foreach (var destination in context.Destinations)
    {
      Console.WriteLine(destination.Name);
    }

    var count = context.Destinations.Local.Count;
    Console.WriteLine("Destinations in memory: {0}", count);
  }
}
```

This new code iterates over the `Destinations` set, causing the data to be loaded from the database. Because the data is loaded when we get the count from the `Local` property, we now see a nonzero result when we run the application:

```
Grand Canyon
Hawaii
Wine Glass Bay
Great Barrier Reef
Destinations in memory: 4
```

Using the Load Method to Bring Data into Memory

Iterating over the contents of a DbSet with a foreach loop is one way to get all the data into memory, but it's a little inefficient to do that just for the sake of loading data. It's also a little unclear what the intent of the code is, especially if the iteration code doesn't directly precede the local query.

Fortunately the DbContext API includes a Load method, which can be used on a DbSet to pull all the data from the database into memory. Go ahead and add the GetLo calDestinationCountWithLoad method (Example 2-19) that uses Load on the Destinations set and then prints out the count of in-memory Destinations.

Example 2-19. Using the Load to bring data into memory

```
private static void GetLocalDestinationCountWithLoad()
{
  using (var context = new BreakAwayContext())
  {
    context.Destinations.Load();

    var count = context.Destinations.Local.Count;
    Console.WriteLine("Destinations in memory: {0}", count);
  }
}
```

Compare this code with the GetLocalDestinationCount method we wrote back in Example 2-18. This updated code makes it much clearer that our intent is to load the contents of the Destinations set and then query the in-memory data.

 Load is actually an extension method on IQueryable<T> and is defined in the System.Data.Entity namespace. If you want to use Load, you will need to have this namespace imported.

Because Load is an extension method on IQueryable<T>, we can also use it to load the results of a LINQ query into memory, rather than the entire contents of a set. For example, let's say we only wanted to load Australian Destinations into memory and then run a few local queries on that subset of data. Let's add the LoadAustralianDesti nations method shown in Example 2-20.

Example 2-20. Loading results of a LINQ query into memory

```
private static void LoadAustralianDestinations()
{
```

```
  using (var context = new BreakAwayContext())
  {
    var query = from d in context.Destinations
                where d.Country == "Australia"
                select d;

    query.Load();

    var count = context.Destinations.Local.Count;
    Console.WriteLine("Aussie destinations in memory: {0}", count);
  }
}
```

This time just the Destinations with Country set to Australia are loaded into memory.
When we run the application, we see that the count we get from Local is reduced to
reflect this.

 Using Load on a LINQ query will bring the results of that query into
memory but it does not remove the results of previous queries. For example if you called Load on a query for Australian destinations and then
Load on a query for American destinations, both Australian and American destinations would be in memory and would be returned from
Local.

Running LINQ Queries Against Local

So far we have just looked at getting the count from Local to make sure that it is returning the correct data that we brought into memory. Because Local is just a collection
of in-memory objects, we can also run queries against it. One of the great things about
LINQ is that it's not specific to Entity Framework. We can use the same LINQ syntax
to query a number of different data sources, including in-memory collections of objects.

Let's add a LocalLinqQueries method that pulls data into memory using a single database query and then runs some in-memory queries using Local (Example 2-21).

Example 2-21. Using LINQ to query Local

```
private static void LocalLinqQueries()
{
  using (var context = new BreakAwayContext())
  {
    context.Destinations.Load();

    var sortedDestinations = from d in context.Destinations.Local
                             orderby d.Name
                             select d;

    Console.WriteLine("All Destinations:");
    foreach (var destination in sortedDestinations)
    {
      Console.WriteLine(destination.Name);
```

```
  }

  var aussieDestinations = from d in context.Destinations.Local
                           where d.Country == "Australia"
                           select d;

  Console.WriteLine();
  Console.WriteLine("Australian Destinations:");
  foreach (var destination in aussieDestinations)
  {
    Console.WriteLine(destination.Name);
  }
 }
}
```

The code loads all Destinations into memory and then runs one query to sort them by Name and another to pull out just the Australian Destinations. Remember that Find also defaults to using in-memory data where possible. So we could also use Find and it would use the data we loaded rather than sending more queries to the database.

While Load and Local are great if you want to reduce the number of queries that get run against the database just remember that pulling all your data into memory may be an expensive operation. If you are running multiple queries that only return a subset of your data you'll probably get better performance by letting these queries hit the database and just pull back the data you actually need.

Differences Between LINQ Providers

There are a few subtle but important differences between querying directly against a DbSet and against Local. These two data sources actually use two different LINQ providers. Querying against DbSet uses LINQ to Entities, which is specific to Entity Framework and uses your model and mapping to turn your query into SQL that is executed in the database. However, querying against Local uses LINQ to Objects, which performs filtering, sorting, and similar operations in memory using the standard .NET operators for testing equality, determining ordering, and the like.

The same query syntax can return different results depending on which one you are using. For example, the database is typically not case-sensitive when comparing string values, but .NET is. If you issued a query for Destination names that contain "great", the database would return "Great Barrier Reef" and "The great wall of China." The same query against Local would return "The great wall of China" but would not return "Great Barrier Reef" because the capitalization of "great" is different.

Most LINQ providers support the same core features, but there are some differences in features between each provider. For example, LINQ to Objects supports the Last operator but LINQ to Entities does not. Therefore, you can use Last when running queries against Local but not when running queries directly against a DbSet.

Working with the ObservableCollection Returned by Local

If you've looked at the API closely you may have noticed that Local returns an Observ ableCollection<TEntity>. This type of collection allows subscribers to be notified whenever objects are added or removed from the collection. ObservableCollection is useful in a number of data-binding scenarios, but it can also be useful if your application needs to know when new data comes into memory.

Local will raise the CollectionChanged event whenever the contents of Local change. This can be when data is brought back from that database via a query, when new objects are added to the DbContext, or when objects previously brought into memory are marked for deletion.

Let's add a ListenToLocalChanges method that uses this functionality to log any changes to Destinations.Local to the console (Example 2-22).

Example 2-22. Using CollectionChanged to print out changes to Local

```
private static void ListenToLocalChanges()
{
  using (var context = new BreakAwayContext())
  {
    context.Destinations.Local
      .CollectionChanged += (sender, args) =>
    {
      if (args.NewItems != null)
      {
        foreach (Destination item in args.NewItems)
        {
          Console.WriteLine("Added: " + item.Name);
        }
      }

      if (args.OldItems != null)
      {
        foreach (Destination item in args.OldItems)
        {
          Console.WriteLine("Removed: " + item.Name);
        }
      }
    };

    context.Destinations.Load();
  }
}
```

The code adds a new event handler to the Local collection of Destinations. This handler looks at items entering or leaving the collection and prints out the name of the affected Destination and indicates if it is being added or removed. Once the event handler is in place, we use Load to pull all the data from the database into memory. If you run the application, you can see the output appearing as items are returned from the database:

```
Added: Grand Canyon
Added: Hawaii
Added: Wine Glass Bay
Added: Great Barrier Reef
```

These events could be handy if you have a screen that needs to be refreshed whenever some data in your context changes. For example, you might have a screen that displays all Destinations and another screen where the user can add a new Destination. You could wire up the screen displaying all Destinations to listen to the Collection Changed event and refresh whenever anything is added or removed.

Some UI frameworks, such as WPF, will take care of this for you so that you don't have to write code to listen to changes. If you bind a WPF ListBox to the contents of Local, whenever any other area of the application adds or removes an entity from the DbSet, the ListBox will be updated to reflect those changes.

> If you use LINQ to query the contents of Local, the result of the query is no longer an ObservableCollection. This means if you run a LINQ query against Local and bind the results to a WPF ListBox, it will no longer get automatically updated for you when entities are added or removed. You would need to write code that listens to OnCollection Changed on DbSet.Local and rerun the query to refresh the ListBox.

Loading Related Data

So far we have looked at accessing data for a single type of entity and everything has been about Destinations. But if we were writing a real application, we would probably want to know something about the Lodging that is available at each Destination. If we want to access the Lodgings associated with a Destination, that means working with related data.

You'll need to pull related data into memory so that we can look at it. There are three approaches you can use to load related data: lazily, eagerly, or explicitly. While they may achieve the same end result, there are some differences between each approach that can have a significant impact on performance. This isn't a one-time decision either. Different approaches may be better at different times. This section will walk through the three available options and help you work out which one is best for you in different situations.

> The "Demystifying Entity Framework Strategies: Loading Related Data" (*http://msdn.microsoft.com/en-us/magazine/hh205756.aspx*) MSDN article gives a detailed look at the pros and cons of the different strategies and some pointers on choosing the right strategy for you.

Lazy Loading

Lazy loading related data is the most transparent to your application and involves letting Entity Framework automatically retrieve the related data for you when you try to access it. For example, you may have the Grand Canyon destination loaded. If you then use the Lodgings property of this Destination, Entity Framework will automatically send a query to the database to load all Lodgings at the Grand Canyon. It will appear to your application code as if the Lodgings property was always populated.

Entity Framework achieves lazy loading using a *dynamic proxy*. Here's how that works. When Entity Framework returns the results of a query, it creates instances of your classes and populates them with the data that was returned from the database. Entity Framework has the ability to dynamically create a new type at runtime that derives from your POCO class. This new class acts as a proxy to your POCO class and is referred to as a dynamic proxy. It will override the navigation properties of your POCO class and include some additional logic to retrieve the data from the database when the property is accessed. Because the dynamic proxy derives from your POCO class, your application can be written in terms of the POCO class and doesn't need to be aware that there may be a dynamic proxy at runtime.

 DbContext has a configuration setting that enables lazy loading: DbCon text.Configuration.LazyLoadingEnabled. This setting is true by default and therefore if you have not changed the default, the dynamic proxy will perform lazy loading.

In order to use dynamic proxies, and therefore lazy loading, there are a couple of criteria your class must meet. If these criteria are not met, Entity Framework will not create a dynamic proxy for the class and will just return instances of your POCO class, which cannot perform lazy loading:

- Your POCO class must be public and not sealed.
- The navigation properties that you want to be lazy loaded must also be marked as virtual (Overridable in Visual Basic) so that Entity Framework can override the properties to include the lazy loading logic.

Before we make any changes to our classes, let's see what the behavior is like without dynamic proxies. Add a TestLazyLoading method that attempts to access the Lodg ings associated with a specific Destination (Example 2-23).

Example 2-23. Method to access related data

```
private static void TestLazyLoading()
{
  using (var context = new BreakAwayContext())
  {
    var query = from d in context.Destinations
                where d.Name == "Grand Canyon"
```

```
        select d;

var canyon = query.Single();

Console.WriteLine("Grand Canyon Lodging:");
if (canyon.Lodgings != null)
{
  foreach (var lodging in canyon.Lodgings)
  {
    Console.WriteLine(lodging.Name);
  }
}
}
}
```

The code locates the Grand Canyon `Destination` and then tests if the `Lodgings` property is populated. If it is populated, the name of each associated `Lodging` is printed to the console. If you update the `Main` method to call `TestLazyLoading` and run the application, you will see that nothing is printed out to the console. This is because the `Lodgings` property on `Destination` isn't marked as `virtual` (`Overridable` in Visual Basic), so Entity Framework can't override the property in a dynamic proxy. Entity Framework is forced to use your implementation of the property (that doesn't perform lazy loading) rather than replacing it with an implementation that includes the lazy loading logic. Let's go ahead and edit the `Destination` class so that the property is marked as `virtual`:

```
public virtual List<Lodging> Lodgings { get; set; }
```

Now Entity Framework can create a dynamic proxy for the `Destination` class. If you run the application again, you'll see that the individual `Lodgings` for the Grand Canyon are displayed because the data was automatically loaded for you when the code encountered the first request for `Lodgings`:

```
Grand Canyon Lodging:
Grand Hotel
Dave's Dump
```

As the code executed, Entity Framework sent two queries to the database (Figure 2-1). The first query retrieves the data for the Grand Canyon `Destination` and was executed when the code called the `Single` method on `query`. Remember that the `Single` method uses a `SELECT TOP (2)` query to ensure there is one result and only one result. The second query selects all `Lodgings` associated with the Grand Canyon. This query was sent at the moment the code first tried to access the `Lodgings` property for the Grand Canyon `Destination`.

```
SELECT TOP (2)   [Extent1].[LocationID] AS [LocationID],   [Extent1].[Loca...
exec sp_executesql N'SELECT   [Extent1].[LodgingId] AS [LodgingId],   CASE...
```

Figure 2-1. Lazy loading query

Multiple Active Result Sets

When Entity Framework runs a query against the database, it doesn't bring all the data back the first time you read data from the query. Each row of data is transferred from the database as it is needed. This means that as you iterate over the results of a query, the query is still active and data is being pulled back from the database as you iterate.

When lazy loading is being used, it's very common for lazy loading to occur while you are iterating the results of a query. For example, you may have queried for all Destina tions. You might then iterate over the results using a foreach loop. Inside the loop you might access the Lodgings property, which will be lazy loaded from the database. This means that the query to load Lodgings is executed while the main query to fetch all Destinations is still active.

Multiple Active Result Sets (MARS) is a SQL Server feature that allows more than one active query against the same connection. When Code First creates a connection by convention, which it has been in our examples, it will enable MARS. If you are supplying your own connection, you will need to ensure that MARS is enabled if you want to be able to have multiple active queries.

If you don't enable MARS and your code tries to run two active queries, you will receive an exception. The exception you receive will depend on the operation that triggers the second query, but the inner exception will be an InvalidOperationException stating "There is already an open DataReader associated with this Command which must be closed first."

Understanding the downsides of lazy loading

Lazy loading is very simple because your application doesn't really need to be aware that data is being loaded from the database. But that is also one of its dangers! Improper use of lazy loading can result in a lot of queries being sent to the database. For example, you might load fifty Destinations and then access the Lodgings property on each. That would result in 51 queries against the database—one query to get the Destinations and then for each of the fifty Destinations, to load that Destination's Lodgings. In cases like this it may be much more efficient to load all that data in a single query, using a SQL join in the database query. This is where eager loading comes into play.

 If you decide that lazy loading is just too much magic, you can choose to disable it altogether by using the DbContext.Configuration.LazyLoa dingEnabled property. If this switch is set to false, lazy loading will never occur, even if a navigation property is marked as virtual.

Eager Loading

Eager loading related data relies on you telling Entity Framework what related data to include when you query for an entity type. Entity Framework will then use a JOIN in the generated SQL to pull back all of the data in a single query. Let's assume we want to run though all Destinations and print out the Lodgings for each. Add a TestEager Loading method that queries for all Destinations and uses Include to also query for the associated Lodgings (Example 2-24).

Example 2-24. Using eager loading to load related data

```
private static void TestEagerLoading()
{
  using (var context = new BreakAwayContext())
  {
    var allDestinations = context
      .Destinations
      .Include(d => d.Lodgings);

    foreach (var destination in allDestinations)
    {
      Console.WriteLine(destination.Name);

      foreach (var lodging in destination.Lodgings)
      {
        Console.WriteLine(" - " + lodging.Name);
      }
    }
  }
}
```

The code uses the Include method to indicate that the query for all destinations should include the related Lodging data. Include uses a lambda expression to specify which properties to include the data for. When the application runs, we see a single query is executed against the database (Figure 2-2). This query uses a join to return the Desti nation and Lodging data as a single result set.

```
SELECT    [Project2].[LocationID] AS [LocationID],    [Project...
```

Figure 2-2. Eager loading returns all data in a single query

There is also a string-based overload of Include that just accepts the name of the property to include data for (Include("Lodgings") in our case). Previous versions of Entity Framework only included this string option. The string-based overload is problematic because it's not strongly typed and therefore there is no compile-time checking of the parameter. This can lead to issues with mistyped property names or failing to update the Include call if the property is renamed in the future.

 The lambda version of the Include method is defined as an extension method in System.Data.Entity. To use the lambda overload you will need to import this namespace.

It is possible to include more than one related set of data in a single query. Say we wanted to query for `Lodgings` and include the `PrimaryContact` plus the associated `Photo`. We do this by "dotting through" the navigation properties in the lambda expression:

```
context.Lodgings
    .Include(l => l.PrimaryContact.Photo)
```

The syntax gets a little more complicated if you have a collection navigation property in the middle of the path to be included. What if you want to query for `Destinations` and include `Lodgings` and also the `PrimaryContact` for each of the related `Lodging` instances? Following the collection, you need to use the LINQ `Select` method to identify which property you want to load:

```
context.Destinations
    .Include(d => d.Lodgings.Select(l => l.PrimaryContact))
```

`Include` can be used multiple times in the same query to identify different data to be loaded. For example, you may want to query the `Lodgings` set and include both `PrimaryContact` and `SecondaryContact`. This requires two separate calls to `Include`:

```
context.Lodgings
    .Include(l => l.PrimaryContact)
    .Include(l => l.SecondaryContact)
```

Eager loading is currently only able to include the entire contents of a navigation property. The ability to only include a subset of the contents of a collection navigation property is a common request, but it is not currently supported by the Entity Framework.

Understanding the downsides of eager loading

One thing to bear in mind with eager loading is that fewer queries aren't always better. The reduction in the number of queries comes at the expense of the simplicity of the queries being executed. As you include more and more data, the number of joins in the query that is sent to the database increases and results in a slower and more complex query. If you need a significant amount of related data, multiple simpler queries will often be significantly faster than one big query that returns all the data.

Using Include in LINQ queries

You can also use `Include` as part of a LINQ query by adding the `Include` method to the `DbSet` being queried. If you are using query syntax, the `Include` goes in the `from` part of the query:

```
var query = from d in context.Destinations.Include(d => d.Lodgings)
            where d.Country == "Australia"
            select d;
```

If you are using method syntax, you can simply put Include in line with the other method calls:

```
var query = context.Destinations
  .Include(d => d.Lodgings)
  .Where(d => d.Country == "Australia");
```

Include is defined as an extension method on IQueryable<T> and can therefore be added to a query at any point. It doesn't have to immediately follow the DbSet from which you are selecting. For example, you can call Include on an existing query for Australian Destinations to specify that Lodgings should also be included:

```
var query = from d in context.Destinations
            where d.Country == "Australia"
            select d;

query = query.Include(d => d.Lodgings);
```

Note that the code doesn't just call Include on the existing query but overrides the query variable with the result of the Include call. This is necessary because Include doesn't modify the query that it is called on, it returns a new query that will include the related data. Remember that Entity Framework doesn't execute any queries until the code uses the results of the query. The above code doesn't use the results of the query, so nothing will be executed against the database until some other code accesses the Destinations from the query variable.

 Although Include is defined as an extension method on IQueryable<T> it will only have an effect when used on a LINQ to Entities query. If another LINQ provider is being used, Include will have no effect unless the implementation of IQueryable<T> exposes an Include method that accepts a single string parameter. If this method exists, it will be called with a string representing the property path that was specified to be included.

Explicit Loading

Another loading option is *explicit loading*. Explicit loading is like lazy loading in that related data is loaded separately, after the main data has been loaded. However, unlike lazy loading, it doesn't automatically happen for you; you need to call a method to load the data.

There are a number of reasons you might opt for explicit loading over lazy loading:

- It removes the need to mark your navigation properties as virtual. To some this may seem like a trivial change, for others, the fact that a data access technology requires you to change your POCO classes is far from ideal.

- You may be working with an existing class library where the navigation properties are not marked as virtual and you simply can't change that.

- Explicit loading allows you to be sure that you know exactly when queries are sent to the database. Lazy loading has the potential to generate a lot of queries; with explicit loading it is very obvious when and where queries are being run.

Explicit loading is achieved using the DbContext.Entry method. The Entry method gives you access to all the information that the DbContext has about an entity. This goes beyond the values that are stored in the properties of the actual entity and includes things such as the state of the entity and the original values for each property when it was retrieved from the database. You'll see a lot more about this information in Chapters 4 and 5. In addition to information about the entity, the Entry method also gives you access to some operations you can perform on the entity, including loading data for navigation properties.

Once we have the entry for a given entity we can use the Collection and Reference methods to drill into the information and operations for navigation properties. One of the operations available is the Load method, which will send a query to the database to load the contents of the navigation property.

Let's take another look at loading the Lodgings available at the Grand Canyon. This time let's add a TestExplicitLoading method that uses the Entry method to load the data (Example 2-25).

Example 2-25. Loading related data with explicit load

```
private static void TestExplicitLoading()
{
  using (var context = new BreakAwayContext())
  {
    var query = from d in context.Destinations
                where d.Name == "Grand Canyon"
                select d;

    var canyon = query.Single();

    context.Entry(canyon)
      .Collection(d => d.Lodgings)
      .Load();

    Console.WriteLine("Grand Canyon Lodging:");
    foreach (var lodging in canyon.Lodgings)
    {
      Console.WriteLine(lodging.Name);
    }
  }
}
```

The first part of the code should be familiar—it uses a LINQ query to locate the Grand Canyon Destination. The code then calls the Entry method, passing in the canyon object. From there the Collection method is used to drill into the Lodgings navigation property. Collection and Reference use a lambda expression to specify the property to drill into. There are also string-based alternatives to these methods, but the lambda version ensures we get compile-time checking of the parameter. Finally, the `Load` method is used to query for the related data and bring it into memory.

If you update the `Main` method to call `TestExplicitLoading` and then run the application, you will see two queries run against the database (Figure 2-3). The first one runs when the code requests the single result of the query for the Grand Canyon, by calling `Sin gle` on query. The second query is asking for all `Lodging` at the Grand Canyon and runs as a result of the call to `Load`.

```
SELECT TOP (2)    [Extent1].[LocationID] AS [LocationID],   [Extent1].[Loca...
exec sp_executesql N'SELECT   [Extent1].[LodgingId] AS [LodgingId],   CASE...
```

Figure 2-3. Explicit loading runs separate queries for related data

You've seen that explicit loading can be used to load the entire contents of a collection navigation property but it can also be used to load just some of the contents, based on a LINQ query. You'll see this in "Explicit Loading a Subset of the Contents of a Navigation Property" on page 41.

Explicit loading of a reference navigation property looks very similar, except you use the `Reference` method rather than `Collection`. For example, if you wanted to load the `PrimaryContact` of some lodging, you could write this:

```
var lodging = context.Lodgings.First();

context.Entry(lodging)
  .Reference(l => l.PrimaryContact)
  .Load();
```

Checking If a Navigation Property Has Been Loaded

The `Reference` and `Collection` methods also give you access to the `IsLoaded` property. The `IsLoaded` method will tell you whether the entire contents of the navigation property have been loaded from the database or not. The `IsLoaded` property will be set to true when lazy, eager, or explicit loading is used to load the contents of the navigation property. Add the `TestIsLoaded` method shown in Example 2-26.

Example 2-26. Testing if a navigation property has been loaded with IsLoaded

```
private static void TestIsLoaded()
{
  using (var context = new BreakAwayContext())
  {
    var canyon = (from d in context.Destinations
                  where d.Name == "Grand Canyon"
                  select d).Single();

    var entry = context.Entry(canyon);
```

```
Console.WriteLine(
  "Before Load: {0}",
  entry.Collection(d => d.Lodgings).IsLoaded);

entry.Collection(d => d.Lodgings).Load();

Console.WriteLine(
  "After Load: {0}",
  entry.Collection(d => d.Lodgings).IsLoaded);
  }
}
```

The code uses a LINQ query to load the Grand Canyon `Destination` from the database. The value assigned to the `IsLoaded` property for the `Lodgings` property is then printed out to the console. Explicit loading is used to load the contents of the `Lodgings` property and the value of `IsLoaded` is printed to the console again. If you update the `Main` method to call `TestIsLoaded` and then run the application, you will see that the value of `IsLoaded` is set to true after the explicit load is performed:

```
Before Load: False
After Load: True
```

If you are performing an explicit load, and the contents of the navigation property may have already been loaded, you can use the `IsLoaded` flag to determine if the load is required or not.

Querying Contents of a Collection Navigation Property

So far you've looked at loading the entire contents of a collection navigation property so that you can work with the data in memory. If you wanted to filter the contents of a navigation property you could do this after you'd brought everything into memory, using LINQ to Objects. However, if you are only interested in a subset of the contents, it may make sense to just bring the bits you are interested in into memory. Or if you just want a count, or some other calculation, it may make sense just to calculate the result in the database and not bring any of the data into memory.

Once you've used `Entry` and `Collection` to drill into a collection navigation property, you can then use the `Query` method to get a LINQ query representing the contents of that property. Because it's a LINQ query, you can then do further filtering, sorting, aggregation, and the like.

Assume you wanted to find all `Lodgings` at the Grand Canyon that are less than ten miles from the nearest airport. You could just use LINQ to query the contents of the `Lodgings` property of the Grand Canyon, something like Example 2-27.

Example 2-27. In-memory query of a navigation property

```
private static void QueryLodgingDistance()
{
  using (var context = new BreakAwayContext())
```

```
  {
    var canyonQuery = from d in context.Destinations
                      where d.Name == "Grand Canyon"
                      select d;

    var canyon = canyonQuery.Single();

    var distanceQuery = from l in canyon.Lodgings
                        where l.MilesFromNearestAirport <= 10
                        select l;

    foreach (var lodging in distanceQuery)
    {
      Console.WriteLine(lodging.Name);
    }
  }
}
```

The problem with this code is that `distanceQuery` is using LINQ to Objects to query the contents of the `Lodgings` navigation property. This will cause the property to be lazy loaded, pulling the entire contents into memory. The code then immediately filters out some of the data, meaning there was no need to pull it into memory. Let's rewrite the `QueryLodgingDistance` method from Example 2-27 to use `Query`, as shown in Example 2-28.

Example 2-28. Database query of a navigation property

```
private static void QueryLodgingDistance()
{
  using (var context = new BreakAwayContext())
  {
    var canyonQuery = from d in context.Destinations
                      where d.Name == "Grand Canyon"
                      select d;

    var canyon = canyonQuery.Single();

    var lodgingQuery = context.Entry(canyon)
      .Collection(d => d.Lodgings)
      .Query();

    var distanceQuery = from l in lodgingQuery
                        where l.MilesFromNearestAirport <= 10
                        select l;

    foreach (var lodging in distanceQuery)
    {
      Console.WriteLine(lodging.Name);
    }
  }
}
```

This updated code uses the `Query` method to create a LINQ to Entities query for the `Lodgings` associated with the Grand Canyon. It then composes on that query to ask for just the `Lodgings` that are within ten miles of an airport. When iterating over this query, Entity Framework takes care of the translation to SQL and performs the filter on `Mile sFromNearestAirport` in the database. This means that only the data you care about is brought back into memory.

Perhaps you want to know how many `Lodgings` are available at the Grand Canyon. You could load all the `Lodgings` and get a count, but why bring all that data into memory just to get a single integer result? Add a `QueryLodgingCount` method that uses `Query` to get the count without loading the data (Example 2-29).

Example 2-29. Using Query to get a count of Lodgings

```
private static void QueryLodgingCount()
{
  using (var context = new BreakAwayContext())
  {
    var canyonQuery = from d in context.Destinations
                where d.Name == "Grand Canyon"
                select d;

    var canyon = canyonQuery.Single();

    var lodgingQuery = context.Entry(canyon)
      .Collection(d => d.Lodgings)
      .Query();

    var lodgingCount = lodgingQuery.Count();

    Console.WriteLine("Lodging at Grand Canyon: " + lodgingCount);
  }
}
```

The code loads the Grand Canyon destination and then uses `Entry` and `Collection` to drill into the `Lodgings` navigation property. From there it uses the `Query` method to get a query representing the contents of the navigation property. It then uses the LINQ `Count` method to materialize just the count of the results of the query. Because it is using the LINQ to Entities provider, it recognizes that you want the count and pushes the entire query to the database so that only the single integer result is returned from the database. If you update the `Main` method to call `QueryLodgingCount` and run the application you will see the count correctly displayed:

```
Lodging at Grand Canyon: 2
```

Explicit Loading a Subset of the Contents of a Navigation Property

You can combine the `Query` and `Load` methods to perform a *filtered explicit load*. That's an explicit load that only loads a subset of the contents of a navigation property. For example, you may want to just load the `Lodgings` at the Grand Canyon that contain the word "Hotel" in their `Name`:

```
context.Entry(canyon)
  .Collection(d => d.Lodgings)
  .Query()
  .Where(l => l.Name.Contains("Hotel"))
  .Load();
```

It's important to remember that calling Load will not clear any objects that are already in the navigation property. So if you loaded Lodgings at the Grand Canyon that contain the word "Hotel" and then also loaded Lodgings that contain the word "Campsite", the Lodgings navigation property will contain both hotels and campsites.

CHAPTER 3

Adding, Changing, and Deleting Entities

In the previous chapter you saw how to get data from the database into memory. But this is only half the story. Most applications also need to make changes to that data and then push those changes back into the database. In this chapter we will take a look at how Entity Framework can be used to make changes to data. These changes fall into three main categories: adding new data, changing existing data and deleting existing data.

While looking at querying, we saw the main benefit of using an Object Relational Mapper (ORM), like Entity Framework, is that application code is written in terms of your object model. As you write your application, you don't need to be looking at the shape of your tables and columns. Nor do you need to know how to write INSERT, UPDATE, and DELETE statements for your database. Entity Framework will take care of translating the operations you perform on your objects into SQL statements that will push these changes into the database.

As you perform operations on your object instances, Entity Framework uses its *change tracker* to keep track of what you have done. When you're ready to commit the changes to the database, you call the SaveChanges method. SaveChanges will invoke the *update pipeline*, which is responsible for translating the changes to your object instances into SQL statements that are executed against your database. If you've developed applications using Entity Framework's ObjectContext, you should be familiar with this process.

Because Entity Framework is aware of the relationships between your entities, if you are saving related objects, it will take care of ordering the SQL statements to ensure changes are applied in the correct order. For example, you may be deleting an existing Destination and also moving the Lodgings associated with that Destination to a different Destination. Entity Framework will determine that the Lodging records must be updated before the Destination record is deleted, regardless of the order that you performed these operations in memory.

Entity Framework allows you to make changes that affect single objects, a relationship between two objects, or an entire graph of objects. In this chapter we are going to take a look at changes affecting a single object and relationships between objects. In the next chapter we'll take a look at some advanced scenarios where operations can affect a whole graph of objects.

Working with Single Entities

There are three types of changes that can affect a single entity—adding a new entity, changing the property values of an existing entity, or deleting an existing entity. In this section you'll learn how to make each of these changes using Entity Framework.

Adding New Entities

Adding a new object with Entity Framework is as simple as constructing a new instance of your object and registering it using the Add method on DbSet. Let's say you wanted to add a Machu Picchu destination to the database. The AddMachuPicchu method shown in Example 3-1 demonstrates this.

Example 3-1. Adding a new Destination

```
private static void AddMachuPicchu()
{
  using (var context = new BreakAwayContext())
  {
    var machuPicchu = new Destination
    {
      Name = "Machu Picchu",
      Country = "Peru"
    };

    context.Destinations.Add(machuPicchu);
    context.SaveChanges();
  }
}
```

The code constructs a new Destination for Machu Picchu and then calls Add on the Destinations set you defined in the BreakAwayContext. Finally, the code calls Save Changes, which will take the changes and save them to the database. We see that a single INSERT statement is executed against our database:

```
exec sp_executesql N'
insert [baga].[Locations]
    ([LocationName], [Country], [Description], [Photo])
    values (@0, @1, null, null)

select [LocationID]
    from [baga].[Locations]
    where @@ROWCOUNT > 0 and [LocationID] = scope_identity()',
```

```
N'@0 nvarchar(max) ,@1 nvarchar(max) ',
@0=N'Machu Picchu',@1=N'Peru'
```

Notice that Entity Framework is using the mapping we supplied as it translates the object changes into SQL. For example, we mapped the `Destination` class in our domain model to the `baga.Locations` table in the database. Entity Framework uses this information to construct an `INSERT` statement that targets the `Locations` table. The key of `Destination` is an identity column, meaning the value is generated by the database when the record is inserted. Because of this, Entity Framework includes some additional SQL to fetch this newly created value after the `INSERT` statement has executed. Entity Framework will then take the returned value and assign it to the `DestinationId` property of the object that was added.

 In this example we used the default constructor of our POCO class to create the new instance to be inserted. A little later in this chapter you'll learn about change tracking proxies and how to create new instances of proxies to insert.

Changing Existing Entities

Changing existing objects is as simple as updating the value assigned to the property(s) you want changed and calling `SaveChanges`. Perhaps we want to change the Grand Canyon `Destination` and assign a `Description` to it so that BAGA customers know just how grand it is. Add the `ChangeGrandCanyon` method shown in Example 3-2.

Example 3-2. Changing an existing Destination

```
private static void ChangeGrandCanyon()
{
  using (var context = new BreakAwayContext())
  {
    var canyon = (from d in context.Destinations
                  where d.Name == "Grand Canyon"
                  select d).Single();

    canyon.Description = "227 mile long canyon.";

    context.SaveChanges();
  }
}
```

This code uses a LINQ query to load the Grand Canyon `Destination` into memory. It then assigns the new value to the `Description` property of the loaded `Destination`. With the changes completed it calls `SaveChanges`, which issues an `UPDATE` statement to the database:

```
exec sp_executesql N'
update [baga].[Locations]
    set [Description] = @0
    where ([LocationID] = @1)
```

```
',N'@0 nvarchar(500),@1 int',
@0=N'227 mile long canyon.',@1=1
```

Again we see Entity Framework using the mapping to construct the appropriate SQL statement. This time it's an UPDATE statement against the baga.Locations table. Entity Framework uses the key of the entity to identify the record to be updated. In our case, that's DestinationId, which is mapped to the LocationId column. This results in a WHERE clause that filters based on the LocationId column with the value from the Des tinationId property in the object being updated.

Deleting Existing Entities

To delete an entity using Entity Framework, you use the Remove method on DbSet. Remove works for both existing and newly added entities. Calling Remove on an entity that has been added but not yet saved to the database will cancel the addition of the entity. The entity is removed from the change tracker and is no longer tracked by the DbContext. Calling Remove on an existing entity that is being change-tracked will register the entity for deletion the next time SaveChanges is called.

 You may be wondering why the Entity Framework team chose to call the method Remove rather than Delete, and for that matter, why they chose Add instead of Insert. The names were chosen for consistency with other collections and sets in the .NET Framework. Other collections all use the Add/Remove pair of methods to bring elements into and out of the collection.

Let's add a DeleteWineGlassBay method that will delete the Wine Glass Bay Destina tion from our database (Example 3-3).

Example 3-3. Deleting an existing Destination

```
private static void DeleteWineGlassBay()
{
  using (var context = new BreakAwayContext())
  {
    var bay = (from d in context.Destinations
               where d.Name == "Wine Glass Bay"
               select d).Single();

    context.Destinations.Remove(bay);
    context.SaveChanges();
  }
}
```

The code uses a LINQ query to load the Wine Glass Bay Destination from the database. It then calls Remove on the Destinations set you have defined on the BreakAwayCon text. Now that Wine Glass Bay is registered for deletion (at least from our database), we call SaveChanges and a DELETE statement is run against our database:

```
exec sp_executesql N'
delete [baga].[Locations]
    where ([LocationID] = @0)',
N'@0 int',
@0=3
```

This is a very simple DELETE statement that uses the key value from the Wine Glass Bay object to build a WHERE clause that identifies the object we are deleting.

DbSet.Remove Versus Remove on a Collection Navigation Property

While calling Remove on a DbSet will mark an entity for deletion, calling Remove on a collection navigation property will not. Removing an entity from a collection navigation property will mark the relationship between the two entities as deleted but not the entities themselves. More information is provided in "Removing a Relationship Between Objects" on page 57.

Deleting without loading from the database

DbSet.Remove follows the same rule that we've always had to contend with for having Entity Framework deleting objects. The object must be tracked by the change tracker and marked as Deleted in order for SaveChanges to construct a DELETE command to send to the database.

If you know you need to delete an entity, but it's not already in memory, it's a little inefficient to retrieve that entity from the database just to delete it. If you know the key of the entity you want to delete, you can attach a *stub* that represents the entity to be deleted, and then delete this stub. A stub is an instance of an entity that just has the key value assigned. The key value is all that's required for deleting entities.

When attaching a stub you use the DbSet.Attach method to let Entity Framework know that it's an existing entity. Once an entity is attached, it behaves just like an entity that was retrieved from the database. So calling DbSet.Remove will cause a DELETE statement to be sent to the database during SaveChanges. For example, the following code would delete the Destination with an ID of 2, without loading it from the database:

```
var toDelete = new Destination { DestinationId = 2 };
context.Destinations.Attach(toDelete);
context.Destinations.Remove(toDelete);
context.SaveChanges();
```

If an entity has been loaded into memory, you won't be able to attach a stub for the entity. Doing so would cause two existing entities with the same key value to be tracked by the context. If you try and do this you will get an InvalidOperationException stating "An object with the same key already exists in the ObjectStateManager."

Another way to delete entities without loading them is to use DbContext.Database.Exe cuteSqlCommand to execute some raw SQL to perform the deletion in the database. For example, the following code would delete the Hawaii Destination without loading it from the database:

```
context.Database.ExecuteSqlCommand(
    "DELETE FROM baga.Locations WHERE LocationName = 'Hawaii'");
```

Because we are using raw SQL, we are bypassing any mapping that is done using Entity Framework. In the above code we needed to remember that the `Destination` class is mapped to the `baga.Locations` table and that the `Name` property is mapped to the `LocationName` column.

Deleting an object with related data

If you are deleting objects that have related data, you may need to update related data for the delete to succeed. The required updates to related data will depend on whether the relationship is optional or required. Optional relationships mean that the child entity can exist in the database without a parent assigned. For example, a `Reservation` can exist in the database without a `Trip` assigned. Required relationships mean the child entity cannot exist without a parent assigned. For example, a `Lodging` cannot exist in the database without being assigned to a `Destination`.

If you delete an entity that is the parent of an optional relationship, the relationship between the parent and any child entities can be deleted, too. This means the child entities will be updated so that they are no longer assigned to a parent—the foreign key column in the database will be set to null. Entity Framework will automatically delete the relationship for you if the child entity has been loaded into memory from the database.

Let's start by seeing what happens if we delete a parent entity of an optional relationship when the child entity isn't loaded into memory. There is an optional relationship between a `Reservation` and a `Trip`: `Trip` is the parent and `Reservation` is the child. Add a method that tries to delete a `Trip` without its child `Reservation` loaded into memory (Example 3-4).

Example 3-4. Deleting a Trip without its child Reservation loaded

```
private static void DeleteTrip()
{
  using (var context = new BreakAwayContext())
  {
    var trip = (from t in context.Trips
                where t.Description == "Trip from the database"
                select t).Single();

    context.Trips.Remove(trip);
    context.SaveChanges();
  }
}
```

If you update the Main method to call DeleteTrip and run the application, you will get a DbUpdateException informing you that there was an error while saving. If you drill into the InnerException properties, you will see that the innermost exception is a SqlEx ception stating that "The DELETE statement conflicted with the REFERENCE con straint 'FK_Reservations_Trips_Trip_Identifier'." You get this exception because there is still a Reservation in the database that has a foreign key pointing to the Trip you are trying to delete. Let's update the DeleteTrip method so that the Reservation that ref erences the Trip we are deleting is loaded into memory (Example 3-5).

Example 3-5. Deleting a Trip with its child Reservation loaded

```
private static void DeleteTrip()
{
  using (var context = new BreakAwayContext())
  {
    var trip = (from t in context.Trips
                where t.Description == "Trip from the database"
                select t).Single();

    var res = (from r in context.Reservations
                where r.Trip.Description == "Trip from the database"
                select r).Single();

    context.Trips.Remove(trip);
    context.SaveChanges();
  }
}
```

The updated code uses a second LINQ query to load the single Reservation that is assigned to the Trip that is being deleted. If you run the application again, it will succeed and two SQL statements are sent to the database (Figure 3-1).

```
exec sp_executesql N'update [dbo].[Reservations]  ...
exec sp_executesql N'delete [dbo].[Trips]  where (...
```

Figure 3-1. Deleting parent entity and optional relationship to child entity

The update statement sets the foreign key column of the Reservation to null, so that it is no longer related to the Trip that is being deleted. The delete statement then deletes the Trip from the database.

Required relationships are a bit different because the foreign key column in the database can't be set to null. If you delete a parent entity, each child must either be deleted or updated to belong to a different parent entity. You can either do this manually or have the child entities automatically deleted, using a cascade delete. Failure to delete or reassign child records when you delete a parent will result in a referential integrity constraint violation when you attempt to SaveChanges.

In our model there is a cascade delete defined between Lodging and Destination. If we delete a Destination, the Lodging instances that are assigned to it will get automatically deleted. In our database there is a Grand Canyon `Destination`, which has two related `Lodgings`. Add the `DeleteGrandCanyon` method shown in Example 3-6.

Example 3-6. Deleting the Grand Canyon with related Lodgings

```
private static void DeleteGrandCanyon()
{
  using (var context = new BreakAwayContext())
  {
    var canyon = (from d in context.Destinations
                  where d.Name == "Grand Canyon"
                  select d).Single();

    context.Entry(canyon)
      .Collection(d => d.Lodgings)
      .Load();

    context.Destinations.Remove(canyon);
    context.SaveChanges();
  }
}
```

The code loads the Grand Canyon `Destination` from the database and then uses eager loading to ensure the related `Lodgings` are also loaded into memory. The code then marks the Grand Canyon for deletion and pushes the changes to the database. If you update the `Main` method to call `DeleteGrandCanyon` and run the application, three SQL commands get sent to the database (Figure 3-2).

```
exec sp_executesql N'delete [dbo].[Lodgings]  ...
exec sp_executesql N'delete [dbo].[Lodgings]  ...
exec sp_executesql N'delete [baga].[Locations]...
```

Figure 3-2. Deleting the parent of a required relationship with cascade delete

Because the related `Lodgings` were loaded into memory, and we had a cascade delete rule configured, Entity Framework has automatically deleted the related `Lodgings`. The first two `delete` statements are deleting the related `Lodgings` and the final `delete` statement deletes the Grand Canyon `Destination`.

Cascade delete is also configured in the database, so we don't need to load the related data for it to be automatically deleted. Modify the `DeleteGrandCanyon` method so that it no longer loads the related `Lodgings` into memory (Example 3-7).

Example 3-7. Deleting Grand Canyon without Lodgings loaded

```
private static void DeleteGrandCanyon()
{
  using (var context = new BreakAwayContext())
  {
    var canyon = (from d in context.Destinations
                  where d.Name == "Grand Canyon"
```

```
            select d).Single();

    context.Destinations.Remove(canyon);
    context.SaveChanges();
  }
}
```

If you run the application again, a single `delete` command is sent to the database, to delete the Grand Canyon `Destination`. Because there is a cascade delete configured on the foreign key constraint between `Lodging` and `Destination`, the database has taken care of deleting the related data. Cascade delete is covered in detail in *Programming Entity Framework, 2e.*

If we didn't have a cascade delete defined, we would need to manually mark each of the related `Lodging` entities as deleted before attempting to save. To mark each of the related `Lodgings` as deleted, you would need to iterate through the `Lodgings` property and call `DbSet.Remove` on each `Lodging`. Because Entity Framework is going to update the `Lodgings` property to remove each `Lodging` as it is marked for deletion, you need to use `ToList` to create a copy of the `Lodgings`. Failure to create a copy will result in the contents of `Lodgings` changing as it is iterated, which is not supported by the .NET Framework:

```
foreach (var lodging in canyon.Lodgings.ToList())
{
    context.Lodgings.Remove(lodging);
}
```

An alternative to deleting the child entities is to assign them to a new parent. For example, we could move the `Lodgings` from Grand Canyon to Hawaii before deleting the Grand Canyon:

```
foreach (var lodging in canyon.Lodgings.ToList())
{
    lodging.Destination = hawaii;
}
```

You'll learn more about changing relationships in "Changing a Relationship Between Objects" on page 56.

Multiple Changes at Once

So far we have looked at making a single change followed by a call to `SaveChanges` to push that change to the database. Your application may want to intersperse many queries and changes and then push all the changes to the database at once. Let's add a `MakeMultipleChanges` method that does just this (Example 3-8).

Example 3-8. Multiple changes in one transaction

```
private static void MakeMultipleChanges()
{
  using (var context = new BreakAwayContext())
```

```
{
  var niagaraFalls = new Destination
  {
    Name = "Niagara Falls",
    Country = "USA"
  };

  context.Destinations.Add(niagaraFalls);

  var wineGlassBay = (from d in context.Destinations
              where d.Name == "Wine Glass Bay"
              select d).Single();

  wineGlassBay.Description = "Picturesque bay with beaches.";

  context.SaveChanges();
  }
}
```

The code creates a new Destination for Niagara Falls and adds it to the Destinations set. It then retrieves the Wine Glass Bay Destination and changes its description. Once these changes are made, SaveChanges is called to push the changes to the database. If you update the Main method to call MakeMultipleChanges and run the application you will see three statements are run against the database (Figure 3-3).

```
SELECT TOP (2)   [Extent1].[LocationID] AS [Lo...
exec sp_executesql N'update [baga].[Locations]...
exec sp_executesql N'insert [baga].[Locations]...
```

Figure 3-3. Multiple changes from one call to SaveChanges

The first is a SELECT statement to fetch the Wine Glass Bay Destination. The next two statements are an UPDATE and an INSERT that are run when we call SaveChanges.

> SaveChanges is transactional, meaning that it either pushes all the changes to the database or none of them. If one change fails, any changes that have already been made are rolled back and the database is left in the state it was in before SaveChanges was called. You can learn more about how Entity Framework uses transactions by default and how to override that default behavior in Chapter 20 of *Programming Entity Framework, 2e.*

The "Find or Add" Pattern

You may have noticed that DbSet.Add returns an object. It returns the same object that you pass into the method. This may seem a little strange at first, but it enables a nice coding pattern that you may find convenient to use in your applications. Your application might allow a user to search for a Person based on his or her SocialSecurityNumber. If the Person is found, your code can use the existing entity. But if the Person isn't located, you want to create a new Person with the supplied SocialSecurityNumber. The FindOrAddPerson method shown in Example 3-9 demonstrates this pattern.

Example 3-9. Adding a new Person if existing record doesn't exist

```
private static void FindOrAddPerson()
{
  using (var context = new BreakAwayContext())
  {
    var ssn = 123456789;

    var person = context.People.Find(ssn)
      ?? context.People.Add(new Person
      {
        SocialSecurityNumber = ssn,
        FirstName = "<enter first name>",
        LastName = "<enter last name>"
      });

    Console.WriteLine(person.FirstName);
  }
}
```

Remember that DbSet.Find is an easy way to locate entities based on their key values. If it finds the entity either in memory or in the database, it will return the correct instance. But if it can't locate the entity, Find will return null. You can combine Find with the ?? operator that allows you to provide an alternate value to return if some code returns null. In the example above, we attempt to locate the entity by using Find based on its key. If Find doesn't locate the entity, we add a new Person to the context instead.

The ?? operator is specific to C#; however, the same logic can be written in VB.NET using the If method:

```
Dim person = If(context.People.Find(ssn), context.People.Add(
  New Person() With {
    .SocialSecurityNumber = ssn,
    .FirstName = "<enter first name>",
    .LastName = "<enter last name>"
    }
))
```

Working with Relationships

Now that you know how to add, change, and delete entities, it's time to look at how we change relationships between those entities. Your domain model exposes relationships using navigation properties and, optionally, a foreign key property. Changing a relationship is achieved by changing the values assigned to those properties.

Given that a relationship can be represented by up to three properties (two navigation properties and a foreign key property), you may be wondering if you need to update all three just to change the relationship. Updating just one of these properties is enough to let Entity Framework know about the change. It is also fine to update more than one of the properties if you want to, provided that the changes represent the same change. When you call SaveChanges, Entity Framework will take care of updating the rest of these properties for you; this is known as *relationship fix-up*. Rather than waiting for SaveChanges to fix up the properties, you can trigger this fix-up on demand by calling DetectChanges or have it happen in real-time by using change tracking proxies. Both of these concepts are described later in this chapter.

While the basics of changing relationships are quite simple, there are a lot of intricate details to be familiar with as you get into more advanced relationship scenarios. These intricacies are not specific to the DbContext API and are well beyond the scope of this book.

 You can find a detailed look at relationships in Chapter 19 of Programming Entity Framework, 2e (*http://shop.oreilly.com/product/9780596807252.do*).

Adding a Relationship Between Objects

To add a new relationship, you need to assign one of the objects in the relationship to the navigation property of the other object. If the navigation property you want to change is a reference (for example, the Destination property of the Resort class), you set the value to the related object. If the navigation property is a collection (for example, the Payments property of the Reservation class), you use the Add method to add it to that collection. Remember that the change can be made at one or both ends of the relationship.

Let's assume you want to add a Lodging record for a new luxury resort that is opening, and you want to associate it with the Grand Canyon. To follow along, add the New GrandCanyonResort method shown in Example 3-10.

Example 3-10. Adding a new relationship

```
private static void NewGrandCanyonResort()
{
  using (var context = new BreakAwayContext())
  {
    var resort = new Resort
    {
      Name = "Pete's Luxury Resort"
    };

    context.Lodgings.Add(resort);
```

```
    var canyon = (from d in context.Destinations
                  where d.Name == "Grand Canyon"
                  select d).Single();

    canyon.Lodgings.Add(resort);

    context.SaveChanges();
  }
}
```

This code creates the new **Resort** and adds it to the **Lodgings** set we defined on **BreakA
wayContext** (remember that **Resort** derives from **Lodging**). Next, the code locates the
Grand Canyon **Destination** that we want to add this new **Resort** to. Then the new
Resort is added to the **Lodgings** collection of the Grand Canyon. This lets Entity Framework know that the two objects are related. **SaveChanges** is then used to push these
changes to the database.

 In Example 3-10, we added the new **Resort** to the **Lodgings** set and then
added it to the **canyon.Lodgings** collection. The example is intentionally
redundant for clarity as you learn about the behaviors. The first call
ensures that the context knows that **resort** is new and needs to be inserted into the database. The second call then specifies that **resort** must
also be related to **canyon**. While this makes it obvious that **resort** is a
new entity, adding it twice is not strictly necessary in this particular
example. If you had skipped adding the new **resort** to the context and
only added it to **canyon**, Entity Framework would have found **resort**
because it is now referenced from the navigation property of an entity
that is tracked by the context (**canyon**). Entity Framework would have
recognized that **resort** was not being tracked and in response would
have assumed the **resort** needed to be in the **Added** state. Therefore we
could have left out the line of code that added **resort** to **context.Lodg
ings** and achieved the same result.

In the code we updated the collection end of a one-to-many relationship. But remember
we can update either end of the relationship. Rather than adding the new **Resort** to the
Destination.Lodgings collection, we could have set the **Lodging.Destination** property
to the desired **Destination** instance:

```
    resort.Destination = canyon;
```

Lodging also exposes a foreign key property, **DestinationId**, to represent the relationship. We could also have updated that instead:

```
    resort.DestinationId = canyon.DestinationId;
```

If you are adding an object to a collection navigation property, you need to make sure
that the collection property will be initialized. Remember that, by default, properties
will be assigned a value of **null**. In our case we enabled lazy loading on the **Lodgings**
property, so Entity Framework took care of creating a collection and assigning it to the

Lodgings property. If you aren't using lazy loading, you will need to include logic in either your classes or the consuming code to initialize the collection.

Changing a Relationship Between Objects

Changing a relationship is actually the same as adding a new relationship. When we add a relationship, we are changing it from "unassigned" to point to an entity. Changing a relationship to point from one entity to another uses exactly the same process. To change a relationship, we locate the entity to be changed and update the navigation property, or foreign key property.

Perhaps we made a mistake while entering some data and the Grand Hotel actually exists at the Great Barrier Reef rather than the Grand Canyon. The ChangeLodgingDes tination method shown in Example 3-11 demonstrates assigning a new relationship that will replace an existing relationship.

Example 3-11. Updating an existing relationship

```
private static void ChangeLodgingDestination()
{
  using (var context = new BreakAwayContext())
  {
    var hotel = (from l in context.Lodgings
                    where l.Name == "Grand Hotel"
                    select l).Single();

    var reef = (from d in context.Destinations
                    where d.Name == "Great Barrier Reef"
                    select d).Single();

    hotel.Destination = reef;

    context.SaveChanges();
  }
}
```

The code locates both the Grand Hotel and the Great Barrier Reef by using LINQ queries. Next it updates the relationship by changing the Destination property of the Grand Hotel to point to the Great Barrier Reef. There is no need to remove the existing relationship between the Grand Hotel and the Grand Canyon. Entity Framework knows that we want the relationship to be updated, which implies it will no longer point to the old value. Running the code will result in a single update statement being sent to the database:

```
exec sp_executesql N'update [dbo].[Lodgings]
set [destination_id] = @0
where ([LodgingId] = @1)
',N'@0 int,@1 int',@0=4,@1=1
```

The update statement looks very similar to the one you saw earlier in this chapter, when we modified a String property of an entity. Entity Framework uses the Locations key value to locate the record to be updated. This time, instead of updating a simple column, it is updating the foreign key column to point to the primary key of the Destination we updated our Location to.

By now you've probably worked out that we could also make the change by adding hotel to the Lodgings property of reef:

```
reef.Lodgings.Add(hotel);
```

We could also make the change by setting the foreign key property:

```
hotel.DestinationId = reef.DestinationId;
```

Removing a Relationship Between Objects

Let's say that Dave is no longer the primary contact for Dave's Dump. In fact, the service is so bad at this lodging that they no longer have a contact at all. This means we simply want to remove the relationship rather than changing it to a new Person.

To remove a relationship, you can remove the target object from a collection navigation property. Alternatively, you can set a reference navigation property to null. If your classes expose a nullable foreign key property for the relationship, a third option is to set the foreign key to null.

 Removing relationships by changing the foreign key is only possible with nullable properties (for example, the PrimaryContactId property of the Lodging class). If your foreign key is an int (for example, the Destina tionId property of the Lodging class), you won't be able to set the value to null and by convention, that relationship would be required. Setting the value to 0 would cause a primary key/foreign key constraint error in the database, as there will be no parent whose primary key is equal to 0.

Add the RemovePrimaryContact method shown in Example 3-12.

Example 3-12. Removing a primary contact for Dave's Dump

```
private static void RemovePrimaryContact()
{
  using (var context = new BreakAwayContext())
  {
    var davesDump = (from l in context.Lodgings
                     where l.Name == "Dave's Dump"
                     select l).Single();

    context.Entry(davesDump)
      .Reference(l => l.PrimaryContact)
      .Load();

    davesDump.PrimaryContact = null;

    context.SaveChanges();
```

```
    }
}
```

The code starts by fetching Dave's Dump from the database with a LINQ query. Next it loads the related `PrimaryContact`. We need to do this so that something is actually changing when we set the value to `null`. Because lazy loading isn't enabled for this property it is already null by default so the code explicitly loads the `PrimaryContact`. Eager loading or enabling lazy loading would achieve exactly the same thing. Once the contact is loaded, the `PrimaryContact` property is set to `null` to let Entity Framework know that we want to delete this relationship. Dave will not be deleted from the database, nor will Dave's Dump, but they will no longer be related to each other. `Save Changes` will update the database to null out the foreign key for the primary contact of Dave's Dump.

This highlights one of the advantages of exposing foreign key properties in your classes. Because we expose a foreign key property for the PrimaryContact relationship, and that property used a nullable integer (`Nullable<int>` or `int?`), then we can set that property to `null` without the need to load the related data. This works because foreign key properties are always populated when you query for an entity, whereas navigation properties are only populated when you load the related data. Let's rewrite the `RemovePrimaryContact` method to modify the foreign key property rather than the navigation property (Example 3-13).

Example 3-13. Removing a primary contact for Dave's Dump using the foreign key

```
private static void RemovePrimaryContact()
{
  using (var context = new BreakAwayContext())
  {
    var davesDump = (from l in context.Lodgings
                     where l.Name == "Dave's Dump"
                     select l).Single();

    davesDump.PrimaryContactId = null;

    context.SaveChanges();
  }
}
```

In this example, we were removing an optional relationship; according to the model we built, it is fine for `Lodging` to exist without a `PrimaryContact`. If we tried to remove a required relationship the outcome would be a little different. Let's say we had tried to remove the relationship between Dave's Dump and the Grand Canyon. According to the BAGA model, `Lodging` can't exist without a `Destination`. Entity Framework would allow us to set the `Lodging.Destination` property to null, but it would throw an exception when we tried to `SaveChanges`. We are allowed to set the property to null provided we set it to another valid `Destination` before we try and `SaveChanges`.

Given that Dave is no longer a contact, we may want to remove him from the database, rather than just removing his relationship as a primary contact for Dave's Dump. If you delete an entity there is no need to delete all the relationships that they participate in: Entity Framework will automatically delete them for you. As discussed in "Deleting Existing Entities" on page 46, if any of the relationships are required you will need to delete or reassign any child entities before saving.

Working with Change Tracking

Throughout this chapter you have seen that Entity Framework keeps track of the changes you make to your objects. Entity Framework uses its *change tracker* to do this. You can access the change tracker information, and some change tracking–related operations, through the DbContext.ChangeTracker property. You'll see more about the Change Tracker API in Chapter 5.

There are two different ways that Entity Framework can track the changes to your objects: *snapshot change tracking* or *change tracking proxies*.

Snapshot change tracking
> The code written so far in this chapter has relied on snapshot change tracking. The classes in our model are all POCO and they don't contain any logic to notify Entity Framework when a property value is changed. Because there is no way to be notified when a property value changes, Entity Framework will take a snapshot of the values in each property when it first sees an object and store the values in memory. This snapshot occurs when the object is returned from a query or when we add it to a DbSet. When Entity Framework needs to know what changes have been made, it will scan each object and compare its current values to the snapshot. This process of scanning each object is triggered through a method of ChangeTracker called DetectChanges.

Change tracking proxies
> The other mechanism for tracking changes is through change tracking proxies, which allow Entity Framework to be notified of changes as they are made. In Chapter 2, you learned about dynamic proxies that are created for lazy loading. Change tracking proxies are created using the same mechanism, but in addition to providing for lazy loading, they also have the ability to communicate changes to the context.

> To use change tracking proxies, you need to structure your classes in such a way that Entity Framework can create a dynamic type at runtime that derives from our POCO class and override every property. This dynamic type, known as a dynamic proxy, includes logic in the overridden properties to notify Entity Framework when those properties are changed. In fact, all of the rules for creating dynamic change tracking proxies from POCOs that you learned about if you read Programming Entity Framework, 2e, are the same when you are using POCOs with DbContext.

Using Snapshot Change Tracking

Snapshot change tracking depends on Entity Framework being able to detect when changes occur. The default behavior of the DbContext API is to automatically perform this detection as the result of many events on the DbContext. DetectChanges not only updates the context's state management information so that changes can be persisted to the database, it also performs relationship fix-up when you have a combination of reference navigation properties, collection navigation properties and foreign keys. It's important to have a clear understanding of how and when changes are detected, what to expect from it and how to control it. This section addresses those concerns.

Understanding When Automatic Change Detection Occurs

The DetectChanges method of ObjectContext has been available since Entity Framework 4 as part of the snapshot change tracking pattern on POCO objects. What's different about DbContext.ChangeTracker.DetectChanges (which in turn, calls ObjectCon text.DetectChanges) is that there are many more events that trigger an automatic call to DetectChanges. Here is the list of the method calls you should already be familiar with that will cause DetectChanges to do its job:

- DbSet.Add
- DbSet.Find
- DbSet.Remove
- DbSet.Local
- DbContext.SaveChanges
- Running any LINQ query against a DbSet

There are more methods that will trigger DetectChanges. You'll learn more about these methods throughout the rest of this book:

- DbSet.Attach
- DbContext.GetValidationErrors
- DbContext.Entry
- DbChangeTracker.Entries

Controlling When DetectChanges Is Called

The most obvious time that Entity Framework needs to know about changes is during SaveChanges, but there are also many others. For example, if we ask the change tracker for the current state of an object, it will need to scan and check if anything has changed. Scanning isn't just restricted to the object in question either. Consider a situation where you query for a Lodging from the database and then add it to the Lodgings collection of a new Destination. This Lodging is now modified because assigning it to a new

Destination changes its DestinationId property. But to know that this change has occurred (or hasn't occurred) Entity Framework needs to scan all of the Destination objects as well. Many of the operations you perform on the DbContext API will cause DetectChanges to be run.

In most cases DetectChanges is fast enough that it doesn't cause performance issues. However, if you have a very large number of objects in memory or you are performing a lot of operations on DbContext in quick succession, the automatic DetectChanges behavior may be a performance concern. Fortunately you have the option to switch off the automatic DetectChanges behavior and call it manually when you know that it needs to be called.

Entity Framework is built on the assumption that you will call DetectChanges before every API call if you have changed any of the entities since the last API call. This includes calling DetectChanges before running any queries. Failure to do this can result in unexpected side effects. DbContext takes care of this requirement for you provided that you leave automatic DetectChanges enabled. If you switch it off, you are responsible for calling DetectChanges.

 Working out when DetectChanges needs to be called isn't as trivial as it may appear. The Entity Framework team strongly recommends that you only swap to manually calling DetectChanges if you are experiencing performance issues. It's also recommended to only opt out of automatic DetectChanges for poorly performing sections of code and to reenable it once the section in question has finished executing.

Automatic DetectChanges can be toggled on and off via the DbContext.Configura tion.AutoDetectChangesEnabled Boolean flag. Let's add a ManualDetectChanges method that disables automatic DetectChanges and observes the effect this has (Example 3-14).

Example 3-14. Manually calling DetectChanges
```
private static void ManualDetectChanges()
{
  using (var context = new BreakAwayContext())
  {
    context.Configuration.AutoDetectChangesEnabled = false;

    var reef = (from d in context.Destinations
                where d.Name == "Great Barrier Reef"
                select d).Single();

    reef.Description = "The world's largest reef.";

    Console.WriteLine(
      "Before DetectChanges: {0}",
      context.Entry(reef).State);

    context.ChangeTracker.DetectChanges();
```

```
  Console.WriteLine(
    "After DetectChanges: {0}",
      context.Entry(reef).State);
  }
}
```

The code switches off automatic `DetectChanges` and then queries for the Great Barrier Reef and changes its description. The next line will write out the current state that the context thinks the `reef` entity is in. We then manually call `DetectChanges` and repeat the process of writing out the current state. Accessing the current state makes use of the `Entry` method from Change Tracker API, which is discussed in Chapter 5. If you update the `Main` method to call `ManualDetectChanges`, you will see the following output:

```
Before DetectChanges: Unchanged
After DetectChanges: Modified
```

As expected, the context doesn't detect that the `reef` entity is modified until after we manually call `DetectChanges`. The reason we get an incorrect result is that we broke the rule of calling DetectChanges before calling an API after we had modified an entity. Because we were simply reading the state of an entity, this didn't have any nasty side effects.

The code we saw in Example 3-9 didn't really buy us anything by switching off automatic `DetectChanges`. Calling the `DbContext.Entry` method would also have automatically triggered `DetectChanges` if the change tracking wasn't disabled.

 If you write tests to check the state of entities and you use this `Entry` method to inspect state, keep in mind that the `Entry` method itself calls `DetectChanges`. This could inadvertently alter your test results. You can use the `AutoDetectChangesEnabled` configuration to have tighter control over `DetectChanges` in this scenario.

However if we were performing a series of API calls on `DbContext` without changing any objects in between, we could avoid some unnecessary execution of the `DetectChanges` process. The `AddMultipleDestinations` method shown in Example 3-15 demonstrates this.

Example 3-15. Adding multiple objects without DetectChanges

```
private static void AddMultipleDestinations()
{
  using (var context = new BreakAwayContext())
  {
    context.Configuration.AutoDetectChangesEnabled = false;

    context.Destinations.Add(new Destination
    {
        Name = "Paris",
        Country = "France"
    });
```

```
  context.Destinations.Add(new Destination
  {
    Name = "Grindelwald",
    Country = "Switzerland"
  });

  context.Destinations.Add(new Destination
  {
    Name = "Crete",
    Country = "Greece"
  });

  context.SaveChanges();
  }
}
```

This code avoids four unnecessary calls to DetectChanges that would have occurred while calling the DbSet.Add and SaveChanges methods. This example is used purely for demonstration purposes and is not a scenario where disabling DetectChanges is going to provide any significant benefit. In Chapter 5 you'll learn about making changes to your objects using the Change Tracker API. The Change Tracker API enables you to make changes to your objects by going through a DbContext API. This approach allows you to change your objects without the need to call DetectChanges.

Using DetectChanges to Trigger Relationship Fix-up

DetectChanges is also responsible for performing relationship fix-up for any relationships that it detects have changed. If you have changed some relationships and would like to have all the navigation properties and foreign key properties synchronized, DetectChanges will achieve this. This can be particularly useful in data-binding scenarios where your UI will change one of the navigation properties (or perhaps the foreign key property) but you then want the other properties in the relationship to be updated to reflect the change. The DetectRelationshipChanges method in Example 3-16 uses DetectChanges to perform relationship fix-up.

Example 3-16. Using DetectChanges to fix up relationships

```
private static void DetectRelationshipChanges()
{
  using (var context = new BreakAwayContext())
  {
    var hawaii = (from d in context.Destinations
                  where d.Name == "Hawaii"
                  select d).Single();

    var davesDump = (from l in context.Lodgings
                     where l.Name == "Dave's Dump"
                     select l).Single();

    context.Entry(davesDump)
```

```
      .Reference(l => l.Destination)
      .Load();

    hawaii.Lodgings.Add(davesDump);

    Console.WriteLine(
      "Before DetectChanges: {0}",
      davesDump.Destination.Name);

    context.ChangeTracker.DetectChanges();

    Console.WriteLine(
      "After DetectChanges: {0}",
      davesDump.Destination.Name);
  }
}
```

The code loads the Hawaii Destination into memory as well as Dave's Dump Lodg
ing. It also uses explicit loading to load the Destination of Dave's Dump—that's the
Grand Canyon. Dave's Dump has such a bad reputation that he has decided to move
the Dump to Hawaii where nobody's heard of him yet. So we add the davesDump instance
to the Lodgings collection of hawaii. Because we are using POCO objects, Entity Framework doesn't know that we've made this change, and therefore it doesn't fix up the
navigation property or foreign key property on davesDump. We could wait until we call
SaveChanges, or any other method, which triggers DetectChanges, but perhaps we want
things fixed up right away. We've added in a call to DetectChanges to achieve this. If
we update the Main method to call DetectRelationshipChanges and run the application
we see this in action:

```
Before DetectChanges: Grand Canyon
After DetectChanges: Hawaii
```

Before the DetectChanges call, Dave's Dump is still assigned to the old Destination.
After we call DetectChanges, relationship fix-up has occurred and everything is back in
sync.

Enabling and Working with Change Tracking Proxies

If your performance profiler has pinpointed excessive calls to DetectChanges as a problem or you prefer relationship fix-up to occur in real time, there is another option—the
change tracking proxies mentioned earlier. With only some minor changes to your
POCO classes, Entity Framework will be able to create change tracking proxies. Change
tracking proxies will allow Entity Framework to track changes as we make them to our
objects and also perform relationship fix-up as it detects changes to relationships.

The rules for allowing a change tracking proxy to be created are as follows:

- The class must be public and not sealed.
- Each property must be marked as virtual.

- Each property must have a public getter and setter.
- Any collection navigation properties must be typed as `ICollection<T>`.

Update the Destination class as shown in Example 3-17 to meet these requirements. Notice that we are also removing the logic from the constructor that initialized the `Lodgings` property. The change tracking proxy will override any collection navigation properties and use its own collection type (`EntityCollection<TEntity>`). This collection type will track any changes to the collection and report them to the change tracker. If you attempt to assign another type to the property, such as the `List<T>` we were creating in the constructor, the proxy will throw an exception.

Example 3-17. Destination class updated to enable change tracking proxies

```
[Table("Locations", Schema = "baga")]
public class Destination
{
  public Destination()
  {
    //this.Lodgings = new List<Lodging>();
  }

  [Column("LocationID")]
  public virtual int DestinationId { get; set; }
  [Required, Column("LocationName")]
  [MaxLength(200)]
  public virtual string Name { get; set; }
  public virtual string Country { get; set; }
  [MaxLength(500)]
  public virtual string Description { get; set; }
  [Column(TypeName = "image")]
  public virtual byte[] Photo { get; set; }
  public virtual string TravelWarnings { get; set; }
  public virtual string ClimateInfo { get; set; }

  public virtual ICollection<Lodging> Lodgings { get; set; }
}
```

In Chapter 2, you learned how Entity Framework creates dynamic proxies for a class when one or more navigation properties in that class are marked virtual. Those proxies, which derive from the given class, allow the virtual navigation properties to be lazy loaded. The change tracking proxies are created in the same way at runtime, but these proxies have more features than those you saw in Chapter 2.

While the requirements for getting a change tracking proxy are fairly simple, it's also very easy to miss one of them. It's even easier to make a change to the class in the future that will unintentionally break one of the rules. Because of this, it's a good idea to add a unit test that ensures Entity Framework can create a change tracking proxy. Let's add a method that will test just this (Example 3-18). You'll also need to add a using for the `System.Data.Objects.DataClasses` namespace.

Example 3-18. Testing for a change tracking proxy

```
private static void TestForChangeTrackingProxy()
{
  using (var context = new BreakAwayContext())
  {
    var destination = context.Destinations.First();

    var isProxy = destination is IEntityWithChangeTracker;

    Console.WriteLine("Destination is a proxy: {0}", isProxy);
  }
}
```

When Entity Framework creates the dynamic proxy for change tracking, it will implement the `IEntityWithChangeTracker` interface. The test in Example 3-18 creates a `Des tination` instance by retrieving it from the database and then checks for this interface to ensure that the `Destination` is wrapped with a change tracking proxy. Note that it's not enough just to check that Entity Framework is creating a proxy class that derives from our class, because lazy loading proxies will also do this. The presence of `IEntity WithChangeTracker` is what causes Entity Framework to listen for changes in real time.

Now that we have a change tracking proxy, let's update Main to call the `ManualDe tectChanges` method we wrote back in Example 3-14 and run the application:

```
Before DetectChanges: Modified
After DetectChanges: Modified
```

This time we see that Entity Framework is aware of changes regardless of whether DetectChanges is called or not. Now update Main to call the `DetectRelationship Changes` method we wrote in Example 3-16 and run the application:

```
Before DetectChanges: Hawaii
After DetectChanges: Hawaii
```

This time we see that Entity Framework detected the relationship change and performed relationship fix-up without `DetectChanges` being called.

 It is not necessary to disable automatic `DetectChanges` when you use change tracking proxies. `DetectChanges` will skip the change detection process for any objects that report changes in real time. Therefore, enabling change tracking proxies is enough to get the performance benefits of avoiding `DetectChanges`. In fact, Entity Framework won't even take a snapshot of the property values when it finds a change tracking proxy. DetectChanges knows it can skip scanning for changes in entities that don't have a snapshot of their original values.

If you have entities that contain complex types (for example, Person.Address), Entity Framework will still use snapshot change tracking for the properties contained in the complex type. This is required because Entity Framework does not create a proxy for the complex type instance. You still get the benefits of automatic change detection on the properties defined directly on the entity itself, but changes to properties on the complex type will only be detected by DetectChanges.

Ensuring the New Instances Get Proxies

Entity Framework will automatically create proxies for the results of any queries you run. However, if you just use the constructor of your POCO class to create new objects, these will not be proxies. In order to get proxies you need to use the DbSet.Create method to get new instances of an entity. This rule is the same as when working with POCOs with ObjectContext and ObjectSet.

If you have enabled change tracking proxies for an entity in your model, you can still create and add nonproxy instances of the entity. Entity Framework will happily work with a mixture of proxied and nonproxied entities in the same set. You just need to be aware that you will not get automatic change tracking or relationship fix-up for instances that are not change tracking proxies. Having a mixture of proxied and nonproxied instances in the same set can be confusing, so it's generally recommended that you use DbSet.Create to create new instances so that all entities in the set are change tracking proxies.

Add the CreatingNewProxies method shown in Example 3-19 to see this in action.

Example 3-19. Creating new proxy instances

```
private static void CreatingNewProxies()
{
  using (var context = new BreakAwayContext())
  {
    var nonProxy = new Destination();
    nonProxy.Name = "Non-proxy Destination";
    nonProxy.Lodgings = new List<Lodging>();

    var proxy = context.Destinations.Create();
    proxy.Name = "Proxy Destination";

    context.Destinations.Add(proxy);
    context.Destinations.Add(nonProxy);

    var davesDump = (from l in context.Lodgings
                    where l.Name == "Dave's Dump"
                    select l).Single();

    context.Entry(davesDump)
```

```
        .Reference(l => l.Destination)
        .Load();

    Console.WriteLine(
      "Before changes: {0}",
      davesDump.Destination.Name);

    nonProxy.Lodgings.Add(davesDump);

    Console.WriteLine(
      "Added to non-proxy destination: {0}",
      davesDump.Destination.Name);

    proxy.Lodgings.Add(davesDump);

    Console.WriteLine(
      "Added to proxy destination: {0}",
      davesDump.Destination.Name);
  }
}
```

The code starts by creating two new `Destination` instances and adding them to the `Destinations` set on the context. One of these `Destinations` is just an instance of our POCO class. The other is created using `DbSet.Create` and is a change tracking proxy. Next, the code queries for Dave's Dump and loads the `Destination` that it currently belongs to using the `Entry` method that you learned about in Chapter 2. We then add Dave's Dump to the `Lodgings` property of the POCO `Destination` and then to the proxy `Destination`. At each stage the code prints out the name of the `Destination` assigned to the `Destination` property on Dave's Dump:

```
Before changes: Grand Canyon
Added to non-proxy destination: Grand Canyon
Added to proxy destination: Proxy Destination
```

You can see that Dave's Dump is initially assigned to the Grand Canyon `Destination`. When it's added to the `Lodgings` collection of the nonproxy `Destination`, the `Destination` property on Dave's Dump is not updated; it's still the Grand Canyon. Because this `Destination` isn't a proxy, Entity Framework isn't aware that we changed the relationship. However, when we add it to the `Lodgings` collection of the proxy `Destination` we get full relationship fix-up instantly.

Creating Proxy Instances for Derived Types

There is also a generic overload of `DbSet.Create` that is used to create instances of derived classes in our set. For example, calling `Create` on the `Lodgings` set will give you an instance of the `Lodging` class. But the `Lodgings` set can also contain instances of `Resort`, which derives from `Lodging`. To get a new proxy instance of `Resort`, we use the generic overload:

```
    var newResort = context.Lodgings.Create<Resort>();
```

Fetching Entities Without Change Tracking

You've probably gathered by now that tracking changes isn't a trivial process and there is a bit of overhead involved. In some areas of your application, you may be displaying data in a read-only screen. Because the data will never get updated, you may want to avoid the overhead associated with change tracking.

Fortunately Entity Framework includes an `AsNoTracking` method that can be used to execute a *no-tracking query*. A no-tracking query is simply a query where the results will not be tracked for changes by the context. Add the `PrintDestinationsWithoutCh` `angeTracking` method shown in Example 3-20.

Example 3-20. Querying data without change tracking

```
private static void PrintDestinationsWithoutChangeTracking()
{
  using (var context = new BreakAwayContext())
  {
    foreach (var destination in context.Destinations.AsNoTracking())
    {
      Console.WriteLine(destination.Name);
    }
  }
}
```

The code uses the `AsNoTracking` method to get a no-tracking query for the contents of the `Destinations` set. The results are then iterated over and printed to the console. Because this is a no-tracking query, the context is not keeping track of any changes made to the `Destinations`. If you were to modify a property of one of the `Destina` `tions` and call `SaveChanges`, the changes would not be sent to the database.

 Fetching data without change tracking will usually only provide a noticeable performance gain when you are fetching larger amounts of data for read-only display. If your application will update and save any of the data, you should not use `AsNoTracking` there.

`AsNoTracking` is an extension method defined on `IQueryable<T>`, so you can use it in LINQ queries also. You can use `AsNoTracking` on the end of the `DbSet` in the `from` line of the query:

```
var query = from d in context.Destinations.AsNoTracking()
            where d.Country == "Australia"
            select d;
```

You can also use `AsNoTracking` to convert an existing LINQ query to be a no-tracking query. Note that the code doesn't just call `AsNoTracking` on the existing query but overrides the query variable with the result of the `AsNoTracking` call. This is required because `AsNoTracking` doesn't modify the query that it is called on, it returns a new query:

```
var query = from d in context.Destinations
            where d.Country == "Australia"
            select d;

query = query.AsNoTracking();
```

Because `AsNoTracking` is an extension method, you will need to have the `System.Data.Entity` namespace imported to use it.

CHAPTER 4

Working with Disconnected Entities Including N-Tier Applications

In the previous chapter you learned how to add new entities and change or delete existing entities. All the examples we looked at involved making changes one at a time to entities that are tracked by the context. Each of the changes affected a single entity or relationship. You saw that you can perform multiple of these single entity operations and then call SaveChanges to push all the changes to the database in a single transaction. In this chapter we will look at making changes to entities that are not being tracked by a context. Entities that are not being tracked by a context are known as *disconnected entities*.

For most single-tier applications, where the user interface and database access layers run in the same application process, you will probably just be performing operations on entities that are being tracked by a context. Operations on disconnected entities are much more common in N-Tier applications. N-Tier applications involve fetching some data on a server and returning it, over the network, to a client machine. The client application then manipulates this data before returning it to the server to be persisted.

The N-Tier pattern makes data access more complex because there is no longer a context tracking changes that are made to each entity. The data is fetched using one context, and returned to the client where there is no context to track changes. The data is then sent back to the server and must be persisted back to the database using a new instance of the context.

 While the majority of content in this chapter is aimed at developers writing N-Tier applications, it's useful information for anyone working with Entity Framework and will give you a deeper understanding of how Entity Framework behaves.

When it comes time to persist the data on the server, you are typically working with a *graph of entities*. A graph of entities is simply a number of entities that reference each other. We've already worked with graphs of entities that are attached to the context. In the last chapter we looked at adding a relationship using a navigation property, which is enough to create a graph, because one entity now references another. In N-Tier scenarios this graph of entities is usually disconnected from the context, though, meaning the context isn't yet tracking any of the entities in the graph.

When it comes time to start performing operations on this disconnected graph, there are some additional behaviors in Entity Framework that you need to be aware of. The entity that you perform the operation on is known as the *root* of the graph. Performing an operation on the root of disconnected graph can have side effects on the rest of the graph, too.

A Simple Operation on a Disconnected Graph

Before we delve into the complexities of N-Tier scenarios, let's take a quick look at an example of the side effects of performing an operation on the root of a disconnected graph. In the previous chapter we saw that `DbSet.Add` can be used to register a new entity to be inserted when `SaveChanges` is called.

 You'll see the term *register* used throughout this chapter. When an entity is registered with the context it means that the context becomes aware of the entity and starts tracking it.

So far the entities we've passed to the `Add` method have been standalone instances with no references to other entities. Now let's see what happens when we pass the root of a newly created graph of entities that isn't yet tracked by the context. Add the `AddSimpleGraph` method that is shown in Example 4-1.

Example 4-1. Method to add a graph of entities

```
private static void AddSimpleGraph()
{
  var essex = new Destination
  {
    Name = "Essex, Vermont",
    Lodgings = new List<Lodging>
    {
      new Lodging { Name = "Big Essex Hotel" },
      new Lodging { Name = "Essex Junction B&B" },
    }
  };

  using (var context = new BreakAwayContext())
  {
    context.Destinations.Add(essex);

    Console.WriteLine(
```

```
    "Essex Destination: {0}",
    context.Entry(essex).State);

  foreach (var lodging in essex.Lodgings)
  {
    Console.WriteLine(
      "{0}: {1}",
      lodging.Name,
      context.Entry(lodging).State);
  }

  context.SaveChanges();
  }
}
```

The code constructs a new Destination instance, which also references two new Lodg
ing instances in its Lodgings property. Then the new Destination is added to a context
using the Add method. Once the Destination is added, the code uses the DbCon
text.Entry method to get access to the change tracking information that Entity Framework has about the new Destination. From this change tracking information the
State property is used to write out the current state of the entity. This process is then
repeated for each of the newly created Lodgings that are referenced from the new Des
tination. If you modify the Main method to call AddSimpleGraph and run the application
you will see the following output:

```
Essex Destination: Added
Big Essex Hotel: Added
Essex Junction B&B: Added
```

It's no surprise that Entity Framework has the new Destination registered as an
Added entity because we used the Add method to add it to the context. What may be a
little less obvious is that Entity Framework looked in the navigation properties of the
Destination instance and saw that it referenced two Lodging instances that the context
wasn't already tracking. Entity Framework also registers these entities as Added and will
insert them into the database when SaveChanges is called. The process of finding related
entities is recursive, so if one of the new Lodging instances referenced a new Person
instance, the Person would also get added to the context. Figure 4-1 attempts to visualize how calling Add on a disconnected Destination will also add other disconnected
entities that are reachable from the Destination.

If a reference is found to an entity that is already tracked by the context, the entity that
is already tracked is left in its current state. For example, if one of our new Lodging
instances referenced an existing Person that had been queried for using the context, the
existing Person would not be marked as Added. The existing Person would remain in the
Unchanged state and the Lodging would be inserted with its foreign key pointing to the
existing Person. Figure 4-2 attempts to visualize how adding a disconnected Destina
tion will also add other disconnected entities, but if an entity that is being tracked by
the context is found, it is left in its current state.

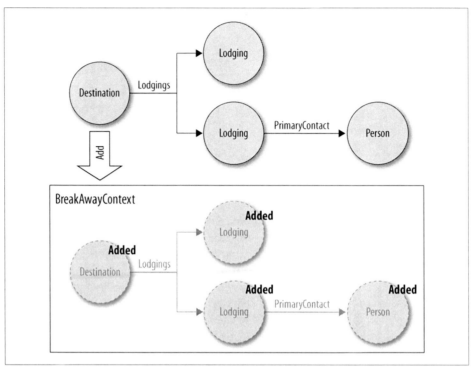

Figure 4-1. Adding a disconnected graph of entities

Exploring the Challenges of N-Tier

Now that you've seen how Entity Framework behaves when it is asked to add the root of a graph of entities to the context, we're going to take a look at how this affects N-Tier applications. Remember that in an N-Tier application the data is queried for in one context, but the changes need to be persisted using another context. For example, on the server side of your application you could expose a `GetDestinationAndLodgings` method that will return a `Destination` with all of its `Lodgings`:

```
public Destination GetDestinationAndLodgings(int destinationId)
```

The client side of the application could then fetch a `Destination` and make some changes to it. These changes could include changing the `Description` of the `Destina tion` and adding a new `Lodging` to its `Lodgings` collection. The server side of the application could then expose a `SaveDestinationAndLodgings` method to push all these changes back to the database:

```
public void SaveDestinationAndLodgings(Destination destination)
```

When it comes time to implement the `SaveDestinationAndLodgings` method, things get a little more complicated. Like the simple graph from Example 4-1, the `Destination` that gets passed in isn't tracked by a context. In fact, because it's been serialized over

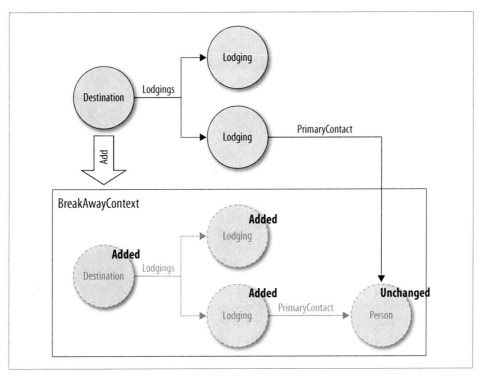

Figure 4-2. Adding a disconnected graph that references a tracked entity

the network on its way to and from the client, it's not even the same instance that was queried for using Entity Framework. The `SaveDestinationAndLodgings` method needs to let Entity Framework know if it's an existing `Destination` or a new `Destination` that needs to be added. If it's an existing `Destination`, some of the properties may have been modified and therefore need to be updated in the database. The `Lodgings` property may also contain instances of `Lodging` that can also be existing or new. Since Entity Framework hasn't been tracking these entities, you need to let it know all of this information.

Your server-side logic could be exposed through a service or perhaps a class that follows the *repository pattern*. Either way, you need to overcome the disconnected nature of the objects that are returned from the client application.

There are a number of different approaches to solving the challenges associated with building N-Tier applications. Covering the details of each approach is well beyond the scope of this book, but we'll take a quick look at the different options that are available to you and how they relate to using Entity Framework.

Using Existing N-Tier Frameworks That Support Graph Modification

In a lot of cases you can save yourself the headache of dealing with the intricacies of N-Tier data access by using a framework that takes care of tracking changes that are made to data on the client and applying those changes on the server. Entity Framework is tightly integrated with WCF Data Services, which is one such framework. WCF Data Services is Microsoft's solution to the N-Tier challenge. There are frameworks available from other vendors as well.

WCF Data Services allows you to choose what data from your model is exposed from the server and what permission clients have for the data (read, append, update, and so on). WCF Data Services also includes a client component that takes care of tracking changes you make to data on the client, pushing those changes back to the database, and saving them using your Entity Framework model. WCF Data Services uses the OData protocol (*http://odata.org*) for exposing data from the server; this allows your service to be accessed by clients other than WCF Data Services, including non .NET Framework platforms.

The WCF Data Services client has a similar "look and feel" to performing data access directly against DbContext. Using WCF Data Services is arguably the simplest approach to N-Tier data access with Entity Framework, and it is the approach the Entity Framework team recommends. You can learn more about using WCF Data Services with DbContext in this article: *http://msdn.microsoft.com/en-us/data/hh272554*.

WCF Data Services is a good option for building N-Tier applications, but there are some reasons it may not be the right tool for your job. WCF Data Services gives you quite a bit of control over how requests are processed on the server, but it is a framework and therefore it is somewhat scoped in what it can handle. Depending on your application, you may have some advanced requirements that are not supported.

You may also be in a situation where the shape of the server operations and/or the protocol to be used for client-server communication are outside of your control. In these situations, authoring your own web services may be the only viable option.

Self-Tracking Entities

Around the time that Entity Framework 4 was released, the Entity Framework team also released a Self-Tracking Entities template for Model First and Database First. This replaced the default code generation with a template that produced entities that would internally track their changes on the client and transfer the information back to the server. The template also generated some helper methods that would take the change tracking information and replay the changes back into a context on the server.

The Entity Framework team hasn't made any significant updates to the Self-Tracking Entities template since it was first released. They are recommending that developers look at using WCF Data Services as a more robust and complete solution.

There is no Self-Tracking Entities template that can be used with the DbContext API. There is also no Self-Tracking Entities solution for use with Code First.

Using Explicit Operations on the Server Side

Another way to avoid the complexity of determining the changes to be made on the server is to expose very granular operations that require the client to identify the exact change to be made. For example, rather than the `SaveDestinationAndLodgings` method we saw earlier in this chapter, you could expose `AddDestination` and `UpdateDestina tion` methods. These methods would only operate on a standalone `Destination` instance rather than a graph of entities. You would expose separate methods for adding and updating `Locations`. Entity Framework makes it simple to implement these methods and you'll find everything you need for this approach in the "Understanding How DbContext Responds to Setting the State of a Single Entity" on page 78 section of this chapter.

While this option makes the server component of your application much easier, it potentially makes the client component more complex. You are also likely to end up with a large number of operations exposed from the server. If you can't use an existing framework, such as WCF Data Services, you will need to weigh up the benefits of this approach and the approach covered in the next section. Granular operations will typically give you a higher quantity of code, but that code will be much simpler to write, test, and debug. Next we'll take a look at a more generalized solution that will probably involve less code, but is inherently more complex.

Replaying Changes on the Server

Another option is to have a more generalized server operation that accepts a graph of entities and then lets Entity Framework know what state each entity in that graph should be in. This is often referred to as *replaying* the changes on the server, because you are walking through each entity and letting Entity Framework know what happened on the client. The process of iterating through each entity and setting its state is also known as *painting the state*.

There are many different ways to implement this logic. You could write code that is strongly tied to the classes in your model and each server operation knows how to navigate the graph that is passed in, look at each entity, and set its state appropriately. You can also come up with a generalized approach that can replay the changes for any graph given any root entity. The generalized approach typically uses a base class or an interface that exposes information to allow your server-side code to work out what state each entity is in. You'll see examples of both of these in the next section of this chapter.

Chapter 18 of *Programming Entity Framework, 2e*, demonstrated this pattern by providing a base class with a State property. The State property could be set on the client side and then read on the server side to determine how to register the class with the context.

Understanding How DbContext Responds to Setting the State of a Single Entity

Now that we've taken a look at the N-Tier challenges and the high-level options for addressing them, it's time to see how to implement those techniques using Entity Framework. We'll start by taking a step back and looking at how to set the state for a single entity. Then we'll take those techniques and use them to set the state for each entity in a graph.

Building an actual N-Tier application is beyond the scope of this book, so we're going to keep working in the console application. We'll implement methods that you could potentially expose from a web service for your client application to consume. Rather than serializing entities, you'll use a temporary context to fetch any data from the database and then manipulate the data to mimic client-side changes. You'll then pass these objects into the pseudo-server-side operations that will use a new context, with no previous knowledge of the entity instances, to persist the changes to the database.

Entity Framework has a list of states that the change tracker uses to record the status of each entity. In this section, you'll see how to move an entity into each of these states. The states that Entity Framework uses when change tracking are the following:

Added
> The entity is being tracked by the context but does not exist in the database. During SaveChanges an INSERT statement will be used to add this entity to the database.

Unchanged
> The entity already exists in the database and has not been modified since it was retrieved from the database. SaveChanges does not need to process the entity.

Modified
> The entity already exists in the database and has been modified in memory. During SaveChanges an UPDATE statement will be sent to the database to apply the changes. A list of the properties that have been modified is also kept to determine which columns should be set in the UPDATE statement.

Deleted
> The entity already exists in the database and has been marked for deletion. During SaveChanges a DELETE statement will be used to remove the entity from the database.

Detached
> The entity is not being tracked by the context.

Setting an entity to the Detached state used to be important before the Entity Framework supported POCO objects. Prior to POCO support, your entities would have references to the context that was tracking them. These references would cause issues when trying to attach an entity to a second context. Setting an entity to the Detached state clears out all the references to the context and also clears the navigation properties of the entity—so that it no longer references any entities being tracked by the context. Now that you can use POCO objects that don't contain references to the context that is tracking them, there is rarely a need to move an entity to the Detached state. We will not be covering the Detached state in the rest of this chapter.

Marking a New Entity as Added

Arguably the simplest operation is to take an entity and mark it as Added; in fact, you saw how to do that in Chapter 3. You can use the DbSet.Add method to tell Entity Framework that an entity is added. Add the AddDestination and TestAddDestination methods shown in Example 4-2.

Example 4-2. Adding a new Destination

```
private static void TestAddDestination()
{
  var jacksonHole = new Destination
  {
    Name = "Jackson Hole, Wyoming",
    Description = "Get your skis on."
  };

  AddDestination(jacksonHole);
}

private static void AddDestination(Destination destination)
{
  using (var context = new BreakAwayContext())
  {
    context.Destinations.Add(destination);
    context.SaveChanges();
  }
}
```

The TestAddDestination method mimics a client application creating a new Destination and passing it to the AddDestination method on the server. The AddDestination method adds the new Destination to a context and then saves it to the database. If you update the Main method to call TestAddDestination and run the application, you will see that the Jackson Hole Destination is added to the database.

There is also another way to write this same method. Earlier in this chapter we saw that we could use DbContext.Entry to get access to the change tracking information for an entity. We used the State property on the change tracking information to read the state of an entity, but we can also set this property, too. Update the `AddDestination` method to use the State property rather than `DbSet.Add` (Example 4-3). You'll need to add a using for the `System.Data` namespace to use the `EntityState` enum.

Example 4-3. Marking a Destination as added using the State property

```
private static void AddDestination(Destination destination)
{
  using (var context = new BreakAwayContext())
  {
    context.Entry(destination).State = EntityState.Added;
    context.SaveChanges();
  }
}
```

Calling `DbSet.Add` and setting the `State` to `Added` both achieve exactly the same thing. If the entity is not tracked by the context, it will start being tracked by the context in the `Added` state. Both `DbSet.Add` and setting the `State` to `Added` are graph operations—meaning that any other entities that are not being tracked by the context and are reachable from the root entity will also be marked as Added. If the entity is already tracked by the context, it will be moved to the `Added` state. So far we've only added entities that aren't tracked by the context, but a little later in this chapter you'll see that being able to set the state of an entity that is already tracked to `Added` is important.

Whether you choose `DbSet.Add` or setting the `State` property is simply a matter of which is more convenient in the code you are writing. For this simple scenario, the code is arguably easier to understand if you stick with `DbSet.Add`. Later in the chapter you'll see that setting the `State` property is cleaner in generalized scenarios where your code calculates the state you are setting the entity to.

Marking an Existing Entity as Unchanged

While `DbSet.Add` is used to tell Entity Framework about new entities, `DbSet.Attach` is used to tell Entity Framework about existing entities. The `Attach` method will mark an entity in the Unchanged state. Add the `AttachDestination` and `TestAttachDestination` methods shown in Example 4-4.

Example 4-4. Attaching an existing Destination

```
private static void TestAttachDestination()
{
  Destination canyon;
  using (var context = new BreakAwayContext())
  {
    canyon = (from d in context.Destinations
              where d.Name == "Grand Canyon"
              select d).Single();
  }

  AttachDestination(canyon);
```

```
}

private static void AttachDestination(Destination destination)
{
  using (var context = new BreakAwayContext())
  {
    context.Destinations.Attach(destination);
    context.SaveChanges();
  }
}
```

The TestAttachDestination method fetches an existing Destination from the database and passes it to the AttachDestination method, which uses DbSet.Attach to register the existing Destination with a context and save the changes. You can also write this method by setting the State property for the entity to Unchanged (Example 4-5).

Example 4-5. Marking a Destination as Unchanged using the State property

```
private static void AttachDestination(Destination destination)
{
  using (var context = new BreakAwayContext())
  {
    context.Entry(destination).State = EntityState.Unchanged;
    context.SaveChanges();
  }
}
```

If you update the Main method to call TestAttachDestination and run your application, you'll discover the AttachDestination is quite pointless because it doesn't do anything. That's because we told Entity Framework that the Destination was Unchanged; therefore SaveChanges just ignores the entity. While this is a bit silly if it's all we do in the method, it will be very useful when we have a graph of entities, some of which may not need any changes pushed to the database.

DbSet.Attach and setting the State property to Unchanged have the same effect. If the entity isn't tracked by the context, it will begin being tracked in the Unchanged state. If it is already tracked, it will be moved to the Unchanged state.

Marking an Existing Entity as Modified

You've seen how to mark an existing entity as Unchanged; now let's look at existing entities that have some changes that need to be pushed to the database. There are a few options that range from marking every property as modified to telling Entity Framework what the original values were for each property and letting it calculate the modifications. For the moment we'll just focus on getting the changes into the database by marking the whole entity as modified. You'll learn about setting individual properties as modified in "Tracking Individually Modified Properties" on page 99.

When you tell Entity Framework that an entire entity is modified, it will send an update statement to the database that sets every column to the values currently stored in the properties of the entity. There isn't an `AttachAsModified` method on `DbSet`, although there are plenty of people asking for one, so don't be surprised if it turns up in the future. For the moment, you need to set the `State` property to `Modified`. Add the `UpdateDestination` and `TestUpdateDestination` methods shown in Example 4-6.

Example 4-6. Attaching an existing entity as modified

```
private static void TestUpdateDestination()
{
  Destination canyon;
  using (var context = new BreakAwayContext())
  {
    canyon = (from d in context.Destinations
              where d.Name == "Grand Canyon"
              select d).Single();
  }

  canyon.TravelWarnings = "Don't fall in!";
  UpdateDestination(canyon);
}

private static void UpdateDestination(Destination destination)
{
  using (var context = new BreakAwayContext())
  {
    context.Entry(destination).State = EntityState.Modified;
    context.SaveChanges();
  }
}
```

The `TestUpdateDestination` simulates a client application that queries for the Grand Canyon `Destination` from the server, modifies the `TravelWarnings` property, and passes the updated `Destination` to the `UpdateDestination` method on the server. The `Update Destination` method marks the incoming `Destination` as `Modified` and saves the changes to the database. If you update the `Main` method to call `TestModifyDestination` and run the application, an update statement is sent to the database:

```
exec sp_executesql N'
update
  [baga].[Locations]
set
  [LocationName] = @0,
  [Country] = @1,
  [Description] = null,
  [Photo] = null,
  [TravelWarnings] = @2,
  [ClimateInfo] = null
where
  ([LocationID] = @3)

',N'@0 nvarchar(200),@1 nvarchar(max) ,@2 nvarchar(max) ,@3 int',
@0=N'Grand Canyon',@1=N'USA',@2=N'Don''t fall in!',@3=1
```

Notice that even though we only updated the `TravelWarnings` property, Entity Framework is updating every column. `TravelWarnings` gets updated to the new value we set; all the other columns get "updated" to the same values they had when we retrieved the `Destination` from the database. This is because Entity Framework doesn't know which properties were updated. We just specified that the entity was `Modified`, so Entity Framework is updating all the columns to match the current property values.

Registering an Existing Entity for Deletion

In the previous chapter you saw that `DbSet.Remove` can be used to delete existing entities. You also learned that calling `Remove` on an entity in the `Added` state will cancel the addition and cause the context to stop tracking the entity. Calling `Remove` on an entity that isn't tracked by the context will cause an `InvalidOperationException` to be thrown. The Entity Framework throws this exception because it isn't clear whether the entity you are trying to remove is an existing entity that should be marked for deletion or a new entity that should just be ignored. For this reason, we can't use just `Remove` to mark a disconnected entity as `Deleted`; we need to `Attach` it first. Add the `DeleteDestination` and `TestDeleteDestination` methods shows in Example 4-7.

Example 4-7. Registering an existing entity for deletion

```
private static void TestDeleteDestination()
{
  Destination canyon;
  using (var context = new BreakAwayContext())
  {
    canyon = (from d in context.Destinations
              where d.Name == "Grand Canyon"
              select d).Single();
  }

  DeleteDestination(canyon);
}

private static void DeleteDestination(Destination destination)
{
  using (var context = new BreakAwayContext())
  {
    context.Destinations.Attach(destination);
    context.Destinations.Remove(destination);
    context.SaveChanges();
  }
}
```

The `TestDeleteDestination` method simulates a client application fetching an existing `Destination` from the server and then passing it to the `DeleteDestination` method on the server. The `DeleteDestination` method uses the `Attach` method to let the context know that it's an existing `Destination`. Then the `Remove` method is used to register the existing `Destination` for deletion.

Having to attach the entity and then delete it is a little confusing and it's not immediately clear what the code is trying to achieve when we look at it. Fortunately we can also set the State property of the entity to Deleted. Because Remove is used in attached scenarios, its behavior is different when used on added, unchanged, or disconnected entities. However, changing the State property is only used for explicitly setting state of an entity, so Entity Framework assumes that setting the state to deleted means you want an existing entity marked for deletion. We can rewrite the DeleteDestination method to use this approach and the intent of the code becomes a lot clearer (Example 4-8).

Example 4-8. Registering an entity for deletion using the State property

```
private static void DeleteDestination(Destination destination)
{
  using (var context = new BreakAwayContext())
  {
    context.Entry(destination).State = EntityState.Deleted;
    context.SaveChanges();
  }
}
```

Using a stub entity to mark for deletion

Entity Framework only needs the key value(s) of an entity to be able to construct a DELETE statement for the entity. Therefore, you can reduce the amount of data that gets sent between the server and client by only sending back the key value of entities that need to be deleted. Add another overload of DeleteDestination that just accepts the key of the Destination to be deleted (Example 4-9).

Example 4-9. Registering an entity for deletion based on its key value

```
private static void DeleteDestination(int destinationId)
{
  using (var context = new BreakAwayContext())
  {
    var destination = new Destination { DestinationId = destinationId };
    context.Entry(destination).State = EntityState.Deleted;
    context.SaveChanges();
  }
}
```

The code constructs a new Destination instance with only the key property set—that's DestinationId. This entity with only the key value set is known as a *stub entity*. The code then sets the State property for this new entity to Deleted, indicating that it is an existing entity to be marked for deletion. Because Entity Framework will only access the DestinationId property when it constructs the DELETE statement, it doesn't matter that the other properties are not populated.

If your entity contains any concurrency tokens, these properties are also used to construct the DELETE statement. You can still use the stub entity approach, but you will need to set values for the concurrency token properties as well.

Working with Relationships with and Without Foreign Keys

If there is one thing you can do to make your life easier in N-Tier scenarios, it's to expose foreign key properties for the relationships in your model. Relationships that include a foreign key property are called *foreign key associations*, and unless you have a very good reason not to expose the foreign key properties you will save yourself a lot of pain by including them.

More detailed information on including foreign keys in your Code First model is available in Chapter 4 of *Programming Entity Framework: Code First*. For Database First and Model First, see Chapter 19 of *Programming Entity Framework, 2e*.

Benefiting from foreign key properties

The good news is that if you include foreign key properties in your model you already know everything you need to know to work with relationships. If you mark the entity as added, it will get inserted with the value currently assigned to its foreign key property. If you mark an entity as modified, the foreign key property will get updated along with all the other properties. To see this in action, add the UpdateLodging and TestUpdate Lodging methods shown in Example 4-10.

Example 4-10. Changing a foreign key value

```
private static void TestUpdateLodging()
{
  int reefId;
  Lodging davesDump;
  using (var context = new BreakAwayContext())
  {
    reefId = (from d in context.Destinations
              where d.Name == "Great Barrier Reef"
              select d.DestinationId).Single();

    davesDump = (from l in context.Lodgings
                 where l.Name == "Dave's Dump"
                 select l).Single();
  }

  davesDump.DestinationId = reefId;
  UpdateLodging(davesDump);
}

private static void UpdateLodging(Lodging lodging)
```

```
{
  using (var context = new BreakAwayContext())
  {
    context.Entry(lodging).State = EntityState.Modified;
    context.SaveChanges();
  }
}
```

The TestUpdateLodging method simulates a client application that fetches a Lodging and changes its DestinationId property. Remember that DestinationId is the foreign key to the Destination that the Lodging belongs to. This time it looks like Dave's reputation has become national, so he is moving his business around the world from Hawaii, USA, to Queensland, Australia. Once the changes are made, the Lodging is passed to the UpdateLodging method on the server. This method looks very much like the UpdateDestination method you wrote back in Example 4-6. As you can see, there is nothing special required to deal with foreign key relationships.

Using navigation properties to define relationships

You aren't restricted to using the foreign key property to change relationships. You can still use the navigation properties, and you'll see this in action a little later in this chapter.

If you chose not to include a foreign key property, you are using *independent associations*. They are called independent associations because Entity Framework reasons about the relationship independently of the entities that the relationship belongs to, and this makes things difficult when it comes to disconnected entities. In fact, foreign keys are so vital in N-Tier scenarios that the Entity Framework team chose not to expose the methods for changing the state of independent relationships on the DbContext API. To work with them, you will need to drop down to the ObjectContext API.

 Delving into the complexities of independent associations in N-Tier scenarios is well beyond the scope of this book. You can find a detailed look at this topic in Chapter 19 of Programming Entity Framework, 2e.

The problem you'll encounter is that change tracking only tracks scalar properties. When you change a foreign key property, such as Lodging.DestinationId, the context is aware of that property. But when you change a navigation property, there's nothing to track. Even if you mark the Lodging as Modified, the context is only aware of the scalar properties. When you use an independent association, the context actually keeps track of the relationship itself. It has an object that contains the keys of the two related instances and this is what the context uses to track relationship modifications and update them in the database and the state of the relationship. When your entity is not connected to the context, the context is unable to do the work of modifying these relationship objects. When you reconnect the entities to a context, you need to manually dig down into the context, find those relationship objects, and modify them. It's pretty complex and very confusing. This is one of the reasons developers convinced the Entity Framework team that we really needed to have foreign key properties available to us after struggling with independent associations in Entity Framework 1.0.

So, given that you simply might find yourself in this same situation, let's take a look at a quick example to give you an idea of the difference in resolving this problem in a disconnected scenario to the simplicity of working with foreign key associations, and hopefully convince you to stay away from them. Let's assume for a moment that we hadn't included the `DestinationId` property on `Lodging` and used an independent association instead. The code for `UpdateLodging` would need to look something like Example 4-11.

Example 4-11. UpdateLodging for independent associations

```
private static void UpdateLodging(
  Lodging lodging,
  Destination previousDestination)
{
  using (var context = new BreakAwayContext())
  {
    context.Entry(lodging).State = EntityState.Modified;
    context.Entry(lodging.Destination).State = EntityState.Unchanged;

    if (lodging.Destination.DestinationId !=
      previousDestination.DestinationId)
    {
      context.Entry(previousDestination).State = EntityState.Unchanged;

      ((IObjectContextAdapter)context).ObjectContext
        .ObjectStateManager
        .ChangeRelationshipState(
          lodging,
          lodging.Destination,
          l => l.Destination,
          EntityState.Added);

      ((IObjectContextAdapter)context).ObjectContext
        .ObjectStateManager
        .ChangeRelationshipState(
          lodging,
          previousDestination,
          l => l.Destination,
          EntityState.Deleted);
    }

    context.SaveChanges();
  }
}
```

The first thing you'll notice is that we now require the `Destination` instance that the `Lodging` used to belong to. This is because changing an independent association requires that the context have an added relationship to the new entity and a deleted relationship to the previous entity. This is a complicated side effect of the way that Entity Framework handles concurrency checks when updating independent associations. The code starts by marking the lodging as `Modified`, to take care of updating any properties that aren't involved in the relationship. The current `Destination` is also marked as an existing entity. The code then checks to see if this call is changing the `Destination` this `Lodging` is assigned to, by comparing the current `Destination` and the previous `Destination`. If the `Destination` does need to be changed, the previous `Destination` is also marked as an existing entity. The code then uses `ObjectContext.ObjectStateManager.ChangeRelationshipState` to mark the relationship to the current `Destination` as `Added` and the previous `Destination` as `Deleted`. With all that taken care of, it's time to call `SaveChanges` and push the changes to the database.

 Many-to-many relationships are always independent associations. If you have many-to-many relationships in your model, you will need to use `ChangeRelationshipState` to mark references as `Added`, `Unchanged`, or `Deleted` when processing changes on the server.

Setting the State for Multiple Entities in an Entity Graph

Now that you know the fundamental building blocks, it's time to plug them together to determine and set the state of each entity in a graph. When a disconnected entity graph arrives on the server side, the server will not know the state of the entities. You need to provide a way for the state to be discovered so that the context can be made aware of each entity's state. This section will demonstrate how you can coerce the context to infer and then apply entity state.

The first step is to get the graph into the context. You do that by performing an operation that will cause the context to start tracking the root of the graph. Once that is done, you can set the state for each entity in the graph.

Getting the Graph into the Context

Back in Example 4-1 you saw that adding the root of a graph will cause every entity in the graph to be registered with the context as a new entity. This behavior is the same if you use `DbSet.Add` or change the `State` property for an entity to `Added`. Once all the entities are tracked by the state manager, you can then work your way around the graph, specifying the correct state for each entity. It is possible to start by calling an operation that will register the root as an existing entity. This includes `DbSet.Attach` or setting the `State` property to `Unchanged`, `Modified`, or `Deleted`. However, this approach isn't recommended because you run the risk of exceptions due to duplicate key values if you have added entities in your graph. If you register the root as an existing entity, every entity in the graph will get registered as an existing entity. Because existing entities should all have unique primary keys, Entity Framework will ensure that you don't register two existing entities of the same type with the same key. If you have a new entity instance that will have its primary key value generated by the database, you probably won't bother assigning a value to the primary key; you'll just leave it set to the default value. This means if your graph contains multiple new entities of the same type, they will have the same key value. If you attach the root, Entity Framework will attempt to mark every entity as Unchanged, which will fail because you would have two existing entities with the same key.

For example, assume you have an existing Destination that includes two new instances of the Lodging class in its Lodgings property. The key of Lodging is the integer property LodgingId, which is generated by the database when you save. This means the two new Lodgings both have zero assigned to their LodgingId property. If you attempt to register the root as an existing entity, the two Lodging instances will also be registered as existing entities. This will fail because that would mean there are two existing Lodgings with a key of zero.

There may be some cases where you have multiple graphs and/or individual entities that need to be registered with the context. This occurs when not all the entities you need to reason about are reachable from one root. For example, we are going to be writing a method that will save a Destination and the Lodgings that it references. Each of these entities will either be a new entity to be added or an existing entity to be updated. The method will also accept a separate list of Lodgings that should be deleted. Because these Lodgings are to be deleted, the client will probably have removed them from the Lodgings collection on the root Destination. Therefore registering the root Destination won't be enough to register the deleted Lodgings; we'll need to register them separately.

Table 4-1 summarizes the options along with the pros and cons that you've read in this section.

Table 4-1. Patterns and warnings for joining graphs to a context

Method	Result	Warnings
Add Root	Every entity in graph will be change tracked and marked with Added state	SaveChanges will attempt to insert data that may already exist in database
Attach Root	Every entity in graph will be change tracked and marked with Unchanged state	New entities will not get inserted into database and have a conflict with matching keys
Add or Attach Root, then paint state throughout graph	Entities will have correct state when painting is complete	It is recommended that you Add the root rather than attaching it to avoid key conflicts for new entities. More information is provided at the start of this section.

Setting the State of Entities in a Graph

We're going to start by looking at an example where we iterate through the graph using our knowledge of the model and set the state for each entity throughout the graph, or *painting the state*. In the next section you'll see how you can generalize this solution so that you don't have to manually navigate the graph set the state of each entity. We're going to write a method that will save a `Destination` and its related `Lodgings`. Deleted entities are tricky in disconnected scenarios. If you delete the entity on the client side, there's nothing to send to the server so that it knows to delete that data in the database as well. This example demonstrates one pattern for overcoming the problem. Add the `SaveDestinationAndLodgings` method shown in Example 4-12.

Example 4-12. Setting state for each entity in a graph

```
private static void SaveDestinationAndLodgings(
  Destination destination,
  List<Lodging> deletedLodgings)
{
  // TODO: Ensure only Destinations & Lodgings are passed in

  using (var context = new BreakAwayContext())
  {
    context.Destinations.Add(destination);

    if (destination.DestinationId > 0)
    {
      context.Entry(destination).State = EntityState.Modified;
    }

    foreach (var lodging in destination.Lodgings)
    {
      if (lodging.LodgingId > 0)
      {
        context.Entry(lodging).State = EntityState.Modified;
      }
    }

    foreach (var lodging in deletedLodgings)
    {
      context.Entry(lodging).State = EntityState.Deleted;
    }

    context.SaveChanges();
  }
}
```

The new method accepts the `Destination` to be saved. This `Destination` may also have `Lodgings` related to it. The method also accepts a list of `Lodgings` to be deleted. These `Lodgings` may or may not be in the `Lodgings` collection of the `Destination` that is being saved. You'll also notice a TODO to ensure that the client calling the method only supplied `Destinations` and `Lodgings`, because that is all that our method is expecting.

If the caller were to reference an unexpected `InternetSpecial` from one of the `Lodgings`, we wouldn't process this with our state setting logic. Validating input is good practice and isn't related to the topic at hand, so we've left it out for clarity.

The code then adds the root `Destination` to the context, which will cause any related `Lodgings` to also be added. Next we are using a check on the key property to determine if this is a new or existing `Destination`. If the key is set to zero, it's assumed it's a new `Destination` and it's left in the added state; if it has a value, it's marked as a modified entity to be updated in the database. The same process is then repeated for each of the `Lodgings` that is referenced from the `Destination`.

Finally the `Lodgings` that are to be deleted are registered in the `Deleted` state. If these `Lodgings` are still referenced from the `Destination`, they are already in the state manager in the added state. If they were not referenced by the `Destination`, the context isn't yet aware of them. Either way, changing the state to `Deleted` will register them for deletion. With the state appropriately set for every entity in the graph, it's time to call Save Changes.

To see the `SaveDestinationAndLodgings` method in action, add the `TestSaveDestinationAndLodgings` method shown in Example 4-13.

Example 4-13. Method to test SaveDestinationAndLodging method

```
private static void TestSaveDestinationAndLodgings()
{
  Destination canyon;
  using (var context = new BreakAwayContext())
  {
    canyon = (from d in context.Destinations.Include(d => d.Lodgings)
              where d.Name == "Grand Canyon"
              select d).Single();
  }

  canyon.TravelWarnings = "Carry enough water!";

  canyon.Lodgings.Add(new Lodging
  {
    Name = "Big Canyon Lodge"
  });

  var firstLodging = canyon.Lodgings.ElementAt(0);
  firstLodging.Name = "New Name Holiday Park";

  var secondLodging = canyon.Lodgings.ElementAt(1);
  var deletedLodgings = new List<Lodging>();
  canyon.Lodgings.Remove(secondLodging);
  deletedLodgings.Add(secondLodging);

  SaveDestinationAndLodgings(canyon, deletedLodgings);
}
```

This method retrieves the Grand Canyon `Destination` from the database, using eager loading to ensure that the related `Lodgings` are also in memory. Next it changes the `TravelWarnings` property of the `canyon`. Then one of the `Lodgings` is modified and another is removed from the `Lodgings` property of the `canyon` and added to a list of `Lodgings` to be deleted. A new `Lodging` is also added to the `canyon`. Finally the `canyon` and the list of `Lodgings` to be deleted are passed to the `SaveDestinationAndLodgings` method. If you update the `Main` method to call `TestSaveDestinationAndLodgings` and run the application, a series of SQL statements will be sent to the database (Figure 4-3).

```
exec sp_executesql N'update [baga].[Locations]...
exec sp_executesql N'update [dbo].[Lodgings]  ...
exec sp_executesql N'delete [dbo].[Lodgings]  ...
exec sp_executesql N'insert [dbo].[Lodgings]([...
```

Figure 4-3. SQL statements during save after setting state for each entity

The first `update` is for the existing Grand Canyon `Destination` that we updated the `TravelWarnings` property on. Next is the `update` for the `Lodging` we changed the name of. Then comes the `delete` for the `Lodging` we added to the list of `Lodgings` to be deleted. Finally, we see the `insert` for the new `Lodging` we created and added to the `Lodgings` collection of the Grand Canyon `Destination`.

Building a Generic Approach to Track State Locally

The `SaveDestination` method we implemented in Example 4-12 isn't overly complex, but if we expose methods to save various parts of our model, we would be repeating the state setting code over and over again in each method. So let's take a look at a more generalized approach to applying changes on the server.

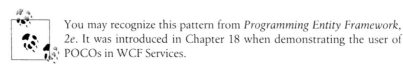 You may recognize this pattern from *Programming Entity Framework*, *2e*. It was introduced in Chapter 18 when demonstrating the user of POCOs in WCF Services.

This approach relies on having a consistent way to determine the state of any entity in your model. The easiest way to achieve that is to have an interface or `abstract` base class that every entity in your model will implement.

Interface Versus Base Class

The decision between using a base class or an interface is entirely up to you. Using a base class means you define the additional properties in one place and then each entity just needs to inherit from the base class. Some developers may prefer the interface because having a common base class for every entity pollutes the shape of the model.

As coauthors we discussed which approach to use in the book and found that there wasn't a clear winner. We opted to use an interface, but the techniques you will learn in this chapter work just as well if you choose to use a base class.

For this example we are going to use an `IObjectWithState` interface that will tell us the current state of the entity. It will have no dependencies on Entity Framework and will be implemented by your domain classes, so it can go in the `Model` project. Go ahead and add the `IObjectWithState` interface to the `Model` project (Example 4-14). Later in this section you'll add this interface to some of your classes.

Example 4-14. Sample interface to determine state of an entity

```
namespace Model
{
  public interface IObjectWithState
  {
    State State { get; set; }
  }

  public enum State
  {
    Added,
    Unchanged,
    Modified,
    Deleted
  }
}
```

Note that we've opted for a new enum to represent state rather than reusing the `Enti tyState` enum from Entity Framework. This ensures our domain model doesn't have any dependencies on types from our data access technology.

Before we get to applying state, it would be useful if any entities we retrieve from the database would have their state automatically set to `Unchanged`. Otherwise the server needs to manually do this before returning the objects to the client. The easiest way to do this is to listen to the `ObjectMaterialized` event on the underlying `ObjectContext`. Add the constructor in Example 4-15 to the `BreakAwayContext` class. You'll need to add a using statement for the `System.Data.Entity.Infrastructure` namespace to get access to the `IObjectContextAdapter` interface.

Example 4-15. Hooking up an event to mark existing entities as Unchanged

```
public BreakAwayContext()
{
  ((IObjectContextAdapter)this).ObjectContext
    .ObjectMaterialized += (sender, args) =>
      {
        var entity = args.Entity as IObjectWithState;
        if (entity != null)
        {
          entity.State = State.Unchanged;
```

```
      }
   };
}
```

The code uses IObjectContextAdapter to get access to the underlying ObjectContext. It then wires up a new handler to the ObjectMaterialized event, which will fire whenever an entity is returned from a query to the database. Because all objects that come from the database are existing objects, we take this opportunity to mark them as Unchanged if they implement our state tracking interface.

In a real-world scenario you would need to implement the change tracking interface on every class in your model. But for the sake of simplicity, we will just use Destination and Lodging for this demonstration. Go ahead and edit the Lodging and Destination classes to implement the IObjectWithState interface:

```
public class Destination : IObjectWithState
```

```
public class Lodging : IObjectWithState
```

You'll also need to add a State property into both of these classes to satisfy the IObjectWithState interface that you just added:

```
public State State { get; set; }
```

Now it's time to write a method that uses all this information to take a disconnected graph and apply the client-side changes to a context by setting the correct state for each entity in the graph.

 One important thing to remember is that this approach is dependent on the client application honoring the contract of setting the correct state. If the client doesn't set the correct state, the save process will not behave correctly.

Add the SaveDestinationGraph and ConvertState methods shown in Example 4-16.

Example 4-16. Setting state based on a state tracking interface

```
public static void SaveDestinationGraph(Destination destination)
{
  using (var context = new BreakAwayContext())
  {
    context.Destinations.Add(destination);

    foreach (var entry in context.ChangeTracker
      .Entries<IObjectWithState>())
    {
      IObjectWithState stateInfo = entry.Entity;
      entry.State = ConvertState(stateInfo.State);
    }

    context.SaveChanges();
  }
```

```
}
public static EntityState ConvertState(State state)
{
  switch (state)
  {
    case State.Added:
      return EntityState.Added;

    case State.Modified:
      return EntityState.Modified;

    case State.Deleted:
      return EntityState.Deleted;

    default:
      return EntityState.Unchanged;
  }
}
```

The code uses DbSet.Add on the root Destination to get the contents of the graph into the context in the Added state. Next it uses the ChangeTracker.Entries<TEntity> method to find the entries for all entities that are tracked by the context and implement IObjectWithState.

> The Entries method will give you access to the same object that you would get by calling DbContext.Entry on each entity. There is a nonge-neric overload of Entries that will give you an entry for every entity that is tracked by the context. The generic overload, which we are using, will filter the entries to those that are of the specified type, derived from the specified type, or implement the specified interface. If you use the generic overload, the Entity property of each entry object will be strongly typed as the type you specified. You'll learn more about the Entries method in Chapter 5.

For each entry, the code converts the state from the entities State property to Entity Framework's EntityState and sets it to the State property for the change tracker entry. Once all the states have been set, it's time to use SaveChanges to push the changes to the database. Now that we have our generalized solution, let's write some code to test it out. We're going to apply the same changes we did back in Example 4-13, but this time using our new method of applying changes. Add the TestSaveDestinationGraph method shown in Example 4-17.

Example 4-17. Testing the new SaveDestinationTest method

```
private static void TestSaveDestinationGraph()
{
  Destination canyon;
  using (var context = new BreakAwayContext())
  {
```

```
    canyon = (from d in context.Destinations.Include(d => d.Lodgings)
              where d.Name == "Grand Canyon"
              select d).Single();
  }

  canyon.TravelWarnings = "Carry enough water!";
  canyon.State = State.Modified;

  var firstLodging = canyon.Lodgings.First();
  firstLodging.Name = "New Name Holiday Park";
  firstLodging.State = State.Modified;

  var secondLodging = canyon.Lodgings.Last();
  secondLodging.State = State.Deleted;

  canyon.Lodgings.Add(new Lodging
  {
    Name = "Big Canyon Lodge",
    State = State.Added
  });

  SaveDestinationGraph(canyon);
}
```

The code simulates a client application that queries for an existing Destination and its
related Lodgings. The Destination is updated and marked as Modified. The first Lodg
ing is also updated and marked as Modified. The second Lodging is marked for deletion
by setting its State property to Deleted. Finally, a new Lodging is put into the Lodg
ings collection with its State set to Added. The graph is then passed to the SaveDestina
tionGraph method. If you update the Main method to call TestSaveDestinationGraph
and run your application, the same SQL statements from Figure 4-3 will be run against
the database.

Creating a Generic Method That Can Apply State Through Any Graph

With some simple tweaks to the SaveDestinationGraph method we wrote in Example 4-16, we can create a method that can work on any root in our model, not just
Destinations. Add the ApplyChanges method shown in Example 4-18.

 The generic method demonstrated in this section is specifically designed
for use with disconnected scenarios where you have a short-lived context. Notice that the context is instantiated in the ApplyChanges method.

Example 4-18. Generalized method for replaying changes from a disconnected graph of entities

```
private static void ApplyChanges<TEntity>(TEntity root)
  where TEntity : class, IObjectWithState
{
  using (var context = new BreakAwayContext())
  {
```

```
context.Set<TEntity>().Add(root);

foreach (var entry in context.ChangeTracker
  .Entries<IObjectWithState>())
{
  IObjectWithState stateInfo = entry.Entity;
  entry.State = ConvertState(stateInfo.State);
}

context.SaveChanges();
    }
}
```

This new method accepts any root that implements `IObjectWithState`. Because we don't know the type of the root until runtime, we don't know which `DbSet` to add it to. Fortunately there is a `Set<T>` method on `DbContext` that can be used to create a set of a type that will be resolved at runtime. We use that to get a set and then add the root. Next we set the state for each entity in the graph and then push the changes to the database. If you want to test this new method out, change the last line of your `TestSaveDestinationGraph` method to call `ApplyChanges` rather than `SaveDestinationGraph`:

```
ApplyChanges(canyon);
```

Running the application will result in the same SQL statements from Figure 4-3 being run again.

There is one potential issue with our `ApplyChanges` method—at the moment it blindly assumes that every entity in the graph implements `IObjectWithState`. If an entity that doesn't implement the interface is present, it will just be left in the `Added` state and Entity Framework will attempt to insert it. Update the `ApplyChanges` method as shown in Example 4-19.

Example 4-19. Checking for entities that don't implement IObjectWithState

```
private static void ApplyChanges<TEntity>(TEntity root)
  where TEntity : class, IObjectWithState
{
  using (var context = new BreakAwayContext())
  {
    context.Set<TEntity>().Add(root);

    CheckForEntitiesWithoutStateInterface(context);

    foreach (var entry in context.ChangeTracker
      .Entries<IObjectWithState>())
    {
      IObjectWithState stateInfo = entry.Entity;
      entry.State = ConvertState(stateInfo.State);
    }

    context.SaveChanges();
  }
}
```

```
private static void CheckForEntitiesWithoutStateInterface(
    BreakAwayContext context)
{
  var entitiesWithoutState =
    from e in context.ChangeTracker.Entries()
    where !(e.Entity is IObjectWithState)
    select e;

  if (entitiesWithoutState.Any())
  {
    throw new NotSupportedException(
      "All entities must implement IObjectWithState");
  }
}
```

The method now calls a CheckForEntitiesWithoutStateInterface helper method that uses the nongeneric overload of ChangeTracker.Entries to get all entities that have been added to the context. It uses a LINQ query to find any of these that don't implement IObjectWithState. If any entities that don't implement IObjectWithState are found, an exception is thrown.

Concurrency Implications

This approach works well with timestamp-style concurrency tokens, where the property that is used as a concurrency token will not be updated on the client. For existing entities, the value of the timestamp property will be sent to the client and then back to the server. The entity will then be registered as Unchanged, Modified, or Deleted with the same value in the concurrency token property as when it was originally queried from the database.

If you need to have concurrency checking in your N-Tier application, timestamp properties are arguably the easiest way to implement this. More information on timestamp properties in Code First models is available in Chapter 3 of *Programming Entity Framework: Code First (http://shop.oreilly.com/product/0636920022220.do)*. For Database First and Model First, see Chapter 23 of *Programming Entity Framework, 2e (http://shop.oreilly.com/product/9780596807252.do)*.

If a property that can be updated on the client is used as a concurrency token, this approach will not suffice. Because this approach does not track the original value of properties, the concurrency token will only have the updated value for the concurrency check. This value will be checked against the database value during save, and a concurrency exception will be thrown because it will not match the value in the database. To overcome this limitation you will need to use the approach described in "Recording Original Values" on page 102.

Tracking Individually Modified Properties

So far, the methods you've seen have focused on changing the state of an entity. For a lot of applications, it's enough to simply track the state at the entity level and update entire objects just as you would when relying on stored procedures. However, you may find yourself wanting to be more granular with the way modified properties are tracked. Rather than marking the entire entity as modified, you might want only the properties that have actually changed to be marked as modified. This is how change tracking works when properties of a tracked entity are modified. It ensures that only the properties that have actually been changed would be included in the update statement. In this section we'll take a quick look at some common approaches to achieving granular property tracking when the entities are disconnected from the context:

- Keeping track of modified properties on the client side and passing that list to the server along with the entities
- Storing the original properties into the entities when they are retrieved from the database before passing them onto the client
- Requerying the database when the entities have been returned to the server from the client

 The samples provided in this section will provide you with a closer look at the Change Tracker API that is tied to the DbContext API. The Entity Framework team worked hard to make our lives easier when dealing with disconnected scenarios. You've already seen some of the benefits we developers can reap from their work, and you'll see more as you read through to the end of this chapter.

Recording Modified Property Names

This first approach is very similar to tracking state at the entity level. In addition to marking an entity as modified, the client is also responsible for recording which properties have been modified. One way to do this would be to add a list of modified property names to the state tracking interface. Update the IObjectWithState interface to include a ModifiedProperties property, as shown in Example 4-20.

Example 4-20. State tracking interface updated to include modified properties

```
using System.Collections.Generic;

namespace Model
{
  public interface IObjectWithState
  {
    State State { get; set; }
    List<string> ModifiedProperties { get; set; }
  }
}
```

```
public enum State
{
  Added,
  Unchanged,
  Modified,
  Deleted
}
}
```

You'll also need to add this property to the Destination and Lodging classes to satisfy this new addition to the IObjectWithState interface:

```
public List<string> ModifiedProperties { get; set; }
```

Now that we have a place to record the modified properties, let's update the Apply Changes method to make use of it, as shown in Example 4-21.

Example 4-21. Updating ApplyChanges to use ModifiedProperties

```
private static void ApplyChanges<TEntity>(TEntity root)
  where TEntity : class, IObjectWithState
{
  using (var context = new BreakAwayContext())
  {
    context.Set<TEntity>().Add(root);

    CheckForEntitiesWithoutStateInterface(context);

    foreach (var entry in context.ChangeTracker
      .Entries<IObjectWithState>())
    {
      IObjectWithState stateInfo = entry.Entity;
      if (stateInfo.State  == State.Modified)
      {
        entry.State = EntityState.Unchanged;
        foreach (var property in stateInfo.ModifiedProperties)
        {
          entry.Property(property).IsModified = true;
        }
      }
      else
      {
        entry.State = ConvertState(stateInfo.State);
      }
    }

    context.SaveChanges();
  }
}
```

The changes to the method are inside the foreach loop where we apply the state. If we find a modified entity in the graph, we mark it as Unchanged, rather than Modified. Once the entity is marked as Unchanged, we loop through the modified properties and mark each of them as modified. We do this using the `Property` method on the entry to get the change tracking information for the given property and then setting the `IsModified` property to `true`. As soon as we mark one of the properties as modified, the state of the entity will also move to `Modified`. But only the properties we marked as modified will be updated when we save.

 There are two overloads of `Property`, one that accepts the name of the property as a string and the other that accepts a lambda expression representing the property. We are using the string property because we don't know the names of the properties we want to access until runtime. If you know the name of the property you want to access, you can use the lambda version so that you get compile-time checking of the supplied value (for example, `context.Entry(destination).Property(d => d.Name).IsModified = true`).

You'll also need to update the `TestSaveDestinationGraph` method to populate `Modified Properties` for the `Destination` and `Lodging` that are modified:

```
canyon.TravelWarnings = "Carry enough water!";
    canyon.State = State.Modified;
    canyon.ModifiedProperties = new List<string> { "TravelWarnings" };

    var firstLodging = canyon.Lodgings.First();
    firstLodging.Name = "New Name Holiday Park";
    firstLodging.State = State.Modified;
    firstLodging.ModifiedProperties = new List<string> { "Name" };
```

If you run the application again, you will see a set of SQL statements similar to the ones in Figure 4-3. This time, however, the `update` statements only set the properties we marked as modified. Here is the SQL from the update statement for the `Destination`:

```
exec sp_executesql N'update [baga].[Locations]
set [TravelWarnings] = @0
where ([LocationID] = @1)
',N'@0 nvarchar(max) ,@1 int',
@0=N'Carry enough water!',@1=1
```

Complex Types

Entity Framework uses a single value to record whether the properties stored inside a complex property are modified or not. If any of the properties are modified, the root complex property is marked as modified and all the properties inside the complex property will be set in the UPDATE statement that is issued during `SaveChanges`. For example, if the `Address.State` property is modified on an existing `Person`, Entity Framework records the entire Address property as modified. All the properties associated with a `Person`s address will be included in the `UPDATE` statement during `SaveChanges`.

The code shown in Example 4-21 assumes that the client uses the same logic when populating the `ModifiedProperties` collection. If the `Address.State` property is modified, the `ModifiedProperties` collection will just contain `"Address"`. The `ApplyChanges` code will then use the change tracker API to mark the `Address` property as modified.

Information on working with the change tracking information of individual properties inside a complex property is provided in "Working with Complex Properties" on page 131.

Concurrency implications

This approach has the same implications for concurrency as the generic approach you saw in the previous section. Timestamp concurrency properties will work well, but concurrency properties that can be modified on the client will cause issues.

Recording Original Values

An alternative to asking the client to record the properties that were modified is to keep track of the original values for existing entities. One of the big advantages of this approach is that you are no longer relying on the client to tell you which properties were modified. This makes the code on the client side much simpler and less error prone. Entity Framework can then check for changes between the original and current values to determine if anything is modified. Let's change the `IObjectWithState` interface to record original values rather than modified properties. Because we are going to calculate whether an entity is modified or not, we no longer need the `Modified` option in the `State` enum, so let's remove that, too. These changes are shown in Example 4-22.

Example 4-22. Change state tracking interface to use original values

```
using System.Collections.Generic;

namespace Model
{
  public interface IObjectWithState
  {
    State State { get; set; }
    Dictionary<string, object> OriginalValues { get; set; }
  }

  public enum State
  {
    Added,
    Unchanged,
    Deleted
  }
}
```

You'll also need to remove the `ModifiedProperties` property from `Destination` and `Lodging` and add in the new `OriginalValues` property:

```
public Dictionary<string, object> OriginalValues { get; set; }
```

We want Entity Framework to automatically populate the OriginalValues property when an entity is retrieved from the database, so let's update the event handler we added to the constructor of our context (Example 4-23). You'll need to add a using statement for the System.Collections.Generic namespace.

Example 4-23. Populating original values after query

```
public BreakAwayContext()
{
  ((IObjectContextAdapter)this).ObjectContext
    .ObjectMaterialized += (sender, args) =>
    {
      var entity = args.Entity as IObjectWithState;
      if (entity != null)
      {
        entity.State = State.Unchanged;

        entity.OriginalValues =
          BuildOriginalValues(this.Entry(entity).OriginalValues);
      }
    };
}

private static Dictionary<string, object> BuildOriginalValues(
  DbPropertyValues originalValues)
{
  var result = new Dictionary<string, object>();
  foreach (var propertyName in originalValues.PropertyNames)
  {
    var value = originalValues[propertyName];
    if (value is DbPropertyValues)
    {
      result[propertyName] =
        BuildOriginalValues((DbPropertyValues)value);
    }
    else
    {
      result[propertyName] = value;
    }
  }
  return result;
}
```

In addition to marking the entity as Unchanged, this updated code will populate the OriginalValues property. It does this by getting the original values from the change tracking entry for the entity and using the BuildOriginalValue helper method to convert them to the required dictionary format. The helper method loops through each of the properties that we have original values for. If the value is just a normal scalar property, it copies the value of the property to into the resulting dictionary. If the value is a DbPropertyValues, this indicates that it is a complex property and the code uses a recursive call to build a nested dictionary of the values in the complex property. More information on nested DbPropertyValues for complex properties is available in "Working with Complex Properties" on page 131.

Because the entity has just been returned from the database, the current and original values are the same, so we could have also used the CurrentValues property to get the values. Now we can update the ApplyChanges method to make use of this property (Example 4-24).

Example 4-24. Using original values in ApplyChanges

```
private static void ApplyChanges<TEntity>(TEntity root)
  where TEntity : class, IObjectWithState
{
  using (var context = new BreakAwayContext())
  {
    context.Set<TEntity>().Add(root);

    CheckForEntitiesWithoutStateInterface(context);

    foreach (var entry in context.ChangeTracker
      .Entries<IObjectWithState>())
    {
      IObjectWithState stateInfo = entry.Entity;
      entry.State = ConvertState(stateInfo.State);
      if (stateInfo.State == State.Unchanged)
      {
        ApplyPropertyChanges(entry.OriginalValues,
          stateInfo.OriginalValues);
      }
    }

    context.SaveChanges();
  }
}

private static void ApplyPropertyChanges(
  DbPropertyValues values,
  Dictionary<string, object> originalValues)
{
  foreach (var originalValue in originalValues)
  {
    if (originalValue.Value is Dictionary<string, object>)
    {
      ApplyPropertyChanges(
        (DbPropertyValues)values[originalValue.Key],
        (Dictionary<string, object>)originalValue.Value);
    }
    else
    {
      values[originalValue.Key] = originalValue.Value;
    }
  }
}
```

After painting the state of entities throughout the graph, the code now checks to see if it's an existing entity. For existing entities the code uses the ApplyPropertyChanges helper method to set the original values for the entity. The helper method loops through the OriginalValues that were captured when the entity was retrieved from the database. If the value is a nested dictionary, indicating a complex property, then it uses a recursive call to apply the changes for the individual properties inside the complex property. If the value is just a scalar value, it updates the original value being stored by the context. Entity Framework will detect if any of the values differ from the values currently assigned to the properties of the entity. If a difference is detected, the property, and therefore the entity, will be marked as modified. We also need to update the Convert State method because we no longer have a Modified option in the State enum (Example 4-25).

Example 4-25. ConvertState updated to reflect removal of Modified state

```
public static EntityState ConvertState(State state)
{
  switch (state)
  {
    case State.Added:
      return EntityState.Added;

    case State.Deleted:
      return EntityState.Deleted;

    default:
      return EntityState.Unchanged;
  }
}
```

To test out the new logic, you can update the TestSaveDestinationGraph method to no longer mark entities as Modified when it changes properties (Example 4-26). This is no longer required because the ApplyChanges method will calculate this for you.

Example 4-26. Updating the test method to test recording of original values

```
private static void TestSaveDestinationGraph()
{
  Destination canyon;
  using (var context = new BreakAwayContext())
  {
    canyon = (from d in context.Destinations.Include(d => d.Lodgings)
              where d.Name == "Grand Canyon"
              select d).Single();
  }

  canyon.TravelWarnings = "Carry enough water!";

  var firstLodging = canyon.Lodgings.First();
  firstLodging.Name = "New Name Holiday Park";

  var secondLodging = canyon.Lodgings.Last();
```

```
    secondLodging.State = State.Deleted;

    canyon.Lodgings.Add(new Lodging
    {
      Name = "Big Canyon Lodge",
      State = State.Added
    });

    ApplyChanges(canyon);
}
```

If you run the application, you will get the familiar set of SQL statements from Figure 4-3. The update statements that are generated will only set properties that were actually modified.

Concurrency implications

This approach offers the best concurrency support because it records the same information that is stored by the change tracker when modifying entities that are attached to a context. Timestamp concurrency properties will work because the value retrieved from the database is sent to the client and then back to the server, to be used when updating existing data. Concurrency properties that can be modified will also work because the original value, which was assigned to the property when it was retrieved from the database, is recorded. Because this value is set as the original value for the property, Entity Framework will use the original value when performing concurrency checks.

Querying and Applying Changes

Another approach that developers sometimes try is to calculate the modified properties by querying the database to get the current entity and then copying the values from the incoming entity. Because this approach requires one query to get the entity from the database and often a second query to update the data, it's usually slower than just marking the entity as modified and updating every column. That said, sending a lot of unnecessary updates to the database isn't ideal. If one of the other techniques in this chapter doesn't work for you, this may be worth looking at.

Entity Framework makes it easy to copy the values from one object to another. Putting graphs aside for a moment, we could implement an UpdateDestination method as follows:

```
    public static void UpdateDestination(Destination destination)
    {
      using (var context = new BreakAwayContext())
      {
        if (destination.DestinationId > 0)
        {
          var existingDestiantion = context.Destinations
            .Find(destination.DestinationId);
```

```
        context.Entry(existingDestiantion)
          .CurrentValues
          .SetValues(destination);
      }
      else
      {
        context.Destinations.Add(destination);
      }

      context.SaveChanges();
    }
  }
```

If the `Destination` has a key value assigned, it's assumed to be an existing `Destina`
`tion`. The `Find` method is used to load the `Destination` from the database. The `SetVal`
`ues` method is used on `CurrentValues` to copy values from the incoming `Destination` to
the existing `Destination` from the database. Entity Framework will automatically detect
if any of the property values are different. If there are differences, the appropriate prop‐
erties will be marked as modified.

This approach falls down when you start working with graphs, though. Let's assume
the incoming `Destination` references a new `Lodging`. We can't query for this `Lodging`
from the database, since it's new, so we need to register this `Lodging` for addition. The
problem is if we try and add the `Lodging` to the context, it will also try and add any other
entities that it references. If the `Lodging` references an existing entity, it's going to end
up in the context in the added state. This gets very complicated, because we now want
to try and take this existing entity back out of the context so that we can query for the
entity from the database and copy its values over.

While it is technically possible to make this work, the code gets very complicated.
Fortunately, there is a better alternative. Rather than getting the existing entity from
the database and copying the values to it, we can attach the incoming entity and then
set its original values to the values from the database. Update the `ApplyChanges` method
as shown in Example 4-27.

Example 4-27. ApplyChanges checks for modification using database values

```
private static void ApplyChanges<TEntity>(TEntity root)
  where TEntity : class, IObjectWithState
{
  using (var context = new BreakAwayContext())
  {
    context.Set<TEntity>().Add(root);

    CheckForEntitiesWithoutStateInterface(context);

    foreach (var entry in context.ChangeTracker
      .Entries<IObjectWithState>())
    {
      IObjectWithState stateInfo = entry.Entity;
      entry.State = ConvertState(stateInfo.State);
```

```
      if (stateInfo.State == State.Unchanged)
      {
        var databaseValues = entry.GetDatabaseValues();
        entry.OriginalValues.SetValues(databaseValues);
      }
    }

    context.SaveChanges();
  }
}
```

Rather than getting the original values that were recorded when the entity was retrieved from the database, the code now gets the current original values from the database. In fact, the OriginalValues property on IObjectWithState is now no longer required. The database values are retrieved using the GetDatabaseValues method. This method returns DbPropertyValues, which is the same type returned from the CurrentValues and Origi nalValues property on an entity. The SetValues method on DbPropertyValues will copy the values from any other DbPropertyValues instance into itself. We use this function- ality to copy the database values into the original values for each entity. If you run the application, SQL statements similar to those from Figure 4-3 will be executed against the database. However, this time the update statements will only set the properties that were actually changed.

Concurrency implications

This approach bypasses concurrency checks because it requeries for the database values just before saving any changes. These new database values are used in place of the values that were originally retrieved from the database when sending data to the client. If you are using concurrency tokens, this approach to replaying changes on the server is not suitable.

Caching Original Entities

Another approach that developers sometimes use is to cache the original entities that are retrieved from the context. These cached entities can then be used to calculate the modified properties when it comes time to save. This approach is effectively the same as the "Query and Apply Changes" method, but it uses cached in-memory entities, instead of querying the database, to calculate changes.

This approach may initially seem attractive because it reduces the round trips to the database and removes the need to include any state information on the entities that are returned to the client application. It is, however, very complex and not recommended unless absolutely required.

In an N-Tier application, the server typically has no way to know which "save data" calls align with which "get data" calls. For example, inside the UpdateDestination method you don't know which call was used to get the data. This makes it hard to know which cached graph to use for comparison. The two common solutions to this are to implement some form of session ID, or to implement a second-level cache.

The session ID approach involves returning a unique identifier to the client alongside any data that is returned. When the client wants to save changes to the data, it must also supply this unique ID that can be used to locate the cached graph for comparison. This gets very complicated when you start to think about server farms where the "get data" and "save data" calls may be processed by different physical servers. Also consider long-running client applications where the user might query for some data, leave the application open overnight, and then save in the morning.

The second-level cache approach involves having a single in-memory cache that is used for all requests on the server. When data is queried from the database, it is stored in the cache ready to be used for comparison. Because multiple queries may return the same data, or at least overlapping data, the cache needs to take care of merging results so that duplicate entities don't exist in the cache. Second-level caches can provide a nice performance improvement because you can also query against the cache to avoid hitting the database to return data. Entity Framework does not have built-in support for a second-level cache, so you need to do a lot of work to wire one up. This gets particularly complicated when you start to think about setting expiration rules for your data so that stale data doesn't remain in the cache when the database gets updated.

If you want to get a deep education on the pros and cons of caching with ORMs, check out this article on the Association for Computing Machinery (ACM) website: "Exposing the ORM Cache: Familiarity with ORM caching issues can help prevent performance problems and bugs" (*http://queue.acm.org/detail.cfm?id=1394141*).

CHAPTER 5

Change Tracker API

So far you have seen how to use Entity Framework to query for data from the database and save changes to those entities back to the database. You've seen how Entity Framework will keep track of any changes you make to entities that are being tracked by a context. It is the responsibility of the Change Tracker to keep track of these changes as you make them.

In this chapter you will learn about using the Change Tracker API to access the information that Entity Framework is storing about the entities it is tracking. This information goes beyond the values stored in the properties of your entities and includes the current state of the entity, the original values from the database, which properties have been modified, and other data. The Change Tracker API also gives you access to additional operations that can be performed on an entity, such as reloading its values from the database to ensure you have the latest data.

You've already seen bits of the Change Tracker API in action in earlier chapters. In Chapter 2 you saw how to perform explicit loading using the DbContext.Entry. In Chapter 3 you saw how to get the Change Tracker to scan your entities for changes using the DbContext.ChangeTracker.DetectChanges method. In Chapter 4 you saw how to set the state of an entity, mark individual properties as modified, and work with original values using the Entry method. You also saw how to look at all entities being tracked by the context using the DbContext.ChangeTracker.Entries method.

We'll start this chapter by taking a tour of all the information and operations that are available in the Change Tracker API. Then we'll wrap up the chapter by looking at how these operations can be combined to save time logging and resolving concurrency conflicts.

Change Tracking Information and Operations for a Single Entity

The easiest way to get access to the change tracking information for an entity is using the Entry method on DbContext. Entry returns a DbEntityEntry instance, which gives you access to the information and operations available for the entity. There are two overloads of `Entry`. One is generic (`Entry<TEntity>`) and will return a strongly typed `DbEntityEntry<TEntity>`:

```
public DbEntityEntry<TEntity> Entry<TEntity>(TEntity entity)
```

The other overload is nongeneric and returns `DbEntityEntry`:

```
public DbEntityEntry Entry(object entity);
```

Both of these provide access to exactly the same information and operations. Because the strongly typed `DbEntityEntry<TEntity>` knows the type of entity it represents, it allows you to use lambda expressions when drilling into property details, so that you get IntelliSense and additional compile-time checks. You don't need to worry about selecting the correct overload—the compiler will take care of this for you. If the entity you pass to `Entry` is typed as `object`, you will get the nongeneric `DbEntityEntry`. If the entity you pass in is typed as something more specific than `object` (for example, `Destination`), you will get the generic `DbEntityEntry<TEntity>`, where `TEntity` is the same type as the entity you pass in. You'll see both of these overloads in action in the next couple of sections.

Working with the State Property

One of the core pieces of change tracking information is what state the entity is currently in: `Added`, `Unchanged`, `Modified`, or `Deleted`. This can be determined using the `State` property on `DbEntityEntry`. To see how this works, add the `PrintState` method shown in Example 5-1.

Example 5-1. Reading the State property

```
private static void PrintState()
{
  using (var context = new BreakAwayContext())
  {
    var canyon = (from d in context.Destinations
                  where d.Name == "Grand Canyon"
                  select d).Single();

    DbEntityEntry<Destination> entry = context.Entry(canyon);

    Console.WriteLine("Before Edit: {0}", entry.State);
    canyon.TravelWarnings = "Take lots of water.";
    Console.WriteLine("After Edit: {0}", entry.State);
  }
}
```

The code retrieves the Grand Canyon destination from the database and then locates the change tracking entry for it. The `canyon` variable is strongly typed as `Destination`, so the compiler selects the generic overload of `Entry` and we get a strongly typed `DbEntityEntry<Destination>` returned. The code then prints out the state of `canyon` as recorded in the change tracker. Next, the `TravelWarnings` property is modified and then the State is printed out again. Update the Main method to call the PrintState method and run the application. The console window will display the following:

```
Before Edit: Unchanged
After Edit: Modified
```

As expected, the canyon object is reported as Unchanged after it is retrieved from the database. After modifying one of its properties, the object is seen by the change tracker as being in the Modified state.

Back in Chapter 3, we enabled Destination as a *change tracking proxy*, meaning that changes to any instances of Destination are reported to the context in real time. Entities that are not change tracking proxies require an explicit or implicit call to DetectCh anges to scan for any changes to the object. Most of the methods on DbContext will automatically call DetectChanges for you. Entry is one of those methods. But reading the State property will not cause an automatic DetectChanges. If Destination was not a change tracking proxy, you would need to call DetectChanges after setting the Trav elWarnings property to get the correct state reported. More information on DetectCh anges is available in the Using Snapshot Change Tracking section of Chapter 3. You can avoid the need to call DetectChanges by calling Entry each time you need the entry, rather than keeping a reference to it. For example, rather than storing the entry in the entry variable as you did in Example 5-1, you could use Entry each time you want the state:

```
Console.WriteLine("Before Edit: {0}", context.Entry(canyon).State);
canyon.TravelWarnings = "Take lots of water.";
Console.WriteLine("After Edit: {0}", context.Entry(canyon).State);
```

 The State property also exposes a public setter, meaning you can assign a state to an entity. Setting the state is useful when you are working with disconnected graphs of entities—typically in N-Tier scenarios. Chapter 4 of this book is dedicated to learning about the various ways to set the state of entities, including setting the State property.

Working with Current, Original, and Database Values

Along with the current state of an entity, DbEntityEntry gives you access to the entity's current, original, and database values. The DbPropertyValues type is used to represent each of these sets of properties. Current values are the values that are currently set in the properties of the entity. Original values are the values for each property when the entity was originally attached to the context; for example, when the entity was first retrieved from the database. Database values are the values currently stored in the database, which may have changed since you queried for the entity. Accessing database values involves Entity Framework performing a behind-the-scenes query for you.

There is a bug in Entity Framework 4.1 and 4.2 that blocks you from using the `GetDatabaseValues` method for an entity that is not in the same namespace as your context. The Entity Framework team has fixed this bug in the Entity Framework 4.3 release. If you are using Entity Framework 4.2 or earlier, you will need to modify the namespace of your context class to be the same as your domain classes. Failure to make this change will result in an `EntitySqlException` if you attempt to retrieve the database values for an entity.

Let's start by writing a method that will output these various values for any given `Lodging`. Add the `PrintChangeTrackingInfo` method shown in Example 5-2.

Example 5-2. Printing change tracking info for a Lodging

```
private static void PrintChangeTrackingInfo(
  BreakAwayContext context,
  Lodging entity)
{
  var entry = context.Entry(entity);

  Console.WriteLine(entry.Entity.Name);

  Console.WriteLine("State: {0}", entry.State);

  Console.WriteLine("\nCurrent Values:");
  PrintPropertyValues(entry.CurrentValues);

  Console.WriteLine("\nOriginal Values:");
  PrintPropertyValues(entry.OriginalValues);

  Console.WriteLine("\nDatabase Values:");
  PrintPropertyValues(entry.GetDatabaseValues());
}

private static void PrintPropertyValues(DbPropertyValues values)
{
  foreach (var propertyName in values.PropertyNames)
  {
    Console.WriteLine(" - {0}: {1}",
      propertyName,
      values[propertyName]);
  }
}
```

The code starts by looking up the change tracking entry for the supplied `Lodging`. Because the `lodging` variable is strongly typed as `Lodging`, the compiler will select the generic overload of `Entry`. The code then prints out the `Name` of the `Lodging`. Of course, we could have just gotten the name from the `lodging` variable, but we are using the `Entity` property on the entry for demonstration purposes. Because the entry is strongly typed, the `Entity` property provides strongly typed access to the `Destination`, which is why we can call `entry.Entity.Name`.

The code then loops through the current, original, and database values and writes the value for each property using the `PrintPropertyValues` helper method. These collections of values are all the `DbPropertyValues` type. Note that there is no way to directly iterate over the values, so you need to iterate over the names of the properties and look up the value for each property. `GetDatabaseValues` will send a query to the database at the time it is called, to determine what values are currently stored in the database. A new query will be sent to the database every time you call the method.

 This method for accessing current, original, and database values uses a string to identify the property to get the value for. In "Working with Individual Properties" on page 128, you will learn about a strongly typed way to specify the property.

Now let's write a method to test out our change tracking logic. Go ahead and add the `PrintLodgingInfo` method shown in Example 5-3.

Example 5-3. Method to test PrintChangeTrackingInfo

```
private static void PrintLodgingInfo()
{
  using (var context = new BreakAwayContext())
  {
    var hotel = (from d in context.Lodgings
                    where d.Name == "Grand Hotel"
                    select d).Single();

    hotel.Name = "Super Grand Hotel";

    context.Database.ExecuteSqlCommand(
      @"UPDATE Lodgings
        SET Name = 'Not-So-Grand Hotel'
        WHERE Name = 'Grand Hotel'");

    PrintChangeTrackingInfo(context, hotel);
  }
}
```

This new method locates an existing `Lodging` from the database and modifies its `Name` property. The code then uses `Database.ExecuteSqlCommand` to run some raw SQL to modify the name of the `Lodging` in the database. You'll learn more about executing raw SQL against the database in Chapter 8. Finally, the `hotel` instance is passed to our `PrintChangeTrackingInfo` method. Update the `Main` method to call `PrintLodgingInfo` and run the application, which will output the following to the console:

```
Super Grand Hotel
State: Modified

Current Values:
 - LodgingId: 1
 - Name: Super Grand Hotel
```

```
        - Owner:
        - MilesFromNearestAirport: 2.50
        - DestinationId: 1
        - PrimaryContactId:
        - SecondaryContactId:

    Original Values:
        - LodgingId: 1
        - Name: Grand Hotel
        - Owner:
        - MilesFromNearestAirport: 2.50
        - DestinationId: 1
        - PrimaryContactId:
        - SecondaryContactId:

    Database Values:
        - LodgingId: 1
        - Name: Not-So-Grand Hotel
        - Owner:
        - MilesFromNearestAirport: 2.50
        - DestinationId: 1
        - PrimaryContactId:
        - SecondaryContactId:
```

As expected, the current name of the hotel is printed out. Since we changed the `Name`, the `State` of the entity is displayed as `Modified`. The current value for `Name` shows the new name that we assigned in `PrintLodgingInfo` ("Super Grand Hotel"). The original value of `Name` shows the value when we retrieved the `Lodging` from the database ("Grand Hotel"). The database value of `Name` shows the new value we assigned in the database using the raw SQL command, after the hotel was retrieved from the database ("Not-So-Grand Hotel").

The code from Example 5-2 works nicely for existing entities, because they have current, original, and database values. But this isn't true for new entities or entities that are marked for deletion. New entities don't have original values or database values. Entity Framework doesn't track current values for entities that are marked for deletion. If you try to access such values, Entity Framework will throw an exception. Let's add some conditional logic in `PrintChangeTrackingInfo` to account for these restrictions. Replace the code that prints out current, original, and database values with the code in Example 5-4.

Example 5-4. Avoiding trying to access invalid values

```
if (entry.State != EntityState.Deleted)
{
  Console.WriteLine("\nCurrent Values:");
  PrintPropertyValues(entry.CurrentValues);
}

if (entry.State != EntityState.Added)
{
  Console.WriteLine("\nOriginal Values:");
```

```
  PrintPropertyValues(entry.OriginalValues);

  Console.WriteLine("\nDatabase Values:");
  PrintPropertyValues(entry.GetDatabaseValues());
}
```

The updated code now checks the State of the entry and skips printing out current values for entities that are marked for deletion. The code also skips printing original and database values for newly added entities. Let's also update the PrintLodgingInfo method so that we can see these changes in action (Example 5-5).

Example 5-5. Modified PrintLodgingInfo method

```
private static void PrintLodgingInfo()
{
  using (var context = new BreakAwayContext())
  {
    var hotel = (from d in context.Lodgings
                 where d.Name == "Grand Hotel"
                 select d).Single();

    PrintChangeTrackingInfo(context, hotel);

    var davesDump = (from d in context.Lodgings
                     where d.Name == "Dave's Dump"
                     select d).Single();

    context.Lodgings.Remove(davesDump);

    PrintChangeTrackingInfo(context, davesDump);

    var newMotel = new Lodging { Name = "New Motel" };

    context.Lodgings.Add(newMotel);

    PrintChangeTrackingInfo(context, newMotel);
  }
}
```

The updated code now also locates Dave's Dump and marks it for deletion. The code also adds New Motel to the context. PrintChangeTrackingInfo is called for both of these entities. If you run the application again, you will see that the relevant change tracking information is successfully displayed for all three locations.

The PrintChangeTrackingInfo method will currently only work for Lodgings, because the entity parameter is strongly typed. But most of the code in the method is not specific to the Lodging type. Let's change the PrintChangeTrackingInfo method to accept any entity type by changing the entity parameter to be typed as object rather than Lodging:

```
private static void PrintChangeTrackingInfo(
    BreakAwayContext context,
    object entity)
```

Since the entity may not be a `Lodging`, the compiler now selects the nongeneric `Entry` method, which returns the nongeneric `DbEntityEntry`. Because we no longer know what type the entity is, we can't be sure that there is a `Name` property to print—in fact, the compiler will give us an error if we try to. Remove the line that printed out the name of the `Lodging` and replace it with a line that prints out the type of the entity instead:

```
Console.WriteLine("Type: {0}", entry.Entity.GetType());
```

Go ahead and run the application. You will see that the updated code continues to successfully display change tracking information.

So far, our examples have used the *indexer* syntax to get the value for a property out of `DbPropertyValues`. The indexer syntax is where you used square braces on an object to specify the key/index of the value you want to retrieve (in other words, `entry.Current Values["Name"]`). Because there is no way to know what type will be returned from each property, the return type of the indexer on `DbPropertyValues` is `object`. There may be times where you do know what type the value will be. Rather than casting the return value to the required type, you can use the `GetValue<TValue>` method to specify the type of the value. For example, you may want to find the original value that was assigned to the `Name` property of a `Lodging` when it was retrieved from the database. Add the `PrintOriginalName` method shown in Example 5-6.

Example 5-6. Using GetValue<TValue> to get a strongly typed original value

```
private static void PrintOriginalName()
{
  using (var context = new BreakAwayContext())
  {
    var hotel = (from d in context.Lodgings
                 where d.Name == "Grand Hotel"
                 select d).Single();

    hotel.Name = "Super Grand Hotel";

    string originalName = context.Entry(hotel)
      .OriginalValues
      .GetValue<string>("Name");

    Console.WriteLine("Current Name: {0}", hotel.Name);
    Console.WriteLine("Original Name: {0}", originalName);
  }
}
```

The code retrieves a `Lodging` from the database and changes its `Name` property. The code then looks up the original value for the `Name` property using the `GetValue` method on the `OriginalValues` for the entity. Because we know that `Name` is a `string` property, the code specifies `string` as the `TValue` when calling `GetValues`. The original value is returned as a `string` and the current and original value for the `Name` property are then printed to the console.

Working with DbPropertyValues for Complex Types

Let's look at how you can work with DbPropertyValues when you have a property on your entity that uses a complex type. Remember that complex types allow you to group multiple scalar values into a class. A property that references a complex type is known as a *complex property*. For example, the BAGA model uses an Address complex type to group address related properties (Example 5-7).

Example 5-7. The existing Address classes

```
[ComplexType]
public class Address
{
  public int AddressId { get; set; }
  [MaxLength(150)]
  [Column("StreetAddress")]
  public string StreetAddress { get; set; }
  [Column("City")]
  public string City { get; set; }
  [Column("State")]
  public string State { get; set; }
  [Column("ZipCode")]
  public string ZipCode { get; set; }
}
```

 Code First convention recognizes complex types when the type has no key property. Since Address has a property that Code First will recognize as a key, AddressId, and therefore will infer this to be an entity type, the class is explicitly marked as a ComplexType.

This complex type is then used by the Address property in the Person class (Example 5-8). Person.Address is therefore a complex property. Note that PersonInfo is also a complex type.

Example 5-8. The existing Person Class

```
[Table("People")]
public class Person
{
  public Person()
  {
    Address = new Address();
    Info = new PersonalInfo
    {
      Weight = new Measurement(),
      Height = new Measurement()
    };
  }

  public int PersonId { get; set; }
  [ConcurrencyCheck]
```

```
  public int SocialSecurityNumber { get; set; }
  public string FirstName { get; set; }
  public string LastName { get; set; }
  public Address Address { get; set; }
  public PersonalInfo Info { get; set; }

  public List<Lodging> PrimaryContactFor { get; set; }
  public List<Lodging> SecondaryContactFor { get; set; }
  [Required]
  public PersonPhoto Photo { get; set; }
  public List<Reservation> Reservations { get; set; }
}
```

To demonstrate how DbPropertyValues handles complex types, let's create a new Person and pass it to our PrintChangeTrackingInfo method. Add the PrintPersonInfo method shown in Example 5-9.

Example 5-9. Printing change tracking information for an entity with a complex property

```
private static void PrintPersonInfo()
{
  using (var context = new BreakAwayContext())
  {
    var person = new Person
    {
      FirstName = "John",
      LastName = "Doe",
      Address = new Address { State = "VT" }
    };

    context.People.Add(person);

    PrintChangeTrackingInfo(context, person);
  }
}
```

When we get the value for a complex property from DbPropertyValues, it's going to return another DbPropertyValues that contains the values from the complex type. Let's update the PrintPropertyValues helper method to account for this (Example 5-10).

Example 5-10. PrintPropertyValues updated to account for complex properties

```
private static void PrintPropertyValues(
  DbPropertyValues values,
  int indent = 1)
{
  foreach (var propertyName in values.PropertyNames)
  {
    var value = values[propertyName];
    if (value is DbPropertyValues)
    {
      Console.WriteLine(
        "{0}- Complex Property: {1}",
        string.Empty.PadLeft(indent),
```

```
      propertyName);

    PrintPropertyValues(
      (DbPropertyValues)value,
      indent + 1);
  }
  else
  {
    Console.WriteLine(
      "{0}- {1}: {2}",
      string.Empty.PadLeft(indent),
      propertyName,
      values[propertyName]);
  }
 }
}
```

For each property being printed, the code now checks if the value is a `DbPropertyVal`ues. If it is, the code prints out the name of the complex property and then recursively calls `PrintPropertyValues` with the values for the complex type. `PrintPropertyValues` also allows an indent level to be supplied, which is used to indent the values of a complex property. If an indent is not supplied, a default indent of 1 is used. Update the `Main` method to call `PrintPersonInfo` and run the application. The console will display the following output:

```
Type: Model.Person
State: Added

Current Values:
  - PersonId: 0
  - SocialSecurityNumber: 0
  - FirstName: John
  - LastName: Doe
  - Complex Property: Address
  - AddressId: 0
  - StreetAddress:
  - City:
  - State: VT
  - ZipCode:
  - Complex Property: Info
  - Complex Property: Weight
   - Reading: 0
   - Units:
  - Complex Property: Height
   - Reading: 0
   - Units:
  - DietryRestrictions:
```

The console output is displaying the property values contained in the `Address` property. You'll also notice that the code works for nested complex types. `Person.Info` is a complex property that references the `PersonInfo` complex type. `PersonInfo` also has complex properties for a `Person`'s `Height` and `Weight`. From the printout you can see that the

DbPropertyValues for the Info complex property returned another DbPropertyValues for its Weight and Height properties.

Copying the Values from DbPropertyValues into an Entity

Having a single object, like DbPropertyValues, that represents a set of values is handy. However, we usually want to write application logic in terms of our domain classes, rather than a type such as DbPropertyValues. For example, we might have a method that defines how we display a Destination for the user of our application to see. We can pass any instance of a Destination into the method to print out its current values, but it would be good if we could use that same method to print out the original and database values as well. Add the PrintDestination method shown in Example 5-11.

Example 5-11. Method to print information about a Destination

```
private static void PrintDestination(Destination destination)
{
  Console.WriteLine("-- {0}, {1} --",
    destination.Name,
    destination.Country);

  Console.WriteLine(destination.Description);

  if (destination.TravelWarnings != null)
  {
    Console.WriteLine("WARNINGS!: {0}", destination.TravelWarnings);
  }
}
```

If you want to display the current values for a Destination, you can pass the actual instance to the method. But there may be scenarios where you want to display the original values fetched from the database or perhaps the current database values to the end user. One such scenario is resolving concurrency conflicts during a save. We'll look at that particular scenario in more detail later in this chapter.

DbPropertyValues includes a ToObject method that will copy the values into a new instance of the entity without overwriting the existing instance as you would with a query to the database. To see how this works, add the TestPrintDestination method shown in Example 5-12.

Example 5-12. Getting an entity representing the values in the database

```
private static void TestPrintDestination()
{
  using (var context = new BreakAwayContext())
  {
    var reef = (from d in context.Destinations
                where d.Name == "Great Barrier Reef"
                select d).Single();

    reef.TravelWarnings = "Watch out for sharks!";
```

```
    Console.WriteLine("Current Values");
    PrintDestination(reef);

    Console.WriteLine("\nDatabase Values");
    DbPropertyValues dbValues = context.Entry(reef)
      .GetDatabaseValues();

    PrintDestination((Destination)dbValues.ToObject());
  }
}
```

The code retrieves the Great Barrier Reef Destination from the database and changes its TravelWarnings property. Then it passes the Destination to the PrintDestination method to print out the current values. Next, it gets the values from the database and uses ToObject to construct a Destination that contains the values from the database. This new Destination is then passed to PrintDestination to print the database values. Update the Main method to call TestPrintDestination and run the application:

```
Current Values
-- Great Barrier Reef, Australia --
Beautiful coral reef.
WARNINGS!: Watch out for sharks!

Database Values
-- Great Barrier Reef, Australia --
Beautiful coral reef
```

The current and database values are printed to the screen and you can see that the updated TravelWarnings property is printed out in the current values. The second instance of Destination, which was created by calling ToObject, is not attached to the context. Any changes to this second instance will not be persisted during SaveChanges.

 ToObject will only clone the values from scalar properties; all navigation properties on the entity will be left unassigned. This makes ToObject useful for cloning a single object, but it will not clone an entire object graph for you.

Changing Values in a DbPropertyValues

DbPropertyValues isn't a read-only type. You can also use it to update values that are stored in an instance. When you set values using CurrentValues or OriginalValues, this will also update the current and original values in the change tracker. Additionally, updating the CurrentValues will change the values that are stored in the properties of your entity instance.

In "Recording Original Values" on page 102, you saw how the OriginalValues could be individually updated. As each value was updated, the Change Tracker worked out which properties had been modified. Let's take a look at setting the current values. Add the ChangeCurrentValue method shown in Example 5-13.

Example 5-13. Changing a current value via the Change Tracker API

```
private static void ChangeCurrentValue()
{
  using (var context = new BreakAwayContext())
  {
    var hotel = (from d in context.Lodgings
                 where d.Name == "Grand Hotel"
                 select d).Single();

    context.Entry(hotel)
      .CurrentValues["Name"] = "Hotel Pretentious";

    Console.WriteLine("Property Value: {0}", hotel.Name);
  }
}
```

The code loads the Grand Hotel Lodging from the database. The code then gets the CurrentValues for the hotel instance and modifies the value stored for the Name property. Finally, the code writes out the value stored in the Name property on the entity. Update the Main method to call ChangeCurrentValue and run the application, which will result in the following output:

```
Property Value: Hotel Pretentious
```

We see from the output that updating the value of a property in the CurrentValues has also updated the value stored in the property of the entity.

Back in "Working with Change Tracking" on page 59, you learned that POCO entities require a call to DetectChanges to scan for changes in the properties of the entity. You also learned that DbContext takes care of calling DetectChanges for you, but that you can disable this behavior if you want to control when DetectChanges is called.

 Remember that in most cases it is best to let DbContext automatically call DetectChanges for you. More information on manually calling DetectChanges and the use of *change tracking proxies* is available in Chapter 4.

If you make changes using the Change Tracker API, there is no need for DetectChanges to be called, because the Change Tracker is aware of the change being made. To see this in action, update the ChangeCurrentValue method, as shown in Example 5-14.

Example 5-14. Updating via the Change Tracker API removes the need for DetectChanges

```
private static void ChangeCurrentValue()
{
  using (var context = new BreakAwayContext())
  {
```

```
    context.Configuration.AutoDetectChangesEnabled = false;

    var hotel = (from d in context.Lodgings
                 where d.Name == "Grand Hotel"
                 select d).Single();

    context.Entry(hotel)
      .CurrentValues["Name"] = "Hotel Pretentious";

    Console.WriteLine("Property Value: {0}", hotel.Name);
    Console.WriteLine("State: {0}", context.Entry(hotel).State);
  }
}
```

The updated code now disables automatic calling of `DetectChanges`. The code also prints out the state of the `hotel` entity, as recorded by the Change Tracker, after the current value for `Name` has been updated. Go ahead and run the application again:

```
Property Value: Hotel Pretentious
State: Modified
```

If we had updated the `Name` property on the entity, we would expect the state to be `Unchanged`, since a call to `DetectChanges` would be required to discover the updated property. However, because the `Name` property was updated using the Change Tracker API, the state is correctly recorded as `Modified` without calling `DetectChanges`.

There may be times when you want to have an editable copy of the current or original values but you don't want changes to be recorded in the Change Tracker. You'll see one such scenario when we look at resolving concurrency conflicts later in this chapter. The `Clone` method will return a copy of any `DbPropertyValues` instance. Be aware that when you clone current or original values, the resulting copy will not be hooked up to the change tracker. Add the `CloneCurrentValues` method shown in Example 5-15 to see how cloning works.

Example 5-15. Cloning current values

```
private static void CloneCurrentValues()
{
  using (var context = new BreakAwayContext())
  {
    var hotel = (from d in context.Lodgings
                 where d.Name == "Grand Hotel"
                 select d).Single();

    var values = context.Entry(hotel).CurrentValues.Clone();

    values["Name"] = "Simple Hotel";

    Console.WriteLine("Property Value: {0}", hotel.Name);
    Console.WriteLine("State: {0}", context.Entry(hotel).State);
  }
}
```

The code loads the Grand Hotel Lodging from the database and then clones its current values. The value stored for the Name property in the cloned values is updated, and then the value of the Name property in the entity is written out. Update the Main method to call CloneCurrentValues and run the application to see the following output in the console:

```
Property Value: Grand Hotel
State: Unchanged
```

As expected, updating the cloned values has no impact on the values or the state of the entity they were cloned from.

Using the SetValues method

In Chapter 4, you learned that you can copy the contents of one DbPropertyValues into another using the SetValues method. For example, you may want users of a client application with access to the change tracker to be able to roll back changes they've made to an entity. The easiest way to do this is to copy the original values (when the entity was retrieved from the database) back into the current values. Add the UndoE dits method shown in Example 5-16.

Example 5-16. Copying original values back into current values

```
private static void UndoEdits()
{
  using (var context = new BreakAwayContext())
  {
    var canyon = (from d in context.Destinations
                  where d.Name == "Grand Canyon"
                  select d).Single();

    canyon.Name = "Bigger & Better Canyon";

    var entry = context.Entry(canyon);
    entry.CurrentValues.SetValues(entry.OriginalValues);
    entry.State = EntityState.Unchanged;

    Console.WriteLine("Name: {0}", canyon.Name);
  }
}
```

The code retrieves the Grand Canyon Destination from the database and changes its Name. The code then undoes this edit by locating the entry and copying the original values back into the current values. Entity Framework isn't smart enough to detect that these new values match the original values, so the code also manually swaps the state back to Unchanged. Finally, the name property is printed out to verify that the changes were reverted. Update the Main method to call UndoEdits and run the application. As expected, the changes to the Name property are reverted and displayed in the console like this:

```
Name: Grand Canyon
```

SetValues doesn't just accept DbPropertyValues, but can accept any object. SetValues will attempt to overwrite the property values with the values in the object that's been passed in. This is done by matching the names of the object's properties with the names of the DbPropertyValues instance. If a property with the same name is found, the value is copied. If the property on the object is not of the same type as the value stored in the DbPropertyValues, an InvalidOperationException is thrown. Any properties in the object that don't match the name of a value already stored in the DbPropertyValues are ignored.

Many applications allow you to enter a new record by cloning an existing record. Let's see how to use SetValues to accomplish this task. You might be a fan of Dave, of Dave's Dump fame, and want to create a new Dave's Campsite Lodging using Dave's Dump as a starting point. Add the CreateDavesCampsite method shown in Example 5-17.

Example 5-17. Copying one entity into another

```
private static void CreateDavesCampsite()
{
  using (var context = new BreakAwayContext())
  {
    var davesDump = (from d in context.Lodgings
                     where d.Name == "Dave's Dump"
                     select d).Single();

    var clone = new Lodging();
    context.Lodgings.Add(clone);
    context.Entry(clone)
      .CurrentValues
      .SetValues(davesDump);

    clone.Name = "Dave's Camp";
    context.SaveChanges();

    Console.WriteLine("Name: {0}",
      clone.Name);

    Console.WriteLine("Miles: {0}",
      clone.MilesFromNearestAirport);

    Console.WriteLine("Contact Id: {0}",
      clone.PrimaryContactId);
  }
}
```

The code retrieves Dave's Dump from the database. Then it creates a new Lodging for Dave's Campsite and adds it to the context. The current values for the new Campsite are then copied from Dave's Dump, using the SetValues method. The code then overwrites the name, since we don't want this new Lodging to have the same name, and saves to the database. Finally, some of the properties of the new Lodging are written out to the console. Update the `Main` method to call `CreateDavesCampsite` and run the application:

```
Name: Dave's Camp
Miles: 32.65
Contact Id: 1
```

As expected, the displayed values are the same as Dave's dump, except for the `Name` property that we overwrote.

Working with Individual Properties

`DbPropertyValues` is a great way to work with complete sets of values, but there may be times when you just want to work with the change tracking information for one property. You can of course access the values of a single property using `DbPropertyValues`, but that uses string-based names for the property. Ideally you should be using strongly typed lambda expressions to identify the property, so that you get compile-time checking, IntelliSense, and refactoring support.

You can use the `Property`, `Complex`, `Reference`, and `Collection` methods on an entry to get access to the change tracking information and operations for an individual property:

- The `Property` method is used for scalar and complex properties.
- The `Complex` method is used to get additional operations that are specific to complex properties.
- The `Reference` and `Collection` methods are used for navigation properties.
- There is also a `Member` method, which can be used for any type of property. The `Member` method is not strongly typed and only provides access to information that is common to all properties.

Working with Scalar Properties

Let's start with the `Property` method. The `Property` method allows you to read and write the original and current value. It also lets you know whether an individual property is marked as `Modified`, something that isn't possible with `DbPropertyValues`. The `WorkingWithPropertyMethod` method shown in Example 5-18 will allow you to begin exploring the `Property` method.

Example 5-18. Accessing change tracking information for a property

```
private static void WorkingWithPropertyMethod()
{
  using (var context = new BreakAwayContext())
  {
    var davesDump = (from d in context.Lodgings
                     where d.Name == "Dave's Dump"
                     select d).Single();
```

```
var entry = context.Entry(davesDump);

entry.Property(d => d.Name).CurrentValue =
    "Dave's Bargain Bungalows";

Console.WriteLine(
    "Current Value: {0}",
    entry.Property(d => d.Name).CurrentValue);

Console.WriteLine(
    "Original Value: {0}",
    entry.Property(d => d.Name).OriginalValue);

Console.WriteLine(
    "Modified?: {0}",
    entry.Property(d => d.Name).IsModified);
  }
}
```

The code retrieves Dave's Dump from the database and locates the representative entry from the context. It then uses the Property method to change the current value for the Name property. Then the code prints out the current and original values plus the IsMo dified flag. The IsModified flag tells us if the property is marked as Modified and will be updated when SaveChanges is called. You can update the Main method to call Work ingWithPropertyMethod and run the application to see these results in the console:

```
Current Value: Dave's Bargain Bungalows
Original Value: Dave's Dump
Modified?: True
```

The current and original values are displayed as expected, since we changed the value of the Name property. You can see that the property is also marked as modified. There is also a weakly typed overload of Property that accepts a string property name rather than a lambda expression. In fact, all the methods you will see in this section have a string-based overload.

The strongly typed lambda overloads are recommended because they give you a compile-time check, but the string-based overloads can be useful when writing generalized code. For example, you might want to find out which properties are currently marked as Modified. You can get the names of all properties using CurrentValues and then check if they are modified using the Property method. The FindModifiedProperties method shown in Example 5-19 demonstrates this.

Example 5-19. Finding the modified properties of an entity

```
private static void FindModifiedProperties()
{
  using (var context = new BreakAwayContext())
  {
    var canyon = (from d in context.Destinations
                  where d.Name == "Grand Canyon"
                  select d).Single();
```

```
    canyon.Name = "Super-Size Canyon";
    canyon.TravelWarnings = "Bigger than your brain can handle!!!";

    var entry = context.Entry(canyon);
    var propertyNames = entry.CurrentValues.PropertyNames;


IEnumerable<string> modifiedProperties = from name in propertyNames
                          where entry.Property(name).IsModified
                          select name;

    foreach (var propertyName in modifiedProperties)
    {
      Console.WriteLine(propertyName);
    }
  }
}
```

The code retrieves the Grand Canyon `Destination` from the database and changes a couple of properties. The code then locates the entry for the Grand Canyon and gets a list of all property names using `CurrentValues`. Then a LINQ query is used to find which of those property names are marked as modified. The `where` section of the LINQ query uses the string-based overload of `Property` to get the change tracking information for the property. Finally, the modified properties are written out to the console. When you run `FindModifiedProperties`, the names of the two edited properties are written out to the console:

```
Name
TravelWarnings
```

The `Property` method also gives you access to the name of the property and the change tracker entry for the entity containing the property. This information is provided in the `Name` and `EntityEntry` properties (Figure 5-1).

prop	{System.Data.Entity.Infrastructure.DbPropertyEntry`2[Model.Destination,System.String]}
base	{System.Data.Entity.Infrastructure.DbPropertyEntry`2[Model.Destination,System.String]}
_internalPropertyEntry	{System.Data.Entity.Internal.InternalEntityPropertyEntry}
CurrentValue	"Bigger than your brain can handle!!!"
EntityEntry	{System.Data.Entity.Infrastructure.DbEntityEntry`1[Model.Destination]}
InternalMemberEntry	{System.Data.Entity.Internal.InternalEntityPropertyEntry}
InternalPropertyEntry	{System.Data.Entity.Internal.InternalEntityPropertyEntry}
IsModified	true
Name	"TravelWarnings"
OriginalValue	null
ParentProperty	null
modifiedProperties	null

Figure 5-1. EntityEntry and Name for the TravelWarnings property

In the code you've seen so far, we've always known this information because we started with the change tracking entry and then the property name to find the information for a property. In Chapters 6 and 7 you will see how the `Name` and `EntityEntry` properties are useful in Validation scenarios.

Working with Complex Properties

When working with complex properties, you use the `ComplexProperty` method to get access to change tracking information and operations. The same operations that you just learned about for scalar properties are all available for complex properties. You can also use the `Property` method to drill into individual scalar properties on the complex type. The `WorkingWithComplexMethod` shown in Example 5-20 demonstrates interacting with the properties of the `Address` complex property in a `Person` instance.

Example 5-20. Accessing change tracking information for a complex property.

```
private static void WorkingWithComplexMethod()
{
  using (var context = new BreakAwayContext())
  {
    var julie = (from p in context.People
                 where p.FirstName == "Julie"
                 select p).Single();

    var entry = context.Entry(julie);

    entry.ComplexProperty(p => p.Address)
      .Property(a => a.State)
      .CurrentValue = "VT";

    Console.WriteLine(
      "Address.State Modified?: {0}",
      entry.ComplexProperty(p => p.Address)
        .Property(a => a.State)
        .IsModified);

    Console.WriteLine(
      "Address Modified?: {0}",
      entry.ComplexProperty(p => p.Address).IsModified);

    Console.WriteLine(
      "Info.Height.Units Modified?: {0}",
      entry.ComplexProperty(p => p.Info)
        .ComplexProperty(i => i.Height)
        .Property(h => h.Units)
        .IsModified);
  }
}
```

The code loads data for Julie from the database and locates the change tracking entry from the context. Next it drills into the `Address` complex property and then into the scalar `State` property within `Address`. The code changes the current value assigned to `Address.State` and then prints out the `IsModified` flag for `Address.State` and for the complex `Address` property. Finally, the code drills into a nested complex property to check the `IsModified` flag for `Info.Height.Units`. You can see that `ComplexProperty` calls can be chained together to drill into a complex property that is defined in another complex property. Following are the console results after running the `WorkingWithCom plexMethod`:

```
Address.State Modified?: True
Address Modified?: True
Info.Height.Units Modified?: False
```

An alternative syntax to access the change tracking information for a complex property is to specify the full path to the property in a single `Property` call. For example, you could also change the current value of `Address.State` using the following code:

```
entry.Property(p => p.Address.State).CurrentValue = "VT";
```

You can also specify the full path if you are using the string-based overload of `Property`:

```
entry.Property("Address.State").CurrentValue = "VT";
```

When working with complex properties, Entity Framework tracks that state for the complex type, but not for its individual properties. If you check the state of any property within the complex type (for example, the `City` property of `Address`), Entity Framework will return the state of the complex type (`Address`). After changing the `Address.State` property, every property of `Address` will be marked as modified.

So far in this section, we have always modified the scalar values of an existing complex type instance. You can also assign a new complex type instance to a complex property. In Example 5-20, instead of editing the `State` property of the existing `Address` instance, we could have replaced it with a new instance:

```
entry.ComplexProperty(p => p.Address)
  .CurrentValue = new Address { State = "VT" };
```

Replacing the value assigned to a complex property with a new instance will mark the entire complex property as modified.

 You may have noticed in Figure 5-1 that a `ParentProperty` is available after calling `Property` or `ComplexProperty`. For properties that are defined directly on an entity, this will always return `null`. For properties that are defined within a complex property, `ParentProperty` will return the change tracking information for the parent complex property. For example, if you are looking at the information for the `City` property inside `Address`, `ParentProperty` will give you the information for `Address`. In the examples in this chapter, we always know the parent property because we started with the entity, then drilled into the complex property, followed by its subproperties.

Working with Navigation Properties

Now it's time to look at how to access the change tracking information and operations associated with a navigation property. Instead of the Property method, you use the `Reference` and `Collection` methods to get to navigation properties:

- `Reference` is used when the navigation property is just a reference to a single entity (for example, `Lodging.Destination`).
- `Collection` is used when the navigation property is a collection (for example, `Destination.Lodgings`).

These methods give you the ability to do several things:

1. Read and write the current value assigned to the navigation property
2. Load the related data from the database
3. Get a query representing the contents of the navigation property

In "Explicit Loading" on page 36, you saw how the `Load` method can be used to load the contents of a navigation property from the database. You also learned that the `IsLoaded` flag can be used to determine if the entire contents of a navigation property (for example, `Destination.Trips`) have already been loaded. In Chapter 2 you also saw how to use the `Query` method to run a LINQ query against the contents of the navigation property. This was in "Querying Contents of a Collection Navigation Property" on page 39.

Modifying the value of a navigation property

The `Reference` method gives you access to change tracking information and operations for a navigation property. One piece of information that is available is the value currently assigned to the navigation property. This is accessed via the `CurrentValue` property. If the navigation property hasn't been loaded from the database, `CurrentValue` will return `null`. You can also set the `CurrentValue` property to change the entity assigned to the navigation property, therefore changing the relationship. Add the code for `WorkingWithReferenceMethod`, shown in Example 5-21.

Example 5-21. Change tracking information for a reference navigation property

```
private static void WorkingWithReferenceMethod()
{
  using (var context = new BreakAwayContext())
  {
    var davesDump = (from d in context.Lodgings
                     where d.Name == "Dave's Dump"
                     select d).Single();

    var entry = context.Entry(davesDump);

    entry.Reference(l => l.Destination)
      .Load();
```

```
var canyon = davesDump.Destination;

Console.WriteLine(
  "Current Value After Load: {0}",
  entry.Reference(d => d.Destination)
    .CurrentValue
    .Name);

var reef = (from d in context.Destinations
            where d.Name == "Great Barrier Reef"
            select d).Single();

entry.Reference(d => d.Destination)
  .CurrentValue = reef;

Console.WriteLine(
  "Current Value After Change: {0}",
  davesDump.Destination.Name);
  }
}
```

The code retrieves Dave's Dump Lodging from the database and locates the change tracking entry from the context. Then it drills into the Destination reference and explicitly loads the related data using Reference().Load(). The name of the Destination that Dave's Dump is assigned is then written out to the console using the Current Value property. Next, we change CurrentValue by assigning the Great Barrier Reef Destination. Finally, we'll write out the name of the Destination that Dave's Dump is assigned again, but this time by accessing the navigation property on the davesDump entity itself.

Update the Main method to call WorkingWithReferenceMethod and run the application to see the following results:

```
Current Value After Load: Grand Canyon
Current Value After Change: Great Barrier Reef
```

CurrentValue allowed you to read and write the Destination that Dave's Dump is assigned to. Changing the CurrentValue also updated the navigation property on the davesDump entity.

Modifying navigation properties with the change tracker

Earlier, when working with scalar properties, you saw that DetectChanges was not required when making changes through the change tracker. The same is true for reference navigation properties. Change detection and relationship fix-up occur without DetectChanges being called. To see this in action, update the WorkingWithReferenceMethod method to disable automatic change detection and lazy loading. Add the following code immediately before the LINQ query that retrieves Dave's Dump from the database:

```
context.Configuration.AutoDetectChangesEnabled = false;
context.Configuration.LazyLoadingEnabled = false;
```

Let's also print some additional information to the console to observe how the context is tracking the changes. Add the following code after the final `Console.WriteLine` call in the existing method:

```
Console.WriteLine(
  "State: {0}",
  entry.State);

Console.WriteLine(
  "Referenced From Current Destination: {0}",
  reef.Lodgings.Contains(davesDump));

Console.WriteLine(
  "Referenced From Former Destination: {0}",
  canyon.Lodgings.Contains(davesDump));
```

The code prints out the state of Dave's Dump as recorded by the change tracker. Then it prints out whether Dave's Dump is present in `Lodgings` collection on the current `Destination` (`reef`) and the former `Destination` (`canyon`). Go ahead and run the application again, which will print these results in the console:

```
After Load: Grand Canyon
After CurrentValue Change: Great Barrier Reef
State: Modified
Referenced From Current Destination: True
Referenced From Former Destination: False
```

The change tracker is aware that Dave's Dump is `Modified` without calling `DetectCh anges`. The change tracker has also taken care of updating the `Destination` reference on Dave's Dump, removing Dave's Dump from the `Lodgings` collection on the former `Destination`, and adding it to the new `Destination`.

> More information on relationship fix-up is available in "Using De-tectChanges to Trigger Relationship Fix-up" on page 63.

Working with collection navigation properties

You've seen many features of working with a reference navigation using the `Refer ence` method. The same operations are available when using the `Collection` method to interact with a collection navigation property. The `WorkingWithCollectionMethod` method, shown in Example 5-22, runs through some of the same tasks, but this time with a navigation property that points to a collection. We're using `Reservation.Pay ments` as our collection navigation property rather than `Destination.Lodgings`. Back in Chapter 3, we set up `Destination` to use a dynamic change tracking proxy so that changes would be automatically reported to the change tracker. But `Reservation` is not

set up to use a change tracking proxy. This will allow us to explore how the `Collec
tion` method behaves with change detection and relationship fix-up.

Example 5-22. Method to explore interacting with a collection property

```
private static void WorkingWithCollectionMethod()
{
  using (var context = new BreakAwayContext())
  {
    var res = (from r in context.Reservations
                where r.Trip.Description == "Trip from the database"
                select r).Single();

    var entry = context.Entry(res);

    entry.Collection(r => r.Payments)
      .Load();

    Console.WriteLine(
      "Payments Before Add: {0}",
      entry.Collection(r => r.Payments).CurrentValue.Count);

    var payment = new Payment { Amount = 245 };
    context.Payments.Add(payment);

    entry.Collection(r => r.Payments)
      .CurrentValue
      .Add(payment);

    Console.WriteLine(
      "Payments After Add: {0}",
      entry.Collection(r => r.Payments).CurrentValue.Count);
  }
}
```

The method loads a `Reservation` from the database and locates its change tracking entry
from the context. Then it drills into the `Payments` property using the `Collection` method
and, just as we did with the `Reference`, uses the `Load` method to explicitly load any
related `Payments` from the database. The method then calls the `Collection.Current
Value.Count` property to count how many payments are in the collection and prints out
the count. Finally, the method adds a new payment and prints out the count again.
Update the `Main` method to call `WorkingWithCollectionMethod` and run the application.
Here is what you'll see in the console:

```
Payments Before Add: 1
Payments After Add: 2
```

With a `Collection`, you can use the `CurrentValue` property to read and write from the
relevant collection navigation property (in this case, `Payments`). `CurrentValue` on collection navigation properties returns the instance of the collection assigned to the navigation property. In the case of `Reservation.Payments`, that's the `List<Payment>` that gets
created in the constructor of `Reservation`. Therefore, adding or removing from the

`CurrentValue` behaves the same as adding or removing from the navigation property itself. This means that unless the entity is a change tracking proxy, you'll need `DetectCh anges` to get change detection and relationship fix-up to occur. Let's see how this affects the results of the `WorkingWithCollectionMethod` method by adding a line of code to disable automatic change detection. Add the following line of code immediately before the LINQ query that retrieves the `Reservation` from the database:

```
context.Configuration.AutoDetectChangesEnabled = false;
```

Also add the following code after the final `Console.WriteLine` call. This new code calls `DetectChanges` after adding the `Payment`. The value assigned to the foreign key on the new `Payment` is printed out to the console on either side of the `DetectChanges` call:

```
Console.WriteLine(
  "Foreign Key Before DetectChanges: {0}",
  payment.ReservationId);

context.ChangeTracker.DetectChanges();

Console.WriteLine(
  "Foreign Key After DetectChanges: {0}",
  payment.ReservationId);
```

Go ahead and run the application again. You can see the effect of setting `AutoDetectCh angesEnabled` to false and the explicit `DetectChanges` call in the console output:

```
Count Before Add: 1
Count After Add: 2
Foreign Key Before DetectChanges: 0
Foreign Key After DetectChanges: 1
```

The addition of the `Payment` to the `Payments` collection of the `Reservation` was not automatically detected. Relationship fix-up was not triggered until `DetectChanges` was called.

Refreshing an Entity from the Database

Throughout this book you have seen how to load data from the database and work with it in-memory. So far, you have only loaded the data one time, but there may be times when you want to refresh or reload a given entity. For example you may have had an entity in memory for a long period of time and want to make sure you have the latest data before displaying it to a user.

Entity Framework includes a Reload method on `DbEntityEntry` that can be used to refresh an entity with the latest data from the database. The `ReloadLodging` method shown in Example 5-23 uses this method.

Example 5-23. Reloading an entity from the database

```
private static void ReloadLodging()
{
```

```
using (var context = new BreakAwayContext())
{
  var hotel = (from d in context.Lodgings
               where d.Name == "Grand Hotel"
               select d).Single();

  context.Database.ExecuteSqlCommand(
    @"UPDATE dbo.Lodgings
      SET Name = 'Le Grand Hotel'
      WHERE Name = 'Grand Hotel'");

  Console.WriteLine(
    "Name Before Reload: {0}",
    hotel.Name);

  Console.WriteLine(
    "State Before Reload: {0}",
    context.Entry(hotel).State);

  context.Entry(hotel).Reload();

  Console.WriteLine(
    "Name After Reload: {0}",
    hotel.Name);

  Console.WriteLine(
    "State After Reload: {0}",
    context.Entry(hotel).State);
  }
}
```

The method retrieves the Grand Hotel Lodging from the database and then, for the sake of demoing this feature, issues a raw SQL query to update its Name in the database. The code then calls Reload to refresh with the latest data from the database. Notice that the code prints out the value assigned to the Name property and the state of the entity before and after calling Reload. Update the Main method to call ReloadLodging and run the application to see the effect. This is the output in the console:

```
Name Before Reload: Grand Hotel
State Before Reload: Unchanged
Name After Reload: Le Grand Hotel
State After Reload: Unchanged
```

You can see that the new value for the Name property was retrieved from the database.

Reload will also overwrite any changes you have in memory. To see this effect, update the ReloadLodging method to edit the Lodging before reloading. Add the following line of code immediately after the LINQ query that populates the hotel variable:

```
hotel.Name = "A New Name";
```

The code now modifies the Name property of the entity in memory before calling Reload. This will now be the output of the method:

```
Name Before Reload: A New Name
State Before Reload: Modified
Name After Reload: Le Grande Hotel
State After Reload: Unchanged
```

Because we edited the Name property, the entity state is Modified before the Reload. After the Reload, the entity is now marked as Unchanged, because any changes were overwritten with data from the database.

Change Tracking Information and Operations for Multiple Entities

So far you have seen how to get access to the DbEntityEntry for a single entity. Sometimes you might want to get access to entries for all entities or a subset of the entries tracked by the context. You can do this using the DbContext.ChangeTracker.Entries method. There is a generic Entries<TEntity> overload that returns a collection of DbEntityEntry<TEntity> records for all entities that are of the type specified for TEntity. The nongeneric overload of Entries does not allow you to specify the type, and it returns a collection of DbEntityEntry records for all of the tracked entities.

We'll start by looking at all entries known by the change tracker using the nongeneric overload using the PrintChangeTrackerEntries method shown in Example 5-24.

Example 5-24. Iterating over all entries from the change tracker

```
private static void PrintChangeTrackerEntries()
{
  using (var context = new BreakAwayContext())
  {
    var res = (from r in context.Reservations
               where r.Trip.Description == "Trip from the database"
               select r).Single();

    context.Entry(res)
      .Collection(r => r.Payments)
      .Load();

    res.Payments.Add(new Payment { Amount = 245 });

    var entries = context.ChangeTracker.Entries();
    foreach (var entry in entries)
    {
      Console.WriteLine(
        "Entity Type: {0}",
        entry.Entity.GetType());

      Console.WriteLine(
        " - State: {0}",
        entry.State);
    }
```

```
    }
}
```

The code retrieves a `Reservation` from the database and then uses explicit loading to bring its related `Payments` into memory. The code also creates a new `Payment` and adds it to the `Payments` collection of the `Reservation`. Then we use the `Entries` method to retrieve all change tracked entries from the context. As the code iterates over the entries, it prints out the type of entity and its current state. Calling `PrintChangeTrackerEn tries` from the `Main` method results in this console output:

```
Entity Type: Model.Payment
  - State: Added
Entity Type: Model.Reservation
  - State: Unchanged
Entity Type: Model.Payment
  - State: Unchanged
```

The `Entries` method returns an entry for the `Reservation` and its existing `Payment`, as well as the new `Payment` we added. You'll notice that the entries aren't returned in the order they began being tracked by the context.

 You shouldn't rely on the order that entries are returned in, as it may change between versions of Entity Framework.

You can also use LINQ to Objects to query the result of the Entries method. Replace the line of code in `PrintChangeTrackerEntries` that populates the `entries` variable to use a LINQ query:

```
var entries = from e in context.ChangeTracker.Entries()
              where e.State == EntityState.Unchanged
              select e;
```

This updated code uses a LINQ query to select only the entries for entities that are tracked in the `Unchanged` state. If you run the application you will see that the information for the `Added` `Payment` is no longer displayed:

```
Entity Type: Model.Reservation
  - State: Unchanged
Entity Type: Model.Payment
  - State: Unchanged
```

Another way to filter is to use the generic overload of `Entries` to specify which types you want entries for. Change the `Entries` call in `PrintChangeTrackerEntries` again along with the code, which writes to the console:

```
var entries = context.ChangeTracker.Entries<Payment>();
foreach (var entry in entries)
{
  Console.WriteLine(
    "Amount: {0}",
    entry.Entity.Amount);
```

```
Console.WriteLine(
    " - State: {0}",
    entry.State);
}
```

The call now uses the generic overload of Entries to specify that we are only interested in entries for the Payment type. Thanks to the generic overload, the Entity property on the returned entries is now strongly typed as Payment. We'll print out the payment Amount instead of the type of the entity. If you run the application again, you will see that only information for the two Payment entities is printed:

```
Amount: 245
 - State: Added
Amount: 150.00
 - State: Unchanged
```

The type that you supply to the generic overload of Entries does not need to be a type that is included in your model. For example, in Chapter 4, you saw the generic overload used to get all entries for entities that implemented a given interface:

```
context.ChangeTracker.Entries<IObjectWithState>()
```

Using the Change Tracker API in Application Scenarios

We've covered a lot of functionality in this chapter, so let's look at a couple of examples of how that functionality can be used in an application.

You'll see how you can use the Change Tracker API to resolve concurrency conflicts and also to log changes that are made during SaveChanges.

Resolving Concurrency Conflicts

A concurrency conflict occurs when you attempt to update a record in the database but another user has updated that same record since you queried for it. By default, Entity Framework will always update the properties that you have modified regardless of whether or not there is a concurrency conflict. However, you can configure your model so that Entity Framework will throw an exception when a concurrency conflict occurs. You do this by specifying that a specific property should be used as a concurrency token.

 How to configure your model for optimistic concurrency is covered in detail in *Programming Entity Framework, 2e (http://shop.oreilly.com/ product/9780596807252.do)* (for EDMX models) and in *Programming Entity Framework: Code First (http://shop.oreilly.com/product/ 0636920022220.do)* (for models defined using Code First).

During `SaveChanges` Entity Framework will check if the value in the corresponding database column has been updated since the record was bought into memory. A concurrency exception is thrown if the value in the database has changed.

The BAGA model includes two examples of concurrency tokens. The `SocialSecurity Number` property on `Person` is marked with the `ConcurrencyCheck` attribute. When updating an existing `Person`, Entity Framework will check that the SSN allocated to the `Person` when the record was retrieved from the database remains the same in the database. If another user has changed the SSN, `SaveChanges` will fail and a `DbUpdateConcur rencyException` will be thrown. The `Trip` class includes a `RowVersion` property that is marked with the `Timestamp` attribute. Timestamp properties are treated the same as other concurrency check properties, except the database will automatically generate a new value for this property whenever any column in the record is updated. This means that when saving changes to an existing `Trip`, a concurrency exception will be thrown if another user has updated any properties since the `Trip` was retrieved from the database.

Let's write a method that will cause a `DbUpdateConcurrencyException` to be thrown when trying to save a change to an existing `Trip`. When the exception is thrown, we'll ask the end user of our application to tell us how they want to resolve the conflict. Go ahead and add the `ConcurrencyDemo` method shown in Example 5-25.

Example 5-25. Causing a concurrency exception.

```
private static void ConcurrencyDemo()
{
  using (var context = new BreakAwayContext())
  {
    var trip = (from t in context.Trips.Include(t => t.Destination)
                where t.Description == "Trip from the database"
                select t).Single();

    trip.Description = "Getaway in Vermont";

    context.Database.ExecuteSqlCommand(
      @"UPDATE dbo.Trips
        SET CostUSD = 400
        WHERE Description = 'Trip from the database'");


    SaveWithConcurrencyResolution(context);
  }
}

private static void SaveWithConcurrencyResolution(
  BreakAwayContext context)
{
  try
  {
    context.SaveChanges();
  }
```

```
  catch (DbUpdateConcurrencyException ex)
  {
    ResolveConcurrencyConflicts(ex);
    SaveWithConcurrencyResolution(context);
  }
}
```

The example retrieves an existing Trip from the database and changes its Description property. It then issues a raw SQL query to update the CostUSD column of the same Trip in the database. Executing this statement will cause the database to generate a new value for the RowVersion column in the database. Issuing a raw SQL statement is not a recommended practice and is just used to simulate another user changing data. Next, the code calls the SaveWithConcurrencyResolution helper method. This helper method calls SaveChanges, which will issue an UPDATE command to apply our changes to the Trip. As part of the update process, Entity Framework will check if the RowVersion column in the database still has the same value as it did when we queried for the Trip. Because of change we made with ExecuteSqlCommand, the RowVersion will have changed and a DbUpdateConcurrencyException will be thrown. The example code catches this exception and attempts to resolve the conflict with a custom method, ResolveConcurrencyConflict. Once the conflict is resolved, the code makes a recursive call to SaveWithConcurrencyResolution. The recursive call is used to ensure that we handle any further concurrency conflicts that occur after the first conflict is resolved. Example 5-26 shows the ResolveConcurrencyConflict method.

Example 5-26. Resolving a concurrency conflict

```
private static void ResolveConcurrencyConflicts(
  DbUpdateConcurrencyException ex)
{
  foreach (var entry in ex.Entries)
  {
    Console.WriteLine(
      "Concurrency conflict found for {0}",
      entry.Entity.GetType());

    Console.WriteLine("\nYou are trying to save the following values:");
    PrintPropertyValues(entry.CurrentValues);

    Console.WriteLine("\nThe values before you started editing were:");
    PrintPropertyValues(entry.OriginalValues);

    var databaseValues = entry.GetDatabaseValues();
    Console.WriteLine("\nAnother user has saved the following values:");
    PrintPropertyValues(databaseValues);

    Console.Write(
      "[S]ave your values, [D]iscard you changes or [M]erge?");

    var action = Console.ReadKey().KeyChar.ToString().ToUpper();
    switch (action)
    {
```

```
      case "S":
        entry.OriginalValues.SetValues(databaseValues);
        break;

      case "D":
        entry.Reload();
        break;

      case "M":
        var mergedValues = MergeValues(
          entry.OriginalValues,
          entry.CurrentValues,
          databaseValues);

        entry.OriginalValues.SetValues(databaseValues);
        entry.CurrentValues.SetValues(mergedValues);
        break;

      default:
        throw new ArgumentException("Invalid option");
      }
    }
  }
}
```

Fortunately, the DbUpdateConcurrencyException gives you access to everything you need to know about the conflict. The exception's Entries property gives you the DbEntityEntry for each of the entities that had a concurrency conflict.

 Because Entity Framework stops at the first exception, the Entries property on DbUpdateConcurrencyException will almost always contain just a single entry. If you have a relationship that does not expose a foreign key property on your entity, Entity Framework treats relationships as separate from the entity; these relationships are known as *independent associations*. SaveChanges also treats the relationships as separate from the entity. If a concurrency conflict occurs when saving the relationship, the resulting exception will include the entry for the entity on each end of the relationship. This is yet one more good reason to always include foreign key properties in your entities.

The ResolveConcurrencyConflicts method iterates through each of the entries in the exception to resolve the conflict. It lets the user know what type of entity the conflict occurred in by checking the type of the entity in the Entity property. Next the user is shown the current, original, and database values using the PrintPropertyValues method you added back in Example 5-10. The code then gives the user three options for resolving the conflict:

"Save your values"
    If the changes that another user has made don't make sense given the changes the current user is making, the user can proceed with saving his or her values to the

database. This option will overwrite any changes that were made by other users, even if those changes were to a property that the user is not trying to update. For example, the drop to $400 that the other user applied might not be applicable now that the Trip is visiting beautiful Vermont.

If the user selects this option, the original values are set to the database values. This updates the RowVersion property with the new value from the database, so that the next save will succeed. Setting the original values will also mark any properties that have a different current value as Modified. In our example, only the Description property was modified. However, the current value for CostUSD is still the value retrieved from the database ($1000), but the database value has been updated ($400). Therefore the CostUSD property will get marked as Modified—to be set back to the value when originally queried ($1000).

"Discard your changes"

If the user's changes no longer make sense, the user can discard his or her changes and accept the new values that the other user has saved. For example, the user might decide that given the price reduction the other user applied, it's better to leave the Trip Description as it was.

The DbEntityEntry.Reload method makes this option very simple to implement. Reload will query the database again for the database values. If you wanted to avoid this additional query, you could also set the original and current values to the database values. Remember that Entity Framework isn't smart enough to move properties back out of the Modified state if you change the current and original value to the same thing. Therefore, you would also need to set the State property on the entry back to Unchanged. Calling Reload has one small advantage; it will always pick up the very latest version of the entity at the time the user decides to discard his or her changes. If another user has modified the affected entity again, after we detected the conflict and queried the database values, then Reload will pick up this latest set of changes.

"Merge"

The user may decide that both sets of changes make sense and they should be merged. The user's change to the Description may be completely unrelated to the drop in price. The price should remain at $400 but the change to Description should also be applied.

We'll use a custom MergeValues method, which we are about to add, to calculate the correct values to save. These merged values are then set to the current values. The database values are set to the original values to ensure the RowVersion property has the new value from the database, so that the next save will succeed.

The final piece of code to add is the MergeValues method that will be used when the user decides to merge his or her changes with the changes another user has applied (Example 5-27).

Example 5-27. The MergeValues method

```
private static DbPropertyValues MergeValues(
  DbPropertyValues original,
  DbPropertyValues current,
  DbPropertyValues database)
{
  var result = original.Clone();

  foreach (var propertyName in original.PropertyNames)
  {
    if (original[propertyName] is DbPropertyValues)
    {
      var mergedComplexValues = MergeValues(
        (DbPropertyValues)original[propertyName],
        (DbPropertyValues)current[propertyName],
        (DbPropertyValues)database[propertyName]);

      ((DbPropertyValues)result[propertyName])
        .SetValues(mergedComplexValues);
    }
    else
    {
      if (!object.Equals(
        current[propertyName],
        original[propertyName]))
      {
        result[propertyName] = current[propertyName];
      }
      else if (!object.Equals(
        database[propertyName],
        original[propertyName]))
      {
        result[propertyName] = database[propertyName];
      }
    }
  }

  return result;
}
```

MergeValues begins by using the Clone method to create a set of values that will store
the merged result. We are cloning from the original values, but you could clone from
any of the three sets of values (current, original, or database). Note that the code is
going to assume that the three sets of supplied values contain exactly the same properties—in our case, we know this is true because they come from the same entity. The
method then loops through each property to perform the merge.

If the property value is a DbPropertyValues, we know it represents a complex type. For
complex types, the code uses a recursive call to merge the values in the complex type.
The merged values for the complex type are then copied into the result using the
SetValues method.

For scalar properties, the code compares the current value to the original value to see if the current user has edited the value. If the current user has edited the value, the current value is copied to the merged result. If the current user hasn't edited the value but another user has changed it in the database, the database value is copied to the result. If nobody has edited the value, all three value collections agree and the value that was originally cloned can be left in the merged result.

If you want to test out the code, update the Main method to call ConcurrencyDemo and run the application.

Logging During Save Changes

The change tracking information that Entity Framework maintains is also useful if you want to log the changes that a user is making during SaveChanges. We'll take a look at an example that writes the changes to the Console, but the techniques could be used for any number of logging or auditing solutions.

The logging output could get annoying if we leave it on for every example in this book, so we are going to introduce a flag that allows us to turn it on when we want to use it. Add the following property to your BreakAwayContext class:

```
public bool LogChangesDuringSave { get; set; }
```

You'll need some helper methods to print out the required logging information. Add the two methods shown in Example 5-28 to your BreakAwayContext class. You'll need to add a using statement for the System, System.Data, and System.Linq namespaces.

Example 5-28. Helper methods for logging

```
private void PrintPropertyValues(
  DbPropertyValues values,
  IEnumerable<string> propertiesToPrint,
  int indent = 1)
{
  foreach (var propertyName in propertiesToPrint)
  {
    var value = values[propertyName];
    if (value is DbPropertyValues)
    {
      Console.WriteLine(
        "{0}- Complex Property: {1}",
        string.Empty.PadLeft(indent),
        propertyName);

      var complexPropertyValues = (DbPropertyValues)value;
      PrintPropertyValues(
        complexPropertyValues,
        complexPropertyValues.PropertyNames,
        indent + 1);
    }
    else
    {
```

```
      Console.WriteLine(
        "{0}- {1}: {2}",
        string.Empty.PadLeft(indent),
        propertyName,
        values[propertyName]);
    }
  }
}

private IEnumerable<string> GetKeyPropertyNames(object entity)
{
  var objectContext = ((IObjectContextAdapter)this).ObjectContext;

  return objectContext
    .ObjectStateManager
    .GetObjectStateEntry(entity)
    .EntityKey
    .EntityKeyValues
    .Select(k => k.Key);
}
```

The `PrintPropertyValues` method is almost the same as the `PrintPropertyValues` you added to the `Program` class back in Example 5-10. The only difference is that this method accepts the names of the properties that should be printed, rather than printing all properties. As the name suggests, the `GetKeyPropertyNames` method will give you the names of the properties that make up the key of an entity. There is no way to get this information from the DbContext API, so the code uses the `IObjectContextAdapter` to get the underlying `ObjectContext`. You'll learn more about `IObjectContextAdapter` in Chapter 8. The code gets the key property names by getting the `EntityKey` for the entity from the `ObjectStateManager`. `ObjectStateManager` is the `ObjectContext` equivalent to the `DbContext.ChangeTracker`.

With the helper methods in place, let's write the logging code. The easiest way to run additional logic during the save process is to override the `SaveChanges` method on your derived context. The `SaveChanges` method on `DbContext` is `virtual` (`Overrideable` in Visual Basic) for exactly this purpose. Add the overridden `SaveChanges` method shown in Example 5-29 to your `BreakAwayContext` class.

Example 5-29. Overriding SaveChanges to perform logging

```
public override int SaveChanges()
{
  if (LogChangesDuringSave)
  {
    var entries = from e in this.ChangeTracker.Entries()
                  where e.State != EntityState.Unchanged
                  select e;

    foreach (var entry in entries)
    {
      switch (entry.State)
      {
```

```
        case EntityState.Added:
          Console.WriteLine(
            "Adding a {0}",
            entry.Entity.GetType());

          PrintPropertyValues(
            entry.CurrentValues,
            entry.CurrentValues.PropertyNames);
          break;

        case EntityState.Deleted:
          Console.WriteLine(
            "Deleting a {0}",
            entry.Entity.GetType());

          PrintPropertyValues(
              entry.OriginalValues,
              GetKeyPropertyNames(entry.Entity));
          break;

        case EntityState.Modified:
          Console.WriteLine(
            "Modifying a {0}",
            entry.Entity.GetType());

          var modifiedPropertyNames =
            from n in entry.CurrentValues.PropertyNames
            where entry.Property(n).IsModified
            select n;

          PrintPropertyValues(
            entry.CurrentValues,
            GetKeyPropertyNames(entry.Entity)
              .Concat(modifiedPropertyNames));
          break;
      }
    }
  }

  return base.SaveChanges();
}
```

The code checks if the LogChangesDuringSave property is set to true—by default the
property is set to false. If logging is enabled, the logging logic is executed. The code
then locates the entries for all entities that are going to be saved—that's all entities that
aren't in the Unchanged state. For each of these entities, the code identifies the change
being performed and the type of entity it is being performed on. Then it prints out the
values of some of the properties of the entity. The set of properties that gets printed
depends on the type of operation being performed:

- For Added entities, the entire set of current values that are going to be inserted are
  printed.

- For Deleted entities, just the key properties are printed out, since this is enough information to identify the record being deleted.

- For Modified entities, the key properties and the properties that are being updated are printed out.

If you want to test the code out, add the TestSaveLogging method shown in Example 5-30.

Example 5-30. Method to test out logging during save

```
private static void TestSaveLogging()
{
  using (var context = new BreakAwayContext())
  {
    var canyon = (from d in context.Destinations
                  where d.Name == "Grand Canyon"
                  select d).Single();

    context.Entry(canyon)
      .Collection(d => d.Lodgings)
      .Load();

    canyon.TravelWarnings = "Take a hat!";

    context.Lodgings.Remove(canyon.Lodgings.First());

    context.Destinations.Add(new Destination { Name = "Seattle, WA" });

    context.LogChangesDuringSave = true;
    context.SaveChanges();
  }
}
```

The code retrieves the Grand Canyon Destination and its related Lodgings from the database. The Grand Canyon Destination is then modified, one of its Lodgings is marked for deletion, and a new Destination is added to the context. The code then enables the logging you just added and calls SaveChanges. Update the Main method to call TestSaveLogging and run the application to see the log information in the console:

```
Adding a new Model.Destination
  - DestinationId: 0
  - Name: Seattle, WA
  - Country:
  - Description:
  - Photo:
  - TravelWarnings:
  - ClimateInfo:
Modifiying an existing
System.Data.Entity.DynamicProxies.Destination_C0312EA59B82EAC711175D8C037E196179
A49BDE8FF3F0D6830DDB66725C841B
  - DestinationId: 1
  - TravelWarnings: Take a hat!
```

```
Deleting an existing Model.Lodging
  - LodgingId: 1
```

As expected, logging information is printed out for the three entities that are affected during SaveChanges. You'll notice that the Lodging we modified has a strange type name—it's not Model.Destination. This is because we enabled Destination as a change tracking proxy. The type name displayed is the type that Entity Framework creates at runtime that derives from the Model.Destination type.

CHAPTER 6

Validating with the Validation API

Developers often spend a lot of time writing validation logic in their applications. Many of the rules for validation are built into their classes, but .NET can't magically verify those rules. Code First allows you to apply some rules directly to properties using Data Annotations or the Fluent API. For example, you can specify the maximum length of a string or the fact that a particular property is required (i.e., can't be null).

Another type of rule that your model describes is relationship constraints. For example, in our model, a `Lodging` is required to have a related `Destination`. Entity Framework has always checked that relationship constraint rules are met before it will push inserts, updates, or deletes to the database.

The `DbContext` adds to this existing validation with the new Validation API that is associated with the `DbContext`. Using the Validation API, the `DbContext` can automatically (or on demand) validate all of the rules that you have defined using mechanisms that the validation will recognize. The API takes advantage of features that already exist in .NET 4—`ValidationAttributes` and the `IValidatableObject`. This integration is a great benefit to developers. Not only does it mean that you can leverage existing experience if you've worked with the features already, but it also means that Entity Framework validation can flow into other tools that use this class or interface.

Validation in the data layer is an important element of data-focused applications. While you may have client-side or business layer validations, you may desire or prefer to have one last bastion of validation before data is pushed into the database. In scenarios where client-side validation is performed in a web application dependent on JavaScript being enabled in a browser, data layer validation plays an important role when the end user has disabled JavaScript.

In this chapter, you'll learn how to take advantage of the built-in validation provided by the `DbContext` and Validation API using its default behaviors.

Defining and Triggering Validation: An Overview

The Validation API checks rules that you can apply in a number of ways:

- Property attribute rules that you can specify using Data Annotations or the fluent API.
- Custom validation attributes that can be defined for properties or types.
- Rules defined in the `Validate` method of any model class that implements `IValidatableObject`. This interface is part of .NET 4, so it's great to see that the `DbContext` was designed to take advantage of this.
- Relationship constraints explicitly defined in the model.
- Additionally, you can inject validations into the validation pipeline.

There are a number of ways to cause the `DbContext` to execute the validations:

- By default, validation will be performed on all tracked `Added` and `Modified` objects when you call `SaveChanges`.
- The `DbEntityEntry.GetValidationResult` method will perform validation on a single object.
- `DbEntityEntry` has a path for validating an individual property.
- `DbContext.GetValidationErrors` will iterate through each `Added` and `Modified` object being tracked by the `DbContext` and validate each object.

 In the next chapter you'll learn how to override `ValidateEntity` as well as change the default that validates only `Added` or `Modified` objects.

At the root of all of these validation methods is the `DbEntityEntry.GetValidationResult` method, which validates the rules defined in property attributes and `IValidatableObjects`. `GetValidationErrors` calls `ValidateEntity` on each [Added or Modified] tracked object, which in turn calls `GetValidationResult`. `SaveChanges` calls `GetValidationErrors`, which means that the validation occurs automatically whenever `SaveChanges` is called. Figure 6-1 shows the waterfall path and different entry points to leverage the Validation API.

The "it just works" approach of having validation implicitly called by `SaveChanges` may be all that some developers need or are interested in. But rather than start with the appearance of magic, we'll use a bottom-up approach to show you the explicit validation functionality so that you can use that to have more control over how and when validation occurs.

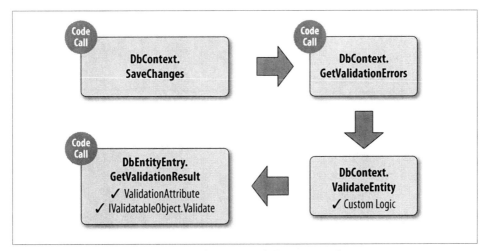

Figure 6-1. Three ways to execute GetValidationResult from your code

Validating a Single Object on Demand with GetValidationResult

Our sample classes already have some attributes that will be checked by the Validation API. For example, in the `Destination` class, you should already have a `MaxLength` annotation on the `Description` property shown here:

```
[MaxLength(500)]
public string Description { get; set; }
```

Refer to the listing for `Destination` shown in Example 2-1.

Testing this rule won't be very easy since breaking it would mean adding a string that is greater than 500 characters. I don't feel like typing that much. Instead, I'll add a new `MaxLength` annotation to another property—the `LastName` property in the `Person` class:

```
[MaxLength(10)]
public string LastName { get; set; }
```

Now let's see what happens when we set the length to a string with more than ten characters. `GetValidationResult` allows you to explicitly validate a single entity. It returns a `ValidationResult` type that contains three important members. We'll focus on just one of those for now, the `IsValid` property, which is a Boolean that indicates if the instance passed its validation rules. Let's use that to validate a `Person` instance. The

`ValidateNewPerson` method in Example 6-1 shows calling the `GetValidationRe` `sult.IsValid` method.

Example 6-1. Method to test validation of LastName.

```csharp
private static void ValidateNewPerson()
{
  var person = new Person
  {
    FirstName = "Julie",
    LastName = "Lerman",
    Photo = new PersonPhoto { Photo = new Byte[] { 0 } }
  };

using (var context = new BreakAwayContext())
{
  if (context.Entry(person).GetValidationResult().IsValid)
  {
    Console.WriteLine("Person is Valid");
  }
  else
  {
    Console.WriteLine("Person is Invalid");
  }
}

}
```

If you run this method from the `Main` method, you will see the message "Person is Valid" in the console windows.

The `GetValidationResult` method calls the necessary logic to validate any `Validatio` `nAttributes` defined on the object's properties. It then looks to see if the type has a `CustomValidationAttribute` or implements the `IValidatableObject` interface and if it does, calls its `Validate` method. You'll see this in action later in this chapter.

 While we strongly recommend against calling data access code directly in the user interface, these examples are solely for the purpose of demonstrating the Validation API features. We are not suggesting that you use the DbContext for performing client-side validation.

Now change the code so that it sets `LastName` to "Lerman-Flynn" instead of Lerman. Run the app again and you will see "Person is Invalid" in the console. The Validation API of the `DbContext` was able to detect that a rule was broken. This is just a high-level look at the method. Let's explore more ways to define rules before we dig further into the result of the validation.

> ## What About Lazy Loading During Validation?
>
> If you have lazy loading enabled on your context, you don't need to worry about adverse effects of lazy loading during validation; `GetValidationResult` will disable lazy loading prior to executing the validations. Then, when it has completed its work, it will restore the `DbContext.Configure.LazyLoadingEnabled` Boolean property to its original state.

Specifying Property Rules with ValidationAttribute Data Annotations

The `MaxLength` Data Annotation is exposed via the `MaxLengthAttribute` class. `MaxLength Attribute` is one of a group of attributes that inherit from a class called `System.Data.Anno tations.ValidationAttribute`. `GetValidationResult` checked `MaxLength` because it's designed to check any rule that is applied using a `ValidationAttribute`.

The Validation API will check any rule that is applied using a `ValidationAttribute`.

Following is a list of the attribute classes that derive from `ValidationAttribute` along with the annotation used to decorate a class property:

`DataTypeAttribute`
    `[DataType(DataType enum)]`

`RangeAttribute`
    `[Range (low value, high value, error message string)]`

`RegularExpressionAttribute`
    `[RegularExpression(@"expression")]`

`RequiredAttribute`
    `[Required]`

`StringLengthAttribute`
    `[StringLength(max length value,`

    `MinimumLength=min length value)]`

`CustomValidationAttribute`
    This attribute can be applied to a type as well as to a property.

For the sake of describing database schema mappings, the Entity Framework team added `MaxLengthAttribute` to the namespace and paired it with a new `MinLengthAttri bute`. They both derive from `ValidationAttribute`, so these too will be checked by the Validation API.

Both `MaxLength` and `Required` are not just ways to define a class property but they are also used to describe a database column to which the properties map. Technically, these are referred to as facets. Therefore, in Entity Framework, these two facets play dual rules—they help Code First understand what the mapped database columns look like and they also participate in the class-level validation. An added benefit is that since you can also define these two facets—MaxLength and Required—with the Fluent API, Entity Framework will take advantage of the relevant ValidationAttribute types under the covers to make sure they get validated as if they had been configured with the Data Annotations.

Entity Framework has been taught to look for the StringLength annotation and use its MaximumLength parameter as a database column facet as well.

Validating Facets Configured with the Fluent API

If you have used the Fluent API to configure your Code First model, you may be familiar with specifying attributes fluently instead of using Data Annotations.

 The *Programming Entity Framework: Code First* book covers fluent API in detail.

Two of the Data Annotations that inherit from ValidationAttribute—MaxLength and Required—have Fluent API counterparts. This is due to the fact that MaxLength and Required are attributes that impact the model's comprehension of the database schema and therefore impact how Entity Framework maps the classes to the database.

The Validation API will check these two rules if you configure them with the Fluent API. For example, you could replace the [MaxLength] annotation on Person.LastName with this code added into the BreakAwayContext.OnModelCreating method:

```
modelBuilder.Entity<Person>()
  .Property(p => p.LastName).HasMaxLength(10)
```

If you return to the ValidateNewPerson method from Example 6-1, ensure the Last Name property is set to "Lerman-Flynn," and then rerun the method, it will result in a message from the console application: "Person is Invalid."

Underneath the covers, Entity Framework is using the StringLengthAttribute (or in the case of a Required scalar, the RequiredAttribute) to validate the HasMaxLength facet of Person.FirstName. Although the example only checks the IsValid property, the details of the error are returned by GetValidationResult, and you'll see how to read these shortly.

Validating Unmapped or "Transient" Properties

It is possible to have properties in your class that do not map to the database. By convention, properties that do not have both a setter and a getter will not be part of the model. These are also known as *transient properties*. You can also configure a property to be unmapped using the `NotMapped` data annotation or the `Ignore` fluent method. By default, unmapped properties will not get validated.

However, if you have applied a `ValidationAttribute` to a transient property (as long as that property is in a class that is part of the model), Entity Framework will validate those rules as well.

Validating Complex Types

Entity Framework's conceptual model supports the use of complex types, also known as value objects. You can configure a complex type both in the Entity Data Model designer as well as with Code First. It is also possible (and feasible) to apply attributes to the properties of complex types. Entity Framework's `GetValidationResult` will validate attributes placed on complex type properties.

Using Data Annotations with an EDMX Model

It's easy to apply data annotations to your class and then use that class with Entity Framework thanks to Code First, but what if you are using the Entity Data Model designer to create your Database First or Code First model and then relying on code generation to create your classes? There's no opportunity to apply Data Annotations to your properties. You might modify the T4 template to apply Data Annotations that follow very common patterns in your classes, but typically this is not the appropriate mechanism for applying property-by-property attributes.

The generated classes are partial classes, which does give you the ability to add more logic to the classes with additional partial classes. However, you cannot add attributes in one partial class to properties that are declared in another partial class.

But all is not lost. There is a feature in .NET called an *associated metadata class* that allows you to add metadata to classes in an external file. These classes are commonly referred to as "buddy classes," although we are more fond of the term "ugly buddy classes" because they feel a little kludgy. However ugly, they are a great way to apply data annotations to generated code. So setting aside illusions of grandeur about our code, let's take a look at a simple example of an associated metadata class.

 David Ebbo has an interesting blog post on other ways to use the `Metadata` attribute: *http://blogs.msdn.com/b/davidebb/archive/2009/07/24/using-an-associated-metadata-class-outside-dynamic-data.aspx*

If you are using the DbContext Generator template to generate classes from an EDMX, the `Person` class will be declared as a partial class:

```
public partial class Person
```

and the scalar properties will be simple. Here is what the `FirstName` property will look like:

```
public string FirstName { get; set; }
```

You can create a new class where you can mimic the property declaration and apply the attribute:

```
class Person_Metadata {
    [MinLength(10)]
    public string FirstName { get; set; }
}
```

Then you need to let the `Person` class know to use the `Person_Metadata` class for the sole purpose of reading the attributes.

You do this by applying the `Metadata` attribute to the `Person` class:

```
[MetadataType(typeof(Person_Metadata))]
    public partial class Person
```

 If you want to try this out in the Code First sample you've been working with, be sure to remove or comment out the `MinLength` annotation on the `FirstName` property in the `Person` class.

Inspecting Validation Result Details

Notice that `GetValidationResult` doesn't simply throw an exception if the validation fails. Instead, it returns a `System.Data.Entity.Validation.DbEntityValidationResult` whether the rule is met or broken, setting `IsValid` to the appropriate value and providing detailed information on any broken rules.

`DbEntityValidationResult` also exposes a `ValidationErrors` property, which contains a collection of more detailed errors in the form of `DbValidationError` types. One final property of `DbEntityValidationResult` is a pointer. In this scenario, it seems redundant to have the `Entry` property when we started with the `Entry` to get the results. However, when one of the higher-level methods calls `GetValidationResult` on your behalf, you may not know which `Entry` is currently being validated; in that scenario, you'll probably be grateful for the `Entry` property.

Figure 6-2 shows getting to the `Entry`, `IsValid`, and `ValidationErrors` properties in the debugger.

⊟ 🔘 context.Entry(personA).GetValidationResult()	{System.Data.Entity.Validation.DbEntityValidationResult}
⊞ 🔲 Entry	{System.Data.Entity.Infrastructure.DbEntityEntry}
🔲 IsValid	false
⊟ 🔲 ValidationErrors	Count = 1
⊟ 🔘 [0]	{System.Data.Entity.Validation.DbValidationError}
🔲 ErrorMessage	"The field LastName must be a string or array type with a maximum length of '10'."
🔲 PropertyName	"LastName"

Figure 6-2. Entry, IsValid and ValidationErrors a validation result

Inspecting Individual Validation Errors

Looking back at Figure 6-2, you'll see that when we set the LastName to Lerman-Flynn, which exceeded the MaxLength(10) specification, the result's ValidationErrors collection contains a single DbValidationError. DbValidationError exposes two properties, the name of the property and the actual error message.

Where did the error message come from? The internal validation logic has a formula that composes a message using the property name and the annotation that failed. This is default behavior.

You can specify your own error message in any ValidationAttribute. For example, if you were writing error messages for an application used by surfers, you might want to specify one like this:

```
[MaxLength(10,
           ErrorMessage= "Dude! Last name is too long! 10 is max.")]
public string LastName { get; set; }
```

Figure 6-3 shows the new ErrorMessage returned in a DbEntityValidationError.

⊟ 🔲 ValidationErrors	Count = 1
⊟ 🔘 [0]	{System.Data.Entity.Validation.DbValidationError}
🔲 ErrorMessage	"Dude! Last name is too long! 10 is max."
🔲 PropertyName	"LastName"

Figure 6-3. ErrorMessage and PropertyName of a DbValidationError

Because the ValidationAttribute type is part of .NET 4 and not specific to Entity Framework, we won't spend a lot of time going into great detail about how to configure the ValidationAttribute types. Other .NET frameworks, such as Managed Extensibility Framework (MEF), ASP.NET MVC, and ASP.NET Dynamic Data, use this functionality, and there is a lot of information available. To start, here is the MSDN Topic on the ValidationAttribute class: *http://msdn.microsoft.com/en -us/library/system.componentmodel.dataannotations.ValidationAttri bute.aspx*.

As mentioned in the earlier note, MEF, MVC, and Dynamic Data are able to leverage the ValidationAttribute. Although the ValidateNewPerson method demonstrated using DbContext to perform the validation, it is also possible to validate ValidationAttributes directly using its Validate method. This is a great benefit for client-side development. However, since the focus of this book is DbContext, we'll focus on how the DbContext works with the ValidationAttributes at the data layer. Remember that DbContext checks more than just ValidationAttributes, so you can benefit from these as well as other rules all at once on the server side with DbContext.

If you are calling GetValidationResults directly, you will have to write your own logic to interact with the DbEntityValidationResult, read the errors, and handle them, whether for logging or returning to the UI to present to the user.

In the case of the validation detected in ValidateNewPerson, there is a single error inside the ValidationErrors property. You could get to it by requesting that first error. For example:

```
var result = context.Entry(person).GetValidationResult();
if (!result.IsValid)
{
  Console.WriteLine(
    result.ValidationErrors.First().ErrorMessage);
}
```

That will work if you only expect or only care about the first error. However, if you have numerous ValidationAttributes defined on a type and more than one is broken, there will be more than one DbEntityValidationError in the ValidationErrors property.

What if the Person class also had a rule that the FirstName property must be at least three characters?

```
[MinLength(3)]
public string FirstName { get; set; }
```

If you were to update the ValidateNewPerson method from Example 6-1 to insert just the letter J as the FirstName, the validation will see two errors, as shown in Figure 6-4.

⊟ ◉ context.Entry(person).GetValidationResult()	{System.Data.Entity.Validation.DbEntityValidationResult}
⊞ 🔧 Entry	{System.Data.Entity.Infrastructure.DbEntityEntry}
🔧 IsValid	false
⊟ 🔧 ValidationErrors	Count = 2
⊟ ◉ [0]	{System.Data.Entity.Validation.DbValidationError}
🔧 ErrorMessage	"The field FirstName must be a string or array type with a minimum length of '3'."
🔧 PropertyName	"FirstName"
⊟ ◉ [1]	{System.Data.Entity.Validation.DbValidationError}
🔧 ErrorMessage	"Dude! Last name is too long! 10 is max."
🔧 PropertyName	"LastName"

Figure 6-4. Two errors inside of the result's ValidationErrors property

It might be wiser, therefore, to iterate through the errors. You'll need to add a using statement for the System.Data.Entity.Validation namespace:

```
foreach (DbValidationError error in result.ValidationErrors)
{
  Console.WriteLine(error.ErrorMessage);
}
```

Simplifying the Console Test Methods

Rather than rewrite the validation result inspection in each method, we've encapsulated that code into a standard method, `ConsoleValidateResults`, which you'll see going forward. Here's that code if you want to use it, too:

```
private static void ConsoleValidationResults(object entity)
{
  using (var context = new BreakAwayContext())
  {
    var result = context.Entry(entity).GetValidationResult();
    foreach (DbValidationError error in result.ValidationErrors)
    {
      Console.WriteLine(error.ErrorMessage);
    }
  }
}
```

Exploring More ValidationAttributes

So far we've looked at the `MaxLength` property, which is not only a `ValidationAttri bute`, but is an attribute that's in the *EntityFramework* assembly. Let's look at an attribute that is not specific to Entity Framework, the `RegularExpressionAttribute`, and verify that the `DbContext.GetValidationResult` will see that as well.

Following is a `RegularExpression` applied to the `Destination.Country` property. This expression specifies that the string can be up to 40 characters and will accept uppercase and lowercase letters:

```
[RegularExpression(@"^[a-zA-Z''-'\s]{1,40}$")]
public string Country { get; set; }
```

The `ValidateDestinationRegEx` method in Example 6-2 creates a new `Destination` and asks the `DbContext` to validate the instance.

 You'll notice that we've also refactored the method to move the call to `GetValidationResult` and `Console.WriteLine` into a separate method called `ConsoleValidationResults`. See the sidebar "Simplifying the Console Test Methods" on page 163 to see this new method.

Example 6-2. The ValidateDestination method

```
public static void ValidateDestination()
{
  ConsoleValidationResults(
```

```
new Destination
{
  Name = "New York City",
  Country = "USA",
  Description = "Big city"
});
}
```

With the Country set to "USA," the property is valid and no errors are displayed. However, if you change the Country value to "U.S.A.," GetValidationResult detects an error because the periods in between the letters do not follow the rule defined by the regular expression. Be aware that the default error message only reports that the value does not match the expression; it does not tell you which part of the expression was broken:

```
The field Country must match the regular expression '^[a-zA-Z''-'\s]{1,40}$'.
```

This is not a problem with how Entity Framework handles the validation. It is simply how the RegularExpressionAttribute behaves by default. You can learn more about controlling this error message in the MSDN documentation referenced above.

Using CustomValidationAttributes

You can build custom validation logic that can be applied to a property using a Custom ValidationAttribute. These too will get checked during Entity Framework validation. Example 6-3 shows an example of a static class, BusinessValidations, which contains a single validation, DescriptionRules, to be used on various description properties in the model. The rule checks for exclamation points and a few emoticons to ensure that trip descriptions or other descriptions don't read as though they were text messages! ☺

Example 6-3. Static custom validations to be used by different classes

```
using System.ComponentModel.DataAnnotations;

namespace Model
{
  public static class BusinessValidations
  {
    public static ValidationResult DescriptionRules(string value)
    {
      var errors = new System.Text.StringBuilder();
      if (value != null)
      {
        var description = value as string;

        if (description.Contains("!"))
        {
          errors.AppendLine("Description should not contain '!'.");
        }
        if (description.Contains(":)") ||
            description.Contains(":("))
        {
          errors.AppendLine(
```

```
          "Description should not contain emoticons.");
        }
      }
      if (errors.Length > 0)
        return new ValidationResult(errors.ToString());
      else
        return ValidationResult.Success;
    }
  }
}
```

 The ValidationResult used here is a System.ComponentModel.DataAnno
tations.ValidationResult, not to be confused with the System.Win
dows.Controls.ValidationResult.

You can apply the validation to properties using the CustomValidationAttribute, as shown in Example 6-4, where we've added the annotation to the Destination.Descrip tion property (which already has a MaxLength annotation). The attribute requires that you specify the class where the validation method exists and then the name of the method as a string.

Example 6-4. Applying the new DescriptionRules validation to a property

```
[MaxLength(500)]
[CustomValidation(typeof(BusinessValidations), "DescriptionRules")]
public string Description { get; set; }
```

If you'd like to test out the validation, you can modify the ValidateDestination method to insert some of the undesirable characters into the Description string, as we've done in Example 6-5.

Example 6-5. Creating a Destination that breaks multiple validation rules

```
public static void ValidateDestination()
{
  ConsoleValidationResults(
    new Destination {
      Name = "New York City",
      Country = "U.S.A",
      Description = "Big city! :) "
    });
}
```

Executing the method will cause the validation to return the following list of errors:

```
The field Country must match the regular expression '^[a-zA-Z''-'\s]{1,40}$'.
Description should not contain '!'.
Description should not contain emoticons.
```

Both the RegularExpression validation on the Country property and the Description Rules custom validation on Description are reported.

Validating Individual Properties on Demand

In addition to providing the GetValidationResults method, DbEntityEntry lets you drill into individual properties, as you've already seen in Chapter 5:

```
context.Entry(trip).Property(t => t.Description);
```

This returns a DbPropertyEntry representing the Description property.

The DbPropertyEntry class has a method for explicitly validating that particular entry— GetValidationErrors—which will return an ICollection<DbValidationError>. This is the same DbValidationError class we've been exploring already in this chapter.

Example 6-6 displays a new method, ValidatePropertyOnDemand, which shows how to validate a property using DbPropertyEntry.GetValidationErrors. You'll first need to apply the DescriptionRules custom attribute to the Trip.Description property, just as you did for Destination.Description in Example 6-4.

Example 6-6. Validating a property

```
private static void ValidatePropertyOnDemand()
{
  var trip=new Trip
          {
              EndDate = DateTime.Now,
              StartDate = DateTime.Now,
              CostUSD = 500.00M,
              Description = "Hope you won't be freezing :)"
      };
  using (var context = new BreakAwayContext())
  {
    var errors = context.Entry(trip)
              .Property(t => t.Description)
              .GetValidationErrors();
    Console.WriteLine("# Errors from Description validation: {0}",
                  errors.Count());
  }
}
```

The method creates a new Trip that has an emoticon in the Description. Based on the custom validation rule you created earlier in this chapter, the emoticon is invalid.

If you were to call this method from the Main method in the console application, the console window would report that there is one error in the Description. Keep this method around, because we'll look at it again in the next section.

Specifying Type-Level Validation Rules

While there are more ways to trigger validations, let's stick with the GetValidationRe sult method while we look at other ways to provide rules that the Validation API will validate. So far you've seen how to apply validation rules on individual properties. You

---

can also define rules for a type that can take multiple properties into account. Two ways to create type-level validation that will be checked by the Entity Framework Validation API are by having your type implement the IValidatableObject interface or defining CustomValidationAttributes for type. This section will explore both of these options.

Using IValidatableObject for Type Validation

In addition to the ValidationAttribute, .NET 4 introduced another feature to help developers with validation logic—the IValidatableObject interface. IValidatableObject provides a Validate method to let developers (or frameworks) provide their own context from which to perform the validation.

If an entity that is being validated implements the IValidatableObject interface, the Validation API logic will recognize this, call the Validate method, and surface the results of the validation in a DbEntityValidationError.

What does IValidatableObject provide that is not satisfied with Data Annotations? The Data Annotations let you specify a limited number of rules for individual properties. With the additional Validate method, you can provide any type of logic that can be constrained to the class. What we mean by constrained is that the validation logic won't rely on external objects since you can't guarantee that they'll be available when the validation is being performed. A typical example is comparing date properties in a class.

Validations and Your Application Architecture

The IValidatableObject.Validate method can be called from any part of your application that has access to the .NET framework. You can even leverage it for client-side validation. In your application architecture, you should be considerate of where you are depending on the DbContext to perform validation logic. Most likely, the context will be on the server side of your application and you would not want to rely on your data access layer for client-side validation in your user interface. Like the ValidationAttributes, IValidatableObject gives you the option to perform your validation in whatever layer of your application makes the most sense for your architecture and scenario.

The Trip type has StartDate and EndDate fields. Let's use IValidatableObject to define a rule that EndDate must be greater than StartDate.

Example 6-7 shows the Trip class after we've added the IValidatableObject implementation that includes the Validate method. Validate compares the dates and returns a ValidationResult if the rule is broken. Notice that we've also added the Description Rules attribute we created in Example 6-3 to the Description field.

Example 6-7. Validating dates in an IValidatableObject.Validate method

```
public class Trip : IValidatableObject
{
  [Key, DatabaseGenerated(DatabaseGeneratedOption.Identity)]
  public Guid Identifier { get; set; }
  public DateTime StartDate { get; set; }
  public DateTime EndDate { get; set; }
  [CustomValidation(typeof(BusinessValidations), "DescriptionRules")]
  public string Description { get; set; }
  public decimal CostUSD { get; set; }
  [Timestamp]
  public byte[] RowVersion { get; set; }

  public int DestinationId { get; set; }
  [Required]
  public Destination Destination { get; set; }
  public List<Activity> Activities { get; set; }

  public IEnumerable<ValidationResult> Validate(
    ValidationContext validationContext)
  {
    if (StartDate.Date >= EndDate.Date)
    {
      yield return new ValidationResult(
        "Start Date must be earlier than End Date",
        new[] { "StartDate", "EndDate" });
    }
  }
}
```

Visual Basic (VB) does not have a yield keyword. Instead, you can create a List<ValidationResult>, add each ValidationResult into that list, and then return it. Example 6-8 shows the Validate method as you would write it in VB.

Example 6-8. The Validate method expressed in Visual Basic

```
Public Function Validate(
 ByVal validationContext As ValidationContext)
 As IEnumerable(Of ValidationResult)
 Implements IValidatableObject.Validate
  Dim results = New List(Of ValidationResult)
  If StartDate.Date >= EndDate.Date Then
    results.Add(New ValidationResult
                ("Start Date must be earlier than End Date",
                 {"StartDate", "EndDate"}))
  End If
  Return result
End Function
```

We've added a new method to the console application called ValidateTrip, shown in Example 6-9.

Example 6-9. The ValidateTrip method to check the new rule

```
private static void ValidateTrip()
{
  ConsoleValidationResults(new Trip
  {
    EndDate = DateTime.Now,
    StartDate = DateTime.Now.AddDays(2),
    CostUSD = 500.00M,
    Destination = new Destination { Name = "Somewhere Fun" }
  });
}
```

When calling `ValidateTrip`, the application displays the error message, "Start Date must be earlier than End Date." But it's listed twice. That's because the Validate method listed this as a problem for both `StartDate` and `EndDate`, so it created two separate errors. The `DbValidationError.ErrorMessage` is the same in both, but one has "EndDate" in its `DbValidationError.PropertyName` while the other has "StartDate."

This is important for data binding with frameworks such as MVC or WPF where you can bind the errors to the displayed properties. If we modify the `ValidateTrip` method to ensure that `EndDate` is a later date than `StartDate`, the `ValidateTrip` method returns no error messages.

 Mapped complex types that implement `IValidatableObject` will be checked in the validation pipeline as well.

Validating Multiple Rules in IValidatableObject

You can add as many class validations as you like in your `Validate` method. With the C# yield keyword, all of the `ValidationResult` types created will be contained within the `IEnumerable` that's returned by the method.

Example 6-10 shows the `Trip.Validate` method with a second validation added that checks against a list of words that are undesirable for describing trips. You could use a `RegularExpression` annotation with the word list, but this method gives you the opportunity to store the list of words in a resource file so that it's not hard-coded into the application. The list is hard-coded into this example only for the simplicity of demonstrating the validation. You'll need to add a using statement for the `System.Linq` namespace.

Example 6-10. Validate method for the Trip type

```
public IEnumerable<ValidationResult> Validate(
  ValidationContext validationContext)
{
  if (StartDate.Date >= EndDate.Date)
  {
```

```
      yield return new ValidationResult(
        "Start Date must be earlier than End Date",
        new[] { "StartDate", "EndDate" });
    }

    var unwantedWords = new List<string>
    {
      "sad",
      "worry",
      "freezing",
      "cold"
    };

    var badwords = unwantedWords
      .Where(word => Description.Contains(word));

    if (badwords.Any())
    {
      yield return new ValidationResult(
        "Description has bad words: " + string.Join(";", badwords),
        new[] { "Description" });
    }
}
```

Now we'll modify the `ValidateTrip` method to add a `Description` (which includes the undesirable words "freezing" and "worry") to the new trip before the validation is performed (Example 6-11).

Example 6-11. ValidateTrip method modified to include Description

```
private static void ValidateTrip()
{
  ConsoleValidationResults(new Trip
    {
      EndDate = DateTime.Now,
      StartDate = DateTime.Now.AddDays(2),
      CostUSD = 500.00M,
      Description="Don't worry about freezing on this trip",
      Destination = new Destination { Name = "Somewhere Fun" }
    });
}
```

When running `ValidateTrip` with this trip that now breaks two rules, both error messages are displayed in the console window:

```
Start Date must be earlier than End Date
Start Date must be earlier than End Date
Description has bad words: worry;freezing
```

In the previous section, "Validating Individual Properties on Demand" on page 166, you created a method to explore the `DbPropertyEntry.GetValidationErrors`. Looking back at Example 6-6, notice that in addition to the emoticon in the description, there is what you now know to be an undesirable word—`freezing`. If you were to run the method again, the console window would still only report a single error, which is a

---

result of the emoticon. It seems to ignore the problem with the word freezing. That's because the validation that checks for the word freezing is defined for the class. DbPropertyEntry.GetValidationErrors can only check ValidationAttributes placed on properties.

Should You Use Validate for Other Purposes?

Applications often track when data was first created or last updated. Updating fields like DateAdded and DateLastModified is something that could demand redundant logic. It may be tempting to place that logic into Validate, but remember that Validate must return an IEnumerable<ValidationResult>. Your code would start to get pretty messy if you had to return fake results. You'd be better off abstracting logic like this elsewhere. In the scope of Entity Framework's Validation API, there's a more important reason to avoid it, which you'll learn about in detail in Chapter 7. Because of the way Save Changes, DetectChanges, and validation interact with one another, you could get unexpected behavior and incorrectly persisted data if you modify values in your validation logic.

Using CustomValidationAttributes for Type Validation

You can also use CustomValidationAttribute on a type rather than an individual property, allowing you to define a validation that takes into account more than a single property. We'll show you how you can define the same validation in the IValidatableObject example above by using CustomValidationAttribute.

The signature of a CustomValidationAttribute has the target type specified in the parameter along with a ValidationContext, which is used in the same way as the ValidationContext parameter of the Validate method. Example 6-12 shows two validation methods that are added into the Trip class. Notice that these methods are both public and static. Also notice that we're using separate methods for each validation. That's because a ValidationAttribute can only return a single ValidationResult.

Example 6-12. Two validation methods to be used as Trip type attributes

```
public static ValidationResult TripDateValidator(
  Trip trip,
  ValidationContext validationContext)
{
  if (trip.StartDate.Date >= trip.EndDate.Date)
  {
    return new ValidationResult(
      "Start Date must be earlier than End Date",
      new[] { "StartDate", "EndDate" });
  }

  return ValidationResult.Success;
}
```

```
public static ValidationResult TripCostInDescriptionValidator(
  Trip trip,
  ValidationContext validationContext)
{
  if (trip.CostUSD > 0)
  {
    if (trip.Description
      .Contains(Convert.ToInt32(trip.CostUSD).ToString()))
    {
      return new ValidationResult(
        "Description cannot contain trip cost",
        new[] { "Description" });
    }
  }

  return ValidationResult.Success;
}
```

The first method, `TripDateValidator`, mimics a validation you used earlier—checking that the `StartDate` is earlier than the `EndDate`. The second method, `TripCostInDescrip tionValidator`, checks to make sure that a user hasn't written the trip cost into the description. The logic in that method could be fine-tuned for a production application, but it should suffice for this demonstration.

There's a notable difference with these methods when comparing them to the `Vali date` method you saw earlier. The Validate method has access to private methods, properties, and fields. But because of the way the `ValidationAttribute` is handled under the covers triggering those methods (which is also why they must be `public` and `static`), it will not have this access.

To have both validations executed, you need to add them as separate attributes on the Trip class, as shown in Example 6-13.

Example 6-13. Applying a type-level CustomValidationAttribute

```
[CustomValidation(typeof(Trip), "TripDateValidator")]
[CustomValidation(typeof(Trip), "TripCostInDescriptionValidator")]
public class Trip: IValidatableObject
```

If you were to run the `ValidateTrip` method, the console window would display this:

```
Start Date must be earlier than End Date
Start Date must be earlier than End Date
Start Date must be earlier than End Date
Start Date must be earlier than End Date
Description has bad words: worry;freezing
```

As a reminder, because the validator creates the `ValidationResult` specifying that it's for both the `StartDate` field and for the `EndDate` property, the error is listed once for each property. If you were to inspect the `ValidationResult` more closely, you would see that the errors are differentiated by their `PropertyName`. You're also seeing the errors generated by the `Validate` method. The `Validate` method is also checking the date range as well as checking the `Description` for unwanted words.

Modify the `ValidateTrip` method to break the `TripCostInDescriptionValidator` rule as follows, changing the value of the `Description`:

```
private static void ValidateTrip()
{
  ConsoleValidationResults(new Trip
  {
    EndDate = DateTime.Now,
    StartDate = DateTime.Now.AddDays(2),
    CostUSD = 500.00M,
    Description = "You should enjoy this 500 dollar trip",
    Destination = new Destination { Name = "Somewhere Fun" }
  });
}
```

Running the application again would result in the two errors from the problem with the date properties as well as the error message from the failed `TripCostInDescription` `Validator` validation:

```
Description cannot contain trip cost
Start Date must be earlier than End Date
Start Date must be earlier than End Date
Start Date must be earlier than End Date
Start Date must be earlier than End Date
```

IValidatableObject or CustomValidationAttribute?

Good question, and it's one that we've been asking the pros so we can relay their advice to you. You have two ways to define type validation rules: which one is best to use? Naturally the question generated some debate. So our best guidance within the context of this book about Entity Framework is that it may simply be a matter of personal preference and coding style. If you are already using Data Annotations in your class, you might want to continue the pattern by using the attribute to provide type validation rules. You may not be a fan of decorating your classes with attributes and find that implementing `IValidatableObject` is more appropriate for your code.

Understanding How EF Combines Validations

Remember the `DescriptionRules` method that we added to the `BusinessValidations` class to validate the `Description` property of `Destination` and `Trip`? Those contain overall rules for writing any description for the company, not just those for destinations.

Now we'll modify the `Description` in the `ValidateTrip` method to include the dreaded smiley face emoticon and exclamation point:

```
Description="Hope you won't be freezing on this trip! :)"
```

Before running the `ValidateTrip` method again, keep in mind that the values of this `Trip` instance break four rules:

1. The `StartDate` is not at least a full calendar day before the `EndDate`.
2. The word `freezing` is in the description.
3. There is an emoticon in the `Description`.
4. There is an exclamation point in the `Description`.

Here is the list of messages returned by the method:

```
Description should not contain '!'.
Description should not contain emoticons.
```

The problems about the dates and the word `freezing` are missing from the messages.

To be sure, let's revert the `Description`, removing the exclamation and emoticon so that it passes the `DescriptionRules` but fails the others. This brings us back to the date problem listed for both the date fields and the message about the word `freezing`:

```
Start Date must be earlier than End Date
Start Date must be earlier than End Date
Start Date must be earlier than End Date
Start Date must be earlier than End Date
Description has bad words: freezing
```

While this looks like there's a problem with the validation, the validation is indeed working as designed. We've defined both property validation and type validation. The property validations check for the emoticons and exclamation point, while the type validations check the dates and look for bad words. The failure of a property validation is short-circuiting the type validations. In other words, the type validation is never performed because problems were found when validating the properties.

Let's update the `ValidateTrip` method so that it no longer supplied a value for the `Destination` property—which is marked with a `Required` attribute:

```
// Destination = new Destination { Name = "Somewhere Fun" }
```

If you rerun the `ValidateTrip` method, which no longer provides a value for the required `Destination` property, the only error message is this:

```
The Destination field is required.
```

The `Required` validation failure is reported, but the type validations are still missing, so the failure of this validation also prevented the type validation. If we added the "! :)" back into the `Description`, you'd see all of the property validation problems listed (Required, "!", and the emoticon) but still no report of the type validation problems.

What's happening is that there are rules that the validation engine follows that prevent it from erroneously reporting errors that might be caused by other validation errors. If the property validation fails, it's possible that the bad attributes might cause the type validation to fail as well.

Borrowing from the Entity Framework team blog post at *http://blogs.msdn.com/b/ado net/archive/2011/05/27/ef-4-1-validation.aspx*, here is a description of the order in which validations are performed:

1. Property-level validation on the entity and the base classes. If a property is complex its validation would also include the following:
2. Property-level validation on the complex type and its base types
3. Type-level validation on the complex type and its base types, including `IValidata bleObject` validation on the complex type
4. Type-level validation on the entity and the base entity types, including `IValidata bleObject` validation

The key point is that type-level validation will not be run if property validation returns an error. In addition to the `IValidatableObject` validations, relationship constraints are validated. Since it's possible that one of the property failures was due to a missing required property, that null value could very easily cause a relationship to be invalid. The Validation API does not allow constraint checking to occur if the properties cannot be validated.

Aligning Validation with the Rest of .NET

ASP.NET MVC, ASP.NET Dynamic Data, WCF RIA Services, and Managed Extensibility Framework have their own mechanisms for leveraging `ValidationAttributes` and `IValidatableObject`. Each of these technologies has similar patterns for determining the order in which to perform validations and how a failure of one validation will impact whether or not other validations are performed.

One of the important patterns is that type validation is not performed if property validations fail. This is mostly due to the possibility of there being a `Required` property. According to Pawel Kadluczka from the Entity Framework team:

> We wanted to be as close as possible to what they (e.g., MVC) do for consistency. The reason why they do it is that none of the built-in validation attributes treat null as an incorrect value—e.g., for `StringLength`, null will not break. This makes sense since null can be treated either as incorrect value or as something that has 0 length. Choosing one of these options arbitrarily would probably make half of the developers using validation unhappy. Now they can choose on their own the behavior they need.

Validating Multiple Objects

In addition to explicitly validating a single object with `GetValidationResult`, you can force the context to validate all of the *necessary* objects it is tracking with a single command: `DbContext.GetValidationErrors`. I've emphasized the word "necessary" because, by default, `GetValidationErrors` only validates `Added` and `Modified` objects since it typically wouldn't be necessary to validate objects that are Unchanged or are marked to be deleted from the database.

When you call this method, the context will internally call DetectChanges to ensure that all of the change tracking information is up-to-date. Then it will iterate through all of the Added and Modified objects that it's tracking and call DbContext.ValidateEntity on each object. ValidateEntity, in turn, will call GetValidationResult on the target object. When all of the objects have been validated, GetValidationErrors returns a collection of DbEntityValidationResult types for every failed object. The collection is returned as an IEnumerable< DbEntityValidationResult > and it only contains DbEntityValidation Result instances for the failed objects.

 In addition to calling GetValidationResult, ValidateEntity can also call custom logic that you specify. The next chapter will focus on customizing ValidateEntity. You'll also learn to modify how Entity Framework decides which entities to validate by overriding the default, which only validates Added and Modified entities.

Example 6-14 displays a method that results in a context tracking

- two new Trips,
- one new Destination,
- and one modified Trip.

If you look closely at the code, you'll see that one of the new trips will be valid while the other three objects are not valid.

Example 6-14. Validating multiple tracked objects

```
private static void ValidateEverything()
{
  using (var context = new BreakAwayContext())
  {
    var station = new Destination
    {
      Name = "Antartica Research Station",
      Country = "Antartica",
      Description = "You will be freezing!"
    };

    context.Destinations.Add(station);

    context.Trips.Add(new Trip
    {
      EndDate = new DateTime(2012, 4, 7),
      StartDate = new DateTime(2012, 4, 1),
      CostUSD = 500.00M,
      Description = "A valid trip.",
      Destination = station
    });
```

```
context.Trips.Add(new Trip
{
  EndDate = new DateTime(2012, 4, 7),
  StartDate = new DateTime(2012, 4, 15),
  CostUSD = 500.00M,
  Description = "There were sad deaths last time.",
  Destination = station
});

var dbTrip = context.Trips.First();
dbTrip.Destination = station;
dbTrip.Description = "don't worry, this one's from the database";

DisplayErrors(context.GetValidationErrors());
  }
}
```

Along with the ValidateEverything method in Example 6-14, add the DisplayErrors custom method (Example 6-15) to the Program class. This will iterate through the DbEntityValidationResult objects returned by the GetValidationErrors method and display them in a console window.

Example 6-15. DisplayErrors method called from Example 5-12

```
private static void DisplayErrors(
  IEnumerable<DbEntityValidationResult> results)
{
  int counter = 0;
  foreach (DbEntityValidationResult result in results)
  {
    counter++;
    Console.WriteLine(
      "Failed Object #{0}: Type is {1}",
      counter,
      result.Entry.Entity.GetType().Name);

    Console.WriteLine(
      " Number of Problems: {0}",
      result.ValidationErrors.Count);

    foreach (DbValidationError error in result.ValidationErrors)
    {
      Console.WriteLine(" - {0}", error.ErrorMessage);
    }
  }
}
```

Modify the Main method to call ValidateEverything, which will execute and display the validation results, as shown in Example 6-16.

Example 6-16. Output from ValidateEverything method

```
Failed Object #1: Type is Destination
 Number of Problems: 1
 - Description should not contain '!'.

Failed Object #2: Type is Trip
 Number of Problems: 5
 - Start Date must be earlier than End Date
 - Start Date must be earlier than End Date
 - Start Date must be earlier than End Date
 - Start Date must be earlier than End Date
 - Description has bad words: sad

Failed Object #3: Type is Trip
 Number of Problems: 1
 - Description has bad words: worry
```

GetValidationErrors does not check relationship constraints unless they are explicitly configured. For example, by default, the Reservation.Traveler property is nullable. There are two ways to force the Reservation to require that a Person type be attached. One is to add an int TravelerId property and configure that to be the foreign key for Traveler. Int is non-nullable by default. ValidateEntity will not check that constraint and therefore GetValidationErrors won't either.

 SaveChanges will detect relationship constraint problems even if they are not defined in a way that ValidateEntity will trap them.

Another way to require that a Person be attached is to configure the Traveler property as required. With a ValidationAttribute (even if you've configured with the Fluent API), ValidateEntity will check this rule and GetValidationErrors will detect the problem.

 In Chapter 3, you learned about DetectChanges, the events that call it by default, and how to disable automatic change detection. If you have disabled change detection, that means GetValidationErrors won't call it either and you should make an explicit call to DetectChanges before calling GetValidationErrors.

Validating When Saving Changes

While you may prefer to have explicit control over when GetValidationResults is called, Entity Framework can automatically perform the validations when you call Save Changes. By default, when you call SaveChanges, each Added and Modified entity that is being tracked by the context will be validated because SaveChanges calls GetValidationErrors.

Reviewing ObjectContext. SaveChanges Workflow

Later in this section, you'll learn how to disable the automatic validation that occurs during SaveChanges. You may already be familiar with how ObjectContext.Save Changes works in the Entity Framework. For a brief overview, it follows this workflow (note that this is not taking DbContext into account yet —only the internal workflow):

1. SaveChanges, by default, calls DetectChanges to update its tracking information on POCO objects.

2. SaveChanges iterates through each tracked entity that requires some modification (those with states Added, Modified, or Deleted).

3. For each of these entities, it checks that their relationship constraints are in a proper state. If not, it will throw an EntityUpdateException for that entity and stop further processing.

4. If all of the entities pass the relationship validation, EF constructs and executes the necessary SQL command(s) to perform the correct action in the database.

5. If the database command fails, the context responds by throwing an EntityUpda teException and stops further processing.

Because SaveChanges uses a DbTransaction by default, in either of the circumstances that causes the routine to throw an exception, any of the commands that succeeded up until that point are rolled back.

Understanding DbContext.SaveChanges Workflow

When you use DbContext to call SaveChanges, one additional step is performed prior to the first step in the ObjectContext.Savechanges workflow. DbContext.SaveChanges calls GetValidationErrors, which runs through the ValidateEntity process. If no errors are found, it then calls ObjectContext.SaveChanges. Because GetValidationErrors has already called DetectChanges, ObjectContext.SaveChanges skips its own call to DetectCh anges.

Figure 6-5 shows the execution path when your code calls DbContext.SaveChanges.

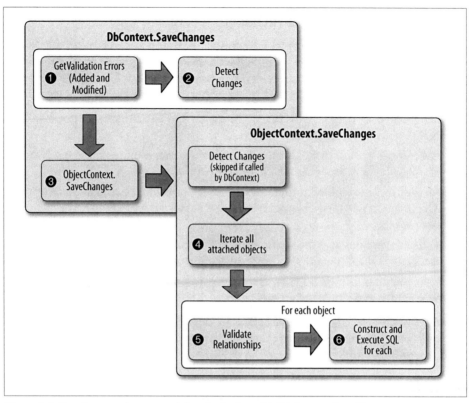

Figure 6-5. Database persistence workflow beginning with DbContext.SaveChanges

What this means to you is that, by default, Entity Framework will validate all of the rules specified with `ValidationAttributes` and `IValidatableObject` automatically when you call `SaveChanges` from a `DbContext`.

If errors are detected during `GetValidationErrors`, `SaveChanges` will throw a `DbEntity ValidationException` with the results of `GetValidationErrors` in its `EntityValidationEr rors` property. In this case, the context will never make the call to `ObjectContext.Save Changes`.

In the previous section, you learned that `ValidationEntity`, called by `GetValidationEr rors`, will not check relationship constraints unless they are specified in configuration. However, `ObjectContext.SaveChanges` has always checked relationship constraints and continues to do so. Therefore, any relationship constraints that were not validated by `GetValidationErrors` will be checked in the next stage of the save. The same applies to null complex properties. Since null complex properties are not supported, `ObjectCon text` always checks if a complex property is not null. Having the `Required` attribute on a complex property makes sense only for consistency reasons (that is, a null complex property violation will be reported the same way as other validation violations).

If you'd like to see this in action, you can modify the ValidateEverything method so that rather than explicitly calling GetValidationErrors, it will call SaveChanges. Replace the final line of the ValidateEverything method from Example 6-14 (i.e., the code line that calls into DisplayErrors) with the code in Example 6-17. You'll call SaveChanges instead and then display information about any validation exceptions.

Example 6-17. ValidateEverything modified to call SaveChanges instead of GetValidationErrors

```
try
{
  context.SaveChanges();
  Console.WriteLine("Save Succeeded.");
}
catch (DbEntityValidationException ex)
{
  Console.WriteLine(
    "Validation failed for {0} objects",
    ex.EntityValidationErrors.Count());
}
```

Because this example contains intentional problems that will be detected during the internal call to GetValidationErrors, ObjectContext.SaveChanges will never be executed and your data will not be persisted to the database. If the validations were to pass, there's still a chance of an UpdateException when the lower-level ObjectContext.Save Changes is called internally, but we're ignoring that possibility in this example.

If you were to run this method, you would find is that a DbEntityValidationExcep tion is thrown. DbEntityValidationException has a property called EntityValidatio nErrors which returns an IEnumerable of something you are already familiar with—EntityValidationResults that were created for each failed entity.

Figure 6-6 shows the DbValidationException in the debug window (with private fields removed for clarity).

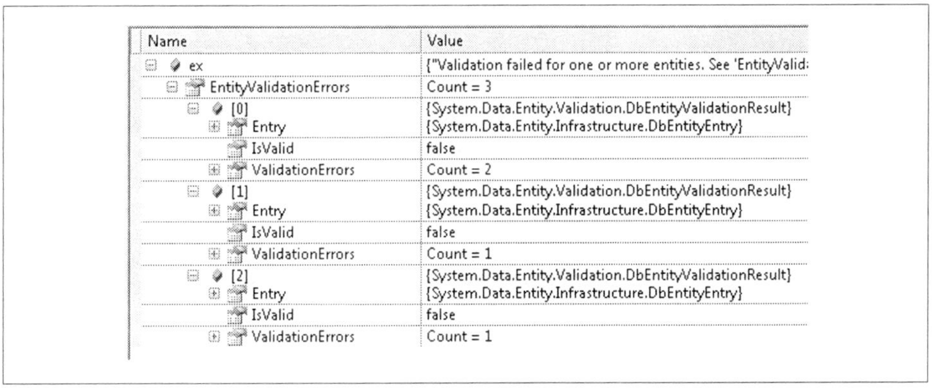

Figure 6-6. Inspecting a DbValidationException

The exception handler in Example 6-17 displays how many `EntityValidationResult` instances are contained in the exception, in other words, how many entities failed validation when `SaveChanges` was called.

Because you already know how to iterate through `EntityValidationResult` objects, you can dig further into the exception if you want to relay the details of the validation errors.

Disabling Validate Before Save

You may want to exert more control over when validation occurs by calling the various validation methods explicitly in your application. You can prevent Entity Framework from triggering the validation during `SaveChanges` thanks to the `DbContext.Configura tion` property. One of the settings you can configure on `DbContext` is `ValidateOnSaveEn abled`. This is set to true by an internal method when you instantiate a new `DbCon text`, which means that it's true by default on any `DbContext` class.

You can disable it in the constructor of your context class so that it's always false whenever you instantiate a new instance of the context.

For example, in `BreakAwayContext` you could add the following constructor:

```
public class BreakAwayContext : DbContext
{
  public BreakAwayContext()
  {
    Configuration.ValidateOnSaveEnabled = false;
  }
  ... rest of class logic
}
```

You can also enable or disable this feature as needed throughout your application by modifying the configuration setting on your context instance.

One benefit of disabling the validation on `SaveChanges` and calling the validation methods explicitly is that it allows you to avoid having an exception thrown. When validations fail inside of the `SaveChanges` call, `SaveChanges` throws the `DbEntityValidationEx ception`. However, as you've seen through this chapter, calling `GetValidationResult` or `GetValidationErrors` explicitly returns something whether the validations pass or fail. `GetValidationResult` returns a `ValidationResult` that will indicate whether or not the validation passed. `GetValidationErrors` returns an `IEnumerable` of `ValidationResults` for failed validations and if there were none, the `IEnumerable` will be empty. When application performance is an important factor in your development process, the expense of exceptions might be the deciding factor for choosing the automatic validation during `SaveChanges` or disabling that and taking control over how and when validation occurs. You'll learn more about taking advantage of this configuration in the next chapter.

CHAPTER 7

Customizing Validations

In the previous chapter you learned many ways that you can apply validation rules so that the DbContext Validation API can find and check them either on demand or automatically. While you can explicitly validate individual classes and properties directly from the DbEntityEntry method, you can also have the context validate all of its tracked entities as a group, either by calling GetValidationErrors or letting SaveChanges call that method for you. GetValidationErrors then calls ValidateEntity on each of the Added and Modified entities in the context. ValidateEntity then triggers logic that checks the ValidationAttribute and IValidatableObject rules you've specified in your classes.

You've seen how ValidateEntity works in Chapter 6. In this chapter, you'll learn how to customize the ValidateEntity method not only by overriding the logic of the method, but also by overriding the method that determines which entities should be validated.

Overriding ValidateEntity in the DbContext

ValidateEntity is a virtual method, meaning that you can override it and add your own custom logic. Like any virtual method, after executing your logic, you can control whether or not it performs the validations it's designed to execute (for example, validating the ValidationAttributes and IValidatableObject rules).

Example 7-1 shows the ValidateEntity method added into the BreakAwayContext class after using the Visual Studio IDE shortcut to add the overridden method.

Example 7-1. Signature of ValidateEntity override

```
protected override
 System.Data.Entity.Validation.DbEntityValidationResult
 ValidateEntity(
  System.Data.Entity.Infrastructure.DbEntityEntry entityEntry,
  System.Collections.Generic.IDictionary<object, object> items)
{
  return base.ValidateEntity(entityEntry, items);
}
```

If you are new to overriding methods in Visual Studio, the IDE has a shortcut to help you insert the method in C# and in VB. In the `BreakAwayContext` class, type the word `override` (`Overrides` for VB) followed by a space. Visual Studio will then show you a list of virtual methods. Select `ValidateEntity` from the list and the method code will be automatically added to the class.

By ensuring that the `System.Data.Entity.Infrastructure`, `System.Data.Entity.Validation`, and `System.Collections.Generic` namespaces are all added to the using statements at the top of the class file, the method signature becomes a little easier to read:

```
protected override DbEntityValidationResult ValidateEntity
  (DbEntityEntry entityEntry,IDictionary<object, object> items)
{
  return base.ValidateEntity(entityEntry, items);
}
```

You can add logic to `ValidateEntity` that performs additional validations on all types or on a subset of types (for example, a particular type or a particular set of types that inherit from another class or implement from an interface).

Another benefit of inserting logic here is that you have access to the `DbContext` and therefore can perform validation that depends on other tracked entities or even checks against data in the database. That's something you can't do in a `ValidationAttribute` or in the `IValidatableObject.Validate` method unless you were to pass a DbContext instance into the type. This would, however, force the type to be aware of the data layer which, if you care about keeping your POCO classes *persistence ignorant*, is undesirable.

You can read more about persistence ignorance (PI) from the perspective of Entity Framework in Chapter 24 of *Programming Entity Framework, 2e*, or in any number of resources on the Internet. Here, for example, is a discussion of PI in the scope of an article on the Unit of Work Pattern and Persistence Ignorance by Jeremy Miller in *MSDN Magazine*: *http://msdn.microsoft.com/en-us/magazine/dd882510.aspx #id0420053*.

An example of a validation that involves multiple entities is a rule for BreakAway Geek Adventures that a payment must made along with a new reservation. You'll find a `Payment` class in the model of the sample download along with a `Payments` navigation property in the `Reservation` class. The two classes are listed in Example 7-2.

Example 7-2. Payment class

```
public class Payment
{
  public Payment()
  {
```

```
    PaymentDate = DateTime.Now;
  }

  public int PaymentId { get; set; }
  public int ReservationId { get; set; }
  public DateTime PaymentDate { get; set; }
  public decimal Amount { get; set; }
}

public class Reservation
{
  public Reservation()
  {
    Payments = new List<Payment>();
  }

  public int ReservationId { get; set; }
  public DateTime DateTimeMade { get; set; }
  public Person Traveler { get; set; }
  public Trip Trip { get; set; }
  public Nullable<DateTime> PaidInFull { get; set; }

  public List<Payment> Payments { get; set; }
}
```

You may want your custom context logic to take precedence over the other validations that would be performed. In other words if the custom logic added in `ValidateEntity` fails, then don't bother validating the rules that are specified in `ValidationAttributes` or `IValidatableObject`. If no errors are detected in the custom context logic, then the `base.ValidateEntity` method will get called to check rules defined with `ValidationAttributes` and `IValidatableObject`. Figure 7-1 helps you visualize this workflow. You'll explore a number of other possible workflows later in the chapter.

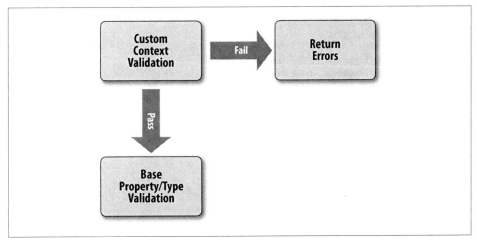

Figure 7-1. Calling base validation only if custom validation finds no errors

The ValidateEntity signature contains an entityEntry parameter. This represents the DbEntityEntry for the object currently being processed by the SaveChanges method. DbEntityEntry allows you to navigate to the actual object instance that it represents. You cast with the as operator to ensure you are working with the correct type:

```
var reservation = entityEntry.Entity as Reservation;
if (reservation !=null)
{
  //logic on reservation goes here
}
```

From here you can use the reservation instance or work directly against the change tracker through entityEntry.

Example 7-3 shows code that validates the new rule for Reservation. The code instantiates a new DbEntityValidationResult for this particular entry. Then, if the entry is for a Reservation and is new (Added) but has no Payments, a new error is added to the DbEntityValidationResult. If the reservation validation results in errors (in which case, result.IsValid will be false), those results are returned from ValidateEntity and the base validation is not called. If the result is valid, the base method is called instead.

 Remember from Chapter 6 that ValidateEntity temporarily disables lazy loading, so the context will not be looking for any payments in the database.

Example 7-3. ValidateEntity calling base validation only if custom validation passes

```
protected override DbEntityValidationResult ValidateEntity
    (DbEntityEntry entityEntry, IDictionary<object, object> items)
{
  var result = new DbEntityValidationResult(entityEntry,
                    new List<DbValidationError>());
  var reservation = entityEntry.Entity as Reservation;
  if (reservation != null)
  {
    if (entityEntry.State == EntityState.Added &&
        reservation.Payments.Count == 0)
    {
      result.ValidationErrors.Add(
        new DbValidationError(
          "Reservation",
          "New reservation must have a payment.")
        );
    }
  }
  if (!result.IsValid)
  {
    return result;
  }
  return base.ValidateEntity(entityEntry, items);
}
```

Keep in mind an important detail of the processing steps described earlier in Chapter 6. GetValidationErrors (called by SaveChanges) will execute ValidateEntity on all of the tracked entities before it begins constructing commands for the database. When designing custom logic for ValidateEntity, don't expect entities that have already been validated to be in the database by the time you reach the next entity.

If you have multiple validations to perform in ValidateEntity, it could get cluttered up pretty quickly. Example 7-4 shows the same logic as Example 7-3, but with the validation specific to the Reservation split out to a separate method.

Example 7-4. ValidateEntity calling base validation only if custom validation passes

```
protected override DbEntityValidationResult ValidateEntity
    (DbEntityEntry entityEntry, IDictionary<object, object> items)
{
  var result = new DbEntityValidationResult(entityEntry,
                   new List<DbValidationError>());

  ValidateReservation(result);

  if (!result.IsValid)
  {
    return result;
  }

  //call base validation
  return base.ValidateEntity(entityEntry, items);
}

private void ValidateReservation(DbEntityValidationResult result)
{
  var reservation = result.Entry.Entity as Reservation;
  if (reservation != null)
  {
    if (result.Entry.State == EntityState.Added &&
                       reservation.Payments.Count == 0)
    {
      result.ValidationErrors.Add(
        new DbValidationError(
          "Reservation",
          "New reservation must have a payment.")
        );
    }
  }
}
```

Considering Different Ways to Leverage ValidateEntity

In the previous example, ValidateEntity executes our context-based business validations. If no errors are found, it continues on to execute the base ValidateEntity method, which checks any rules defined with type validation (`IValidatableObject` rules) and property validation (`ValidateAttribute` rules). That's just one execution path you could set up in `ValidateEntity`.

 Throughout this chapter, we'll present different forms of the `Valida teEntity` method. If you are following along with the code samples, you might want to retain each version of `ValidateEntity` in the `BreakAway Context` class. What we did while developing our samples was to wrap a complier directive around the methods that we don't want to use anymore. This is cleaner than commenting out code. In C# you can add `#if false` before the beginning of the method and then `#endif` after the end of the method.

```
#if false
protected override DbEntityValidationResult
 ValidateEntity(DbEntityEntry entityEntry,
              IDictionary<object, object> items)
{
    ...method code
}
#endif
```

The code inside the directive will be grayed out and ignored by the compiler. Change the directive to `#if true` to reengage it.

In Visual Basic the directive looks like this:

```
#If False Then
#End If
```

You could reverse this logic, returning the base `ValidateEntity` results first and, if there are none, executing your custom logic as visualized in Figure 7-2.

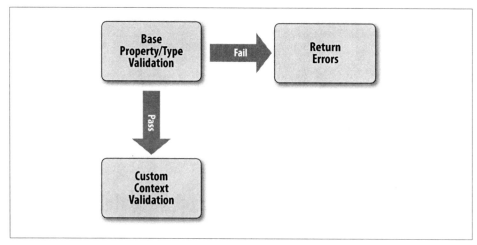

Figure 7-2. Calling custom validation only if base validation finds on errors

As an example, you might want to check a value for uniqueness in the database, perhaps to ensure that new Lodgings have a unique Name and Destination combination. You can do this in ValidateEntity because you have access to the context and therefore can execute a query such as

```
Lodgings.Any(l => l.Name == lodging.Name &&
    l.DestinationId == lodging.DestinationId);
```

But Lodging.Name already has a number of ValidationAttribute rules applied: Required, MinLength, and MaxLength. You might prefer to ensure that these three attributes are satisfied before wasting the trip to the database to check for a duplicate lodging. You could run the base ValidateEntity method first and return its errors if there are any. If there are no errors found in the base validation, continue on to the new validation logic, which checks the database for an existing lodging with the name and destination of the one about to be added. Example 7-5 demonstrates this logic. First, base.ValidateEn tity is called. If its results are valid, a custom validation method, ValidateLodging, is called and its errors, if any, are added to the results collection, which is returned at the end.

Example 7-5. Executing context validation only if property and type validation pass

```
protected override DbEntityValidationResult ValidateEntity
 (DbEntityEntry entityEntry, IDictionary<object, object> items)
{
  var result = base.ValidateEntity(entityEntry, items);

  if (result.IsValid)
  {
    ValidateLodging(result);
  }
  return result;
}

private void ValidateLodging(DbEntityValidationResult result)
{
  var lodging = result.Entry.Entity as Lodging;
  if (lodging != null && lodging.DestinationId != 0)
  {
    if (Lodgings.Any(l => l.Name == lodging.Name &&
                          l.DestinationId == lodging.DestinationId))
    {
      result.ValidationErrors.Add(
        new DbValidationError(
          "Lodging",
          "There is already a lodging named " + lodging.Name +
          " at this destination.")
        );
    }
  }
}
```

Checking for uniqueness in Example 7-5 may have made you wonder about a simpler way to define unique validations. The Entity Framework team is working on a feature that would allow you to define Unique Constraints directly in the model. You can read more details about this in their March 2011 blog post at *http://blogs.msdn.com/b/efdesign/ archive/2011/03/09/unique-constraints-in-the-entity-framework.aspx*.

We created a method in the console app called `CreateDuplicateLodging` to test this validation, shown in Example 7-6.

Example 7-6. Inserting Lodgings to test validations

```
private static void CreateDuplicateLodging()
{
  using (var context = new BreakAwayContext())
  {
    var destination = context.Destinations
      .FirstOrDefault(d => d.Name == "Grand Canyon");

    try
    {
      context.Lodgings.Add(new Lodging
      {
        Destination = destination,
        Name = "Grand Hotel"
      });

      context.SaveChanges();
      Console.WriteLine("Save Successful");
    }
    catch (DbEntityValidationException ex)
    {
      Console.WriteLine("Save Failed: ");
      foreach (var error in ex.EntityValidationErrors)
      {
        Console.WriteLine(
          string.Join(Environment.NewLine,
          error.ValidationErrors.Select(v => v.ErrorMessage)));
      }

      return;
    }
  }
}
```

The critical part of this method inserts Grand Hotel at the Grand Canyon while the bulk of the method is code to display errors for this demonstration. Our seed data includes a `Lodging` called Grand Hotel at the `Destination` Grand Canyon. So our new `Lodging` will be a duplicate. If you run this method from the console application's main method, `ValidateEntity` will call `ValidateLodging` and discover the duplication. The console will report the error:

```
Save Failed:
There is already a lodging named Grand Hotel at this destination.
```

Now let's add in a validation that will fail the base.ValidateEntity check. Modify the Lodging to add a data annotation to the MilesFromNearestAirport property. The RangeAttribute specifies a valid value range for the property. Here we'll say that anything from .5 to 150 miles will be valid:

```
[Range(.5,150)]
public decimal MilesFromNearestAirport { get; set; }
```

If you run the application again, you'll see this message in the console window:

```
Save Failed:
The field MilesFromNearestAirport must be between 0.5 and 150.
```

There's no mention of the duplication. That's because the ValidateEntity method is designed to check the property and type rules first and return the exception right away if any are found—before it has called ValidateLodging.

Let's return to the ValidateEntity method and force it to return the combination of validation errors checked in the custom logic and in the logic check by base.ValidateEntity, as visualized in Figure 7-3.

Figure 7-3. Combining errors from custom and base validation

Example 7-7 demonstrates code that will allow you to collect the results of the base validation and then add any additional errors found in the custom logic to that result before returning the combined errors from ValidateEntity.

Example 7-7. Combing type and property validation results with context results

```
protected override DbEntityValidationResult ValidateEntity
  (DbEntityEntry entityEntry, IDictionary<object, object> items)
{
  var result = base.ValidateEntity(entityEntry, items);
  ValidateLodging(result);
  return result;
}
```

Running the CreateDuplicateLodging method one last time will now display both errors:

```
Save Failed:
The field MilesFromNearestAirport must be between 0.5 and 150.
There is already a lodging named Grand Hotel at this destination.
```

You can include multiple validation checks in ValidateEntity. These examples only contain one at a time for the sake of brevity.

Now that you've seen a few possible workflows for executing validations in ValidateEntity, you can mimic these or define your own workflow when customizing ValidateEntity.

Further Refactoring

As you implement this custom logic into your own application, you may have many custom validations defined in your DbContext class. Rather than having to call Vali dateReservation, ValidateLodging, and any others from ValidateEntity, you could combine them into a single method such as IsValid and call that from ValidateEn tity instead. For example:

```
private void IsValid(DbEntityValidationResult result)
{
  ValidateLodging(result);
  ValidateReservation(result);
}
```

Updating Data During SaveChanges

Quite often, there are last-minute modifications that you want to make to data before it's sent to the database. One example is setting DateAdded and DateModified values in your classes. While there are a number of ways to achieve this in .NET code, you may wish to perform this logic in the data layer. Because the context is already iterating through all of its Added and Modified entities when it calls ValidateEntity, it's tempting to add this logic into ValidateEntity rather than perform an additional enumeration in the SaveChanges method.

It's possible to do this, but it is not recommended. The following are some downsides to putting this type of logic inside of ValidateEntity:

- The ValidateEntity method is designed for performing validations. Using it for other purposes infringes on the principle of Singular Responsibility—a coding principle that exists to help you in the quest for maintainable code.

- You might not want to bother with modifying data before you know it's valid and headed for the database. You could call base.ValidateEntity prior to the update logic as shown in Example 7-5, but a later entity might be invalid, rendering all modifications moot.

- By the time you're in the ValidateEntity method, DetectChanges has already been called and you need to be careful about how you update values.

One alternative is to override SaveChanges and iterate through entities to apply the dates before base.SaveChanges does a second iteration to validate the entities. Keep in mind that after this, there is a third iteration—the one that creates and executes the commands for each Added, Modified, and Deleted entity to the database.

If you override SaveChanges to apply the date values, ValidateEntity will be called afterwards, during base.SaveChanges. If invalid data is found, the effort and processing time taken to update the date properties was wasted.

In the next section, we'll look at pros and cons of the options you have to perform the date modifications during SaveChanges and then show you an efficient example of modifying ModifiedDate and AddedDate properties during SaveChanges.

Overriding SaveChanges When Validation Occurs

If you want to set values inside of SaveChanges and you are leveraging the Validation API, you have a number of choices:

- Update the data values in SaveChanges and let base.SaveChanges perform the validation (through ValidateEntity) as it normally would.
- Turn off ValidateOnSaveEnabled and iterate through entities, calling GetValidation Result and then the date fix-up for each entity.
- Turn off ValidateOnSaveEnabled and iterate through entities, fixing up the dates for each entity and then calling GetValidationResult.
- Turn off ValidateOnSaveEnabled. Call GetValidationErrors (which will iterate through entities) and then iterate again performing the date fix-ups.
- Turn off ValidateOnSaveEnabled. Iterate through entities to perform the date fix-ups, and then call GetValidationErrors (which will iterate through entities). This would be no different than the first option in this list.

There are pros and cons to each approach. We'll walk through one of them and present the pros and cons of the others. In the end, you should be able to choose the approach that best fits your application.

For this example, we'll perform validations by calling GetValidationErrors and then update two date fields for any entity that inherits a new base class, Logger. In this scenario, we have confidence that updating the date fields won't break any validation rules, so it is safe to perform this task after the validations have been checked by the API. In a real-world application, you should have automated tests in place to ensure that future modifications to the application don't break this assertion.

Example 7-8 shows a new abstract class called Logger, which exposes two new date fields. It also has a public method, UpdateModificationLogValues, for updating those fields. This method may be used by any number of business logic methods that access your classes.

Example 7-8. Logger base class

```
public abstract class Logger
{
  public DateTime LastModifiedDate { get; set; }
  public DateTime AddedDate { get; set; }

  public void UpdateModificationLogValues(bool isAdded)
  {
    if (isAdded)
    {
      AddedDate = DateTime.Now;
    }
    LastModifiedDate = DateTime.Now;
  }
}
```

Modify the `Activity` class to inherit from `Logger`:

```
public class Activity : Logger
```

Now you can override `SaveChanges`, as shown in Example 7-9. Back in Chapter 5 you overrode `SaveChanges` to perform logging; you should replace the logging implementation with this new implementation. Notice that the first action in the method is to store the current setting of `AutoDetectChangesEnabled`. That's because we're going to temporarily set it to `false` and want to reset it before exiting the method. The reason we're setting it to `false` is to control exactly when `DetectChanges` is called.

Example 7-9. SaveChanges overridden to perform validation and updates

```
public override int SaveChanges()
{
  var autoDetectChanges = Configuration.AutoDetectChangesEnabled;

  try
  {
    Configuration.AutoDetectChangesEnabled = false;
    ChangeTracker.DetectChanges();
    var errors = GetValidationErrors().ToList();
    if (errors.Any())
    {
      throw new DbEntityValidationException
        ("Validation errors found during save.", errors);
    }

    foreach (var entity in this.ChangeTracker.Entries()
                          .Where(e =>
                                 e.State ==EntityState.Added ||
                                 e.State == EntityState.Modified))
    {
      ApplyLoggingData(entity);
    }
    ChangeTracker.DetectChanges();

    Configuration.ValidateOnSaveEnabled = false;
```

```
    return base.SaveChanges();
  }
  finally
  {
    Configuration.AutoDetectChangesEnabled = autoDetectChanges;
  }
}
```

The `ApplyLoggingData` method shown in Example 7-10 will call `UpdateModification
LogValues` on any entities that inherit from `Logger`, passing in a Boolean to signal
whether or not the `AddedDate` needs to be set. Once all the dates have been updated,
we call `DetectChanges` to ensure that Entity Framework is aware of any changes that
were made.

Example 7-10. ApplyLoggingData method in BreakAwayContext class

```
private static void ApplyLoggingData(DbEntityEntry entityEntry)
{
  var logger = entityEntry.Entity as Logger;
  if (logger == null) return;
  logger.UpdateModificationLogValues
    (entityEntry.State == EntityState.Added);
}
```

Now we'll test that the date fields get changed by adding a new, valid `Activity` using
the `InsertActivity` method (added into the console application) shown in Example 7-11. The code displays the dates after `SaveChanges` has been called. After the first
call to `SaveChanges`, the code makes a modification and saves again, displaying the dates
a second time.

Example 7-11. Console method to observe Logger properties updated in SaveChanges

```
private static void InsertActivity()
{
  var activity = new Activity { Name = "X-C Skiing" };
  using (var context = new BreakAwayContext())
  {
    context.Activities.Add(activity);
    try
    {
      context.SaveChanges();
      Console.WriteLine("After Insert:   Added={0}, Modified={1}",
                        activity.AddedDate, activity.LastModifiedDate);
      //pause 2 seconds
      System.Threading.Thread.Sleep(2000);
      activity.Name = ("X-C Skating");
      context.SaveChanges();
      Console.WriteLine("After Modified: Added={0}, Modified={1}",
                        activity.AddedDate, activity.LastModifiedDate);
    }
    catch (DbEntityValidationException ex)
    {
      Console.WriteLine("Save Test Failed: " +
```

```
                    ex.EntityValidationErrors.FirstOrDefault()
                       .ValidationErrors.First().ErrorMessage);
      }
    }
}
```

When you run this, you'll see that the newly inserted activity has its `AddedDate` and `LastModifiedDate` values populated after being saved. Then when the activity is edited and saved again, you can see that its `LastModifiedDate` value has been updated again, thanks to the combined logic in `SaveChanges` and the `Logger` class:

```
After Insert:   Added=12/9/2011 12:16:27 PM, Modified=12/9/2011 12:16:27 PM
After Modified: Added=12/9/2011 12:16:27 PM, Modified=12/9/2011 12:16:33 PM
```

This works because by the time we're calling `ApplyLoggingData`, the context is already aware that these are either `Added` or `Modified` entities and is already planning to persist them to the database.

You can avoid the need to call `DetectChanges` by changing properties directly through the change tracker. That's logic that you won't be able to (or want to) embed into your domain classes (which we prefer to not have any knowledge of Entity Framework). So you'll have to do that within the context. Example 7-12 shows what the `ApplyLogging Data` would look like if you were to set the properties through the change tracker.

Example 7-12. Using the change tracker to update scalar properties

```
private static void ApplyLoggingData(DbEntityEntry entityEntry)
{
  var logger = entityEntry.Entity as Logger;
  if (logger == null) return;
  entityEntry.Cast<Logger>()
   .Property(l => l.ModifiedDate).CurrentValue = DateTime.Now;
  if (entityEntry.State==EntityState.Added)
  {
    entityEntry.Cast<Logger>()
      .Property(l => l.AddedDate).CurrentValue = DateTime.Now;
  }
}
```

In Chapter 5, you learned how to work with scalars as well as collection and reference navigation properties through the change tracker. If you want to make changes to navigation properties at the data layer, you should do so using the change tracker, as shown with the scalar property changes made in Example 7-12. If you used the navigation properties of the class directly, whether you do that in the context code or call into code in the type you are modifying (for example, `Logger.UpdateModificationLogValues`), you run a substantial risk of those changes not being persisted to the database. Again, this is dependent on where in the workflow `DetectChanges` is being called. If you are in the habit of using the change tracker to make the changes, you don't have to worry about `DetectChanges`.

Comparing ValidateEntity to SaveChanges for Custom Logic

If you've been using Entity Framework for a few years, you might be familiar with various options we've had for applying validation logic and wondering how ValidateEntity fits into the picture. The first version of Entity Framework gave us the ObjectContext.SavingChanges event, which let developers execute validation or other logic when SaveChanges was called. Your logic added into SavingChanges would be executed and then Entity Framework would execute its internal logic. Entity Framework 4 brought us the added benefit of a virtual SaveChanges method so we could not only have Entity Framework execute our custom logic when calling SaveChanges, but we had the option of completely halting the internal code.

You can also override SaveChanges when it is called from DbContext. DbContext doesn't have a SavingChanges event because with the virtual SaveChanges, the former approach is redundant. The only reason SavingChanges still exists as a method of ObjectContext is for backward compatibility. But if you need to, you can get to ObjectContext from DbContext by first dropping down to the ObjectContext using the IObjectContextAdapter, as you've seen previously in this book.

ValidateEntity is yet another extensibility point that is available during SaveChanges. But as you've seen in this chapter, you should be considerate of when your code makes use of ValidateEntity or SaveChanges to insert your logic.

ValidateEntity by default is executed on every Added or Modified object being tracked. It is a good replacement for code that you may have put in SaveChanges where you iterate through each tracked object and perform some validation logic on it.

A big caveat with the ValidateEntity method, however, is that it is executed after DetectChanges has been called, so you have to be careful about how you go about setting properties. You can safely set properties using the DbEntityEntry, but our preference is to avoid adding nonvalidation logic into a method that is designated for performing validations.

The SaveChanges method is a good place to execute logic where you want to do something with a group of objects. For example, you might want to log how many reservations are added in a particular update. While you do have access to this in the ValidateEntity method, this is something you want to execute only once during a save.

Microsoft's guidance is to use ValidateEntity to perform validation logic (rule checking) only. Their primary reason for this guidance is concern over incorrectly coded property modifications that won't get picked up by the context if the developer is unaware of the fact that DetectChanges was already called—and will not be called again. Another is that in ValidateEntity, the team has ensured that lazy loading won't have unexpected effects on the validation.

From a perspective of architectural guidance, yet another reason is that by not forcing ValidateEntity to perform non-validation logic, you follow the principle of Single Responsibility (*http://msdn.microsoft.com/en-us/magazine/cc546578.aspx#id0390008*).

`ValidateEntity` is for validating. Single Responsibility helps to keep in mind the fact that if you introduce other features into that method, you'll increase the difficulty of maintaining your application as it grows and evolves.

Using the IDictionary Parameter of ValidateEntity

So far we've focused on the `entityEntry` parameter of `ValidateEntity`. There is also an `IDictionary<object, object>` parameter available:

```
protected override DbEntityValidationResult ValidateEntity
    (DbEntityEntry entityEntry, IDictionary<object, object> items)
```

By default, the value of this parameter is null, but you can use the parameter to pass additional values to custom implementations of `IValidatableObject.Validate` or `Vali dationAttributes`.

 Watch for a change to the `IDictionary` parameter in a future version of Entity Framework: it may be changed to default to an empty dictionary rather than null. That would make coding against it simpler. As of Entity Framework 4.3, the parameter is still null.

For example, recall the signature of `IValidatableObject.Validate`:

```
public IEnumerable<ValidationResult>
    Validate(ValidationContext validationContext)
```

`ValidationContext` implements `iDictionary`. Entity Framework passes the `items` defined in `ValidateEntity` to this `validationContext` parameter. It's also possible to use a `ValidationContext` when creating overrides of the `ValidationAttribute` class. (See the MSDN Library documentation topic `ValidationAttribute` Class for more information about this feature: *http://msdn.microsoft.com/en-us/library/system.componentmodel.da taannotations.validationattribute.aspx*)

You can create a dictionary of objects in the `ValidateEntity` method and pass them along in the base `ValidateEntity` call by assigning the dictionary to the `items` variable. Those objects would then be available for you to use in validations that accept a `Vali dationContext`.

For example, you may want to be sure that a newly added or modified payment does not cause the saved payments to exceed the cost of the trip on which the reservation is booked. To validate this rule, you would need the data layer to access the database when it's validating new or modified payment objects. But rather than performing all of the calculations in the data layer, you could have the data layer provide the necessary information to the payment so that the rule can be included in the business logic for the `Payment` itself.

I've seen examples where the DbContext itself is passed back into the ValidationContext of IValidatable.Validate or ValidationAttributes from ValidateEntity. Neither of us are fans of this pattern because it forces the object to be aware of the context, of the data layer, and of Entity Framework. Not only is the class no longer POCO, but it also removes another quality that I have learned to admire, persistence ignorance.

Example 7-13 shows the Validate method for Payment after we've modified Payment to implement the IValidatableObject interface. There are two validations in the method. The method first checks to see if there are PaymentSum and TripCost items in the validationContext. The method expects that the method that has triggered Validate will have created these items in the dictionary passed in as the validationContext parameter. If they are there, the method will use those to compare the payments to the trip cost.

Example 7-13. IValidatableObject.Validate method using ValidationResult

```
public IEnumerable<ValidationResult> Validate(
  ValidationContext validationContext)
{
  var vc = validationContext; //for book readability

  if (vc.Items.ContainsKey("DbPaymentTotal")
    && vc.Items.ContainsKey("TripCost"))
  {
    if (Convert.ToDecimal(vc.Items["DbPaymentTotal"]) + Amount >
      Convert.ToDecimal(vc.Items["TripCost"]))
    {
      yield return new ValidationResult(
        "Oh horrors! The client has overpaid!",
        new[] { "Reservation" });
    }
  }
}
```

This example is to demonstrate the use of the IDictionary and not meant as the de facto pattern for checking for overpayments in a production application. There are many more factors to take into consideration for this particular use case regardless of whether you are using Entity Framework validation or any other validation pattern.

Given that the Payment class validation expects to be provided with a ValidationContext that supplies the sum of Payments for a single Reservation that are already in the database and the cost of the trip for which the payment and reservation are made, the ValidateEntity method needs to add those values into the IDictionary.

Example 7-14 does just that—retrieving the total of payments for the Reservation and the TripCost from the database, and then adding them to the _items IDictionary. This example also places the particular validation logic, FillPaymentValidationItems, in a separate method in order to keep the ValidateEntity method cleaner.

Example 7-14. ValidateEntity passing values using the IDictionary

```
protected override DbEntityValidationResult ValidateEntity
    (DbEntityEntry entityEntry, IDictionary<object, object> items)
{
  var _items = new Dictionary<object, object>();
  FillPaymentValidationItems(entityEntry.Entity as Payment, _items);
  return base.ValidateEntity(entityEntry, _items);
}

private void FillPaymentValidationItems(Payment payment, Dictionary<object, object> _items)
{
  if (payment == null)
  {
    return;
  }
  //calculate payments already in the database
  if (payment.ReservationId > 0)
  {
    var paymentData = Reservations
      .Where(r => r.ReservationId == payment.ReservationId)
      .Select(r => new
      {
        DbPaymentTotal = r.Payments.Sum(p => p.Amount),
        TripCost = r.Trip.CostUSD
      }).FirstOrDefault();
    _items.Add("DbPaymentTotal", paymentData.DbPaymentTotal);
    _items.Add("TripCost", paymentData.TripCost);
  }
}
```

Notice that ValidateEntity doesn't check the type of the entityEntry.Entity. Instead it leverages the performance benefit of casting with as, which will return a null if the entity is not a Payment. Then the helper method does a quick check for a null before bothering with the inner logic. This is simply a design decision made on our part.

The method first ensures that the ReservationId has been set. If the user is adding a new Reservation and Payment together, then the Reservation won't have a ReservationId yet and therefore it won't have been set on the Payment.

Controlling Which Entities Are Validated in ValidateEntity

As we've pointed out earlier, by default, Entity Framework will only send Added and Modified entities to the ValidateEntity method. Internal code checks the state before calling ValidateEntity in a virtual (Overridable in VB) method of DbContext called ShouldValidateEntity.

After some internal evaluation, ShouldValidateEntity returns a Boolean based on this line of code which checks to see if the state is either Modified or Added:

```
return ((entityEntry.State &
(EntityState.Modified | EntityState.Added)) != 0);
```

Because ShouldValidateEntity is virtual, you can override the default logic and specify your own rules for which entities are validated. You may want only certain types to be validated or you may want validation performed on Deleted objects.

As an example, it wouldn't make sense to delete Reservations for Trips that are in the past. If you want to capture deleted Reservations in the data layer and check to make sure they aren't for past Trips, you'll have to make sure the deleted Reservation makes it to the ValidateEntity method. You don't have to send all deleted objects. Instead you can "open up" the pipeline only for deleted Reservations.

Add the ShouldValidateEntity method to the BreakAwayContext. You can use the same steps to override the method explained in the earlier note when adding the ValidateEntity method.

Example 7-15 shows the ShouldValidateEntity method after we've added additional logic to allow deleted Reservation objects to be validated as well. If the entity being evaluated is a deleted Reservation, ShouldValidateEntity will return true. If not, it will perform its default logic to determine whether or not to validate the entity.

Example 7-15. Overriding ShouldValidateEntity

```
protected override bool ShouldValidateEntity(DbEntityEntry entityEntry)
{
  return base.ShouldValidateEntity(entityEntry)
      || ( entityEntry.State == EntityState.Deleted
           && entityEntry.Entity is Reservation);
}
```

Once you've allowed the entry to pass through to ValidateEntity, you'll need to add logic to ValidateEntity to perform the new validation.

CHAPTER 8

Using DbContext in Advanced Scenarios

The focus of this book so far has been to get you up and running with using the DbContext, along with its partner APIs—Validation and Change Tracking. Now it's time to look at some advanced and less commonly used features of DbContext, the DbSet and the Database classes, as well as moving between a DbContext and ObjectContext. Even though this book is not an application patterns book, we will also take a look at two interesting application scenarios. One will be a discussion of defining your DbContext and taking into consideration the use of multiple contexts in your application to target only the sets of model classes that are needed in any given scenario. The other will be a look at leveraging the IDbSet to create abstractions that will allow you to build more flexible applications. In *Programming Entity Framework, 2e*, you'll find an extensive sample that uses ObjectSet, automated unit testing, and repositories. This IDbSet example will be a slice of that, explaining how you can replicate the pattern using the DbContext API.

Moving Between ObjectContext and DbContext

As you've learned, the DbContext is a smaller API exposing the most commonly used features of the ObjectContext. In some cases, those features are mirrored in the DbContext API. In other cases, the Entity Framework team has simplified more complex coding by providing us with methods like Find or properties like DbSet.Local. But there's a big API lurking underneath that you may still need access to. For example, you might want to work directly with the MetadataWorkspace to write generic code against classes because that API can read the model more efficiently than reflection. Additionally, the MetadataWorkspace is able to provide more information about the metadata than you can discover with reflection, for example, for Key properties. Or you might want to take advantage of a database-specific function that is exposed through Entity SQL, which you can't access from LINQ to Entities. Or you may already have an application written using the `ObjectContext` and you want to leverage the `DbContext` in future updates without replacing all of the `ObjectContext` code.

All of these scenarios are achievable.

 You can learn about `MetadataWorkspace`, mentioned above, in Chapter 18 of *Programming Entity Framework, 2e.*

Accessing ObjectContext Features from a DbContext

If you are starting with a `DbContext`, you can access the `ObjectContext` features very easily through the `IObjectContextAdapter`. In fact, you've seen this done a few times in this book already. In Chapter 4 we used this to access the `ObjectMaterialized` event that is not available directly on `DbContext`.

 The Entity Framework team refers to the procedure of accessing the `ObjectContext` from `DbContext` as "dropping down to `ObjectContext`." You have seen this expression used a few times already in this book.

The pattern to get to the `ObjectContext` is to cast the `DbContext` instance to this `IObjectContextAdapter` and, from there, access its `ObjectContext` property. `DbContext` is implemented as an explicit interface of `IObjectContextAdapter`, which is why you need to explicitly cast it:

```
((IObjectContextAdapter)context).ObjectContext
```

Once you have the `ObjectContext` in hand, you can work directly against that. This is not a new instance. `DbContext` wraps `ObjectContext`; the `ObjectContext` instance returned from `IObjectContextAdapter` is the instance that your `DbContext` was already using internally.

If you are writing a layered application and don't want other developers on your team to worry about this implementation detail, you could create a property to allow them to get directly from the `DbContext` to the underlying `ObjectContext`.

For example, they may be aware that there are more advanced features available when they need them. You could wrap those into a property called `Core`. Here's an example of a `Core` property that casts with the `as` operator:

```
public ObjectContext Core
{
  get
  {
    return (this as IObjectContextAdapter).ObjectContext;
  }
}
```

Now you can simply call Core from the DbContext instance to get at the desired features.

Adding DbContext into Existing .NET 4 Applications

What if you have an existing .NET 4 application that uses ObjectContext, but now you are extending the features of the application and would like to take advantage of the DbContext for new code? You can do this thanks to one of the overloads for instantiating a new DbContext. The overload allows you to pass in an existing ObjectContext instance.

The overload takes two parameters. The first is an ObjectContext instance and the second is a Boolean indicating whether or not the DbContext can dispose of the Object Context when the DbContext is disposed:

```
public DbContext(ObjectContext objectContext,
                 bool dbContextOwnsObjectContext)
{}
```

If you were to call this overload directly from the code that uses this context, that code would need to provide an ObjectContext instance each time as well as the bool value. Rather than force this onto the developer who is consuming the context, you can create a DbContext class that will do this automatically as well as expose the DbSets necessary for querying, updating, change tracking etc.

For the sake of demonstrating, we'll start with a sample download from *Programming Entity Framework, 2e (http://shop.oreilly.com/product/9780596807252.do)*. The WPF application from Chapter 26 uses a database-first EDMX with generated POCO classes and a hand-built ObjectContext class. This model is based on the BreakAway domain, as is the model we've used throughout this book.

The ObjectContext class, BAEntities, exposes a number of ObjectSets. Example 8-1 displays a subset of its code listing.

Example 8-1. A portion of the original BAEntities ObjectContext class

```
public partial class BAEntities : ObjectContext
{
  public const string ConnectionString = "name=BAEntities";
  public const string ContainerName = "BAEntities";

  public BAEntities()
    : base(ConnectionString, ContainerName)
  {
    this.ContextOptions.LazyLoadingEnabled = false;
    Initialize();
  }

  partial void Initialize();

  public ObjectSet<Activity> Activities
  {
    get { return _activities ??
          (_activities = CreateObjectSet<Activity>("Activities")); }
```

```
  }
  private ObjectSet<Activity> _activities;

  public ObjectSet<Contact> Contacts
  {
    get { return _contacts ??
          (_contacts = CreateObjectSet<Contact>("Contacts")); }
  }
  private ObjectSet<Contact> _contacts;

  public ObjectSet<Trip> Trips
  {
    get { return _trips ??
          (_trips = CreateObjectSet<Trip>("Trips")); }
  }
  private ObjectSet<Trip> _trips;

  public ObjectSet<Destination> Destinations
  {
    get { return _destinations ??
          (_destinations =
            CreateObjectSet<Destination>("Destinations")); }
  }
  private ObjectSet<Destination> _destinations;
}
```

In the project that contains this BAEntities class, we've added the EntityFramework
package reference and a new class file, *BAEntitiesDbContext.cs*, that contains the BAEn
titiesDbContext class. This new class does three important things:

1. Inherits from DbContext
2. Has a default constructor that calls a private constructor with the ObjectContext
   overload.
3. Exposes DbSets to code against using the DbContext API.

Example 8-2 shows the listing for BaEntitiesDbContext. It includes DbSet properties to
expose the classes exposed by the ObjectSet properties shown in Example 8-1. There
are other DbSet properties in the class but they are not relevant to this example.

Example 8-2. DbContext class that wraps the BAEntities ObjectContext

```
using System.Data.Entity;
using System.Data.Objects;

namespace BAGA
{
  public class BAEntitiesDbContext: DbContext
  {
    public BAEntitiesDbContext():this(new BAEntities(),
                                dbContextOwnsObjectContext:true)
    {
    }
    public DbSet<Activity> Activities{get;set;}
```

```
  public DbSet<Contact> Contacts {get;set;}
  public DbSet<Trip> Trips {get;set;}
  public DbSet<Destination> Destinations {get;set;}
 }
}
```

The constructor is a default constructor that takes no parameters, but its declaration invokes the base DbContext constructor overload that uses an ObjectContext.

The automated tests listed in Example 8-3 verify that, using this DbContext, we can retrieve, insert, and edit entities. Notice that the third test uses the DbSet.Find method as well. Because the database generates new key values for Trip, the second test verifies that the inserted Trip has a TripId greater than 0. The third test uses a similar assertion for the inserted Payment. The third test also re-retrieves the reservation from the database to check that its ModifiedDate value was updated.

Example 8-3. Automated tests to exercise the DbContext that wraps an existing ObjectContext

```
using System.Linq;
using System.Transactions;
using BAGA;
using Microsoft.VisualStudio.TestTools.UnitTesting;
using System;

namespace DbContextTests
{
    [TestMethod]
    public void CanRetrieveTripViaDbContext()
    {
      using (var context = new BAEntitiesDbContext())
      {
        Assert.IsNotNull(context.Trips.FirstOrDefault());
      }
    }

    [TestMethod]
    public void CanInsertTripViaDbContext()
    {
      using (new TransactionScope())
      {
        var trip = new Trip
                      {
                          DestinationID = 55,
                          LodgingID = 1,
                          StartDate = new DateTime(2012, 1, 1),
                          EndDate = new DateTime(2012, 2, 1),
                          TripCostUSD = 1000
                      };
        using (var context = new BAEntitiesDbContext())
        {
          context.Trips.Add(trip);
          context.SaveChanges();
          Assert.IsTrue(trip.TripID > 0);
        }
```

```
      }
  }

  [TestMethod]
  public void CanRetrieveandModifyReservationandAddPayment()
  {
    using (new TransactionScope())
    {
      DateTime reservationDate;
      using (var context = new BAEntitiesDbContext())
      {
        //4 is a known reservation in the database
        var res = context.Reservations.Find(4);
        reservationDate = res.ReservationDate.AddDays(-1);
        res.ReservationDate = reservationDate;
        var payment = new Payment
                      {
                          Amount = 100,
                          ModifiedDate = DateTime.Now,
                          PaymentDate = DateTime.Now.Date
                      };
        res.Payments.Add(payment);
        context.SaveChanges();
        Assert.IsTrue(payment.PaymentID > 0);
      }
      using (var context = new BAEntitiesDbContext())
      {
        Assert.AreEqual(reservationDate,
            context.Reservations.Find(4).ReservationDate);
      }
    }
  }
}
```

If you want to take advantage of DbContext when adding new features to an existing application that uses an ObjectContext, you can do so with the addition of a DbContext in the style of the BaEntitiesDbContext. Be sure to test your logic!

Leveraging SQL Server Operators Exposed in SqlFunctions

One scenario that we've been asked about recently was the ability to detect numeric data in some type of string column in the database. SQL Server has an IsNumeric function but there's no way to express that in LINQ to Entities. A set of SQL Server specific functions was wrapped into System.Data.Objects.SQLClient.SqlFunctions in .NET4. These can be used in LINQ to Entities queries against the ObjectContext and against DbContext.

In the BreakAway domain, perhaps you need to search for numeric zip codes. Because postal codes can be alphanumeric in many parts of the world, the zip code field is a string and in the database, it's an nvarchar.

To use IsNumeric in your query, you'll need a using statement for the Sys tem.Data.Objects.SqlClient namespace at the top of your code file.

Then you can use SqlFunctions directly in the query expression. Example 8-4 demonstrates using the IsNumeric function to return a list of people with numeric zip codes. IsNumeric returns 1 for valid numbers, which is why the query searches for IsNumeric is equal to 1.

Example 8-4. Using SQL Server IsNumeric in LINQ to Entities

```
private static void UseSqlFunctions()
{
  using (var context = new BreakAwayContext())
  {
    var query=from p in context.People
             where SqlFunctions.IsNumeric(p.LastName)==1
             select p;
    var results=query.ToList();
  }
}
```

If you look at the query in a profiler, you can see that the IsNumeric function is used in the SQL query. Here are the last two lines of the SQL executed in the database:

```
FROM [dbo].[People] AS [Extent1]
WHERE 1 = (ISNUMERIC([Extent1].[ZipCode]))
```

Just be sure to keep in mind that this is specifically designed for use in SQL Server databases, though other providers could make similar functionality available for their databases.

Querying Derived Types with DbSet

If you have been working with ObjectContext and ObjectSet, you should be aware of another benefit of DbSet when working with derived types. You can create DbSets that encapsulate derived types. When working with ObjectSet, you are only able to create sets from a base type. So if you had a hierarchy such as Person with a derived type, Customer, any time you wanted to query Customer you would have to express a query starting with

```
context.People.OfType<Customer>()
```

This can get pretty tedious.

The DbContext API lets you create DbSet properties from derived types without having to declare the base type or set the OfType method to access the derived type. If you want to expose the derived type as a DbSet, you simply add it as you would any other entity in the model:

```
public DbSet<Customer> Customers { get; set; }
```

You can expose DbSet properties for base types and their derived types in your context. As with ObjectSet, querying a DbSet of the base type (for example, DbSet<Person>) will return all of the types in the hierarchy, including derived types that are exposed by their own DbSet property.

Understanding the Interface Property Limitation

Entity Framework is unable to create schema from interfaces. That means if you have any properties (complex type properties or navigation properties) that are interface types, Code First will not build those into the model. Your code may run without throwing an exception, but the database won't have any schema to represent that type and therefore its data will not be persisted.

For example, you might have an IDestination interface and the Destination class and some other classes implementing that interface:

```
public class Destination : IDestination
public class EliteDestination : IDestination
public class RoughingItDestination : IDestination
```

Then consider the Destination property in Lodging class. Rather than always returning a Destination instance, you might want to return any of those types:

```
[Required]
public IDestination Destination { get; set; }
```

Unfortunately, this scenario is just not supported.

We've seen some workarounds for this limitation, but they typically end up using one of the concrete implementations of the interface somewhere in the workaround and doing so means that you won't be able to use any other implementations of the interface.

 Currently, providing support for mapped interface properties in Entity Framework is not high on the team's priority list because there have been so few requests for this. If you want to get more attention to making Code First recognize interface properties, vote on (or submit) a suggestion at data.uservoice.com (*http://data.uservoice.com*). Be sure you're in the feedback area for Entity Framework.

Considering Automated Testing with DbContext

In this book, we've used a console application to demonstrate many of the features that you've learned about. This is to ensure that readers using the Express and Standard versions of Visual Studio are able to follow along. Our personal preference when building applications, however, is to include automated tests, whether we use the testing tools built into Visual Studio Professional and Visual Studio Ultimate, or third-party tools such as XUnit, NUnit, or the testing features in JetBrain's Resharper.

To be able to build flexible tests, you'll want to leverage the IDbSet interface. The DbSet class you've worked with throughout this book implements IDbSet. And the IDbSet interface is where the Add, Attach, Remove, and Create methods come from. IDbSet also implements IQueryable<T>, which enables LINQ and brings along the extension methods: Find, Include, and AsNoTracking.

First, let's look at examples of automated tests that you can build and run with the existing BreakAwayContext class and without having to work with the IDbSet.

Testing with DbSet

You can build unit tests to validate that your classes work as expected without engaging Entity Framework or the database.

For example, the simple test listed in Example 8-5 checks that the FullName property in the Person type functions as expected.

Example 8-5. Ensuring that FullName works as expected

```
[TestMethod()]
public void PersonFullNameReturnsFirstNamePlusLastName()
{
    var person = new Person
                 {
                     FirstName = "Roland",
                     LastName = "Civet"
                 };
    Assert.AreEqual(person.FullName, "Roland Civet");
}
```

You can also write integrated tests that check to make sure some of your Entity Framework–related logic works as expected. Example 8-6 displays a test method that ensures you've configured your class correctly to cause Entity Framework validation to notice that a related Photo property is missing from a new Person.

Example 8-6. An integration test to ensure that your code and Entity Framework work together

```
[TestMethod]
public void ValidationDetectsMissingPhotoInPerson()
{
    var person = new Person
    {
        FirstName = "Mikael",
        LastName = "Eliasson"
    };
    DbEntityValidationResult result;
    using (var context = new BreakAwayContext())
    {
        result = context.Entry(person).GetValidationResult();
```

```
  }
  Assert.IsFalse(result.IsValid);
  Assert.IsTrue(result.ValidationErrors
    .Any(v => v.ErrorMessage.ToLower()
      .Contains("photo field is required")));
}
```

You can also write integration tests against custom logic that executes database queries or saves data back to the database to make sure the persistence is working as expected.

But there's one area of testing that's a bit trickier with Entity Framework, which is testing logic that uses the context to query and save data but does not necessarily need to make the trip to the database.

Exploring a Scenario That Unnecessarily Queries the Database

A simplistic example is a method that performs a database query based on some other logic. Perhaps you have a repository method to retrieve customers who have reservations for a trip, but *only* if that trip is in the future. Example 8-7 shows a single method from a repository class, GetTravelersOnFutureTrip. The class declaration and constructor are included in the listing for clarity.

Example 8-7. The GetTravelersOnFutureTrip method in the TripRepository class

```
public class TripRepository
{
  BreakAwayContext _context;

  public TripRepository(BreakAwayContext context)
  {
    _context = context;
  }
  public List<Person> GetTravelersOnFutureTrip(Trip trip)
  {
    if (trip.StartDate <= DateTime.Today)
    {
      return null;
    }

    return _context.Reservations
      .Where(r => r.Trip.Identifier == trip.Identifier)
      .Select(r => r.Traveler)
      .ToList();
  }
}
```

If a past trip is passed into the method, the method will return null. If a future trip is passed in, the method will query for the travelers on the trip and return a list of those travelers. Recall that the Reservation.Traveler property returns a Person type. If no reservations have been made for the trip, the list will contain zero items.

It would be feasible to test that the GetTravelersOnFutureTrip returns a null if the past trip is passed in and that it doesn't return a null (regardless of the size of the list returned) if the trip is in the future.

Example 8-8 displays two tests to check both bits of logic.

Example 8-8. Testing logic of GetTravelersOnFutureTrip

```
[TestMethod]
public void GetCustomersOnPastTripReturnsNull()
{
  var trip = new Trip { StartDate = DateTime.Today.AddDays(-1) };
  using (var context = new BreakAwayContext())
  {
    var rep = new TripRepository(context);
    Assert.IsNull(rep.GetTravelersOnFutureTrip(trip));
  }
}


[TestMethod]
public void GetCustomersOnFutureTripDoesNotReturnNull()
{
  Database.SetInitializer(new
    DropCreateDatabaseIfModelChanges<BreakAwayContext>());
  var trip = new Trip { StartDate = DateTime.Today.AddDays(1) };
  using (var context = new BreakAwayContext())
  {
    var rep = new TripRepository(context);
    Assert.IsNotNull(rep.GetTravelersOnFutureTrip(trip));
  }
}
```

The first method, GetTravelersOnPastTripReturnsNull, will not hit the database. It creates a minimally populated trip instance with a past StartDate. The GetCustomersOnFutureTrip method sees that the StartDate is in the past and returns null, never reaching the query. Because the database will never be hit by the repository method, there's no need to even worry about database initialization in this test.

In the second test, we expect to query the database, so we're setting the initializer to DropCreateDatabaseIfModelChanges to ensure that the database exists. Since the test doesn't care about the actual data, there's no need to seed the database. We again create a minimal Trip, this time with a future StartDate. The repository method will execute the database query, requesting all Reservations where the TripIdentifier is 00000000-0000-0000-0000-000000000000 because we didn't set that value in the Trip instance. There will be no results and the method will return an empty List<Person>. The test passes because an empty list is not equal to null. You can see that for this test, what's in the database is of no consequence, so the trip to the database is a wasted effort. You only want to make sure that the method responds correctly to a future or past date. However, with the BreakAwayContext and its DbSets, there's no avoiding the query if a future trip is passed in as a parameter.

If we build some more logic into the solution using the `IDbSet` interface, we'll be able to take the database out of the picture for the tests.

Reducing Database Hits in Testing with IDbSet

If you want to test a method such as `GetTravelersOnFutureTrip` without hitting the database, you'll need to use abstractions of the context and sets that do not involve database interaction. What we'll show you is the key parts of a more abstracted solution so that we can focus on the `IDbSet` interface.

As an alternative to the `BreakAwayContext` class, we'll create another context that can create entities on the fly without depending on the database. But in order for us to use this alternative context with the repository, it will need to let us execute the code in the `GetTravelersOnFutureTrip` method. That means it will need, for example, the ability to create and execute queries. `IDbSet` gives us the capabilities that we need.

Not only does the `DbSet` class we've been using implement `IDbSet`, it also inherits from `DbQuery`. And it's the `DbQuery` class that adds in the reliance on the database. In our alternative context, we'll use properties that implement `IDbSet` but are not derived from `DbQuery`. That means we'll need a concrete implementation of `IDbSet`, giving us the ability to perform set logic and queries without interacting with a database, effectively "faking" the database interaction. So let's start by creating this concrete class.

Creating an IDbSet Implementation

Because `IDbSet` implements `IQueryable` and `IEnumerable`, this new class will need to implement members of all three interfaces. Example 8-9 shows the entire listing of the `FakeDbSet` class including namespaces used by the class.

 The Visual Studio IDE, as well as third-party productivity tools, can help implement the interface members to reduce the typing.

Example 8-9. The FakeDbSet implementation of IDbSet

```
using System;
using System.Collections;
using System.Collections.Generic;
using System.Collections.ObjectModel;
using System.Data.Entity;
using System.Linq;
using System.Linq.Expressions;

namespace Testing
{
    public abstract class FakeDbSet<T> : IDbSet<T>
```

```
  where T : class, new()
{
  readonly ObservableCollection<T> _items;
  readonly IQueryable _query;

  public FakeDbSet()
  {
    _items = new ObservableCollection<T>();
    _query = _items.AsQueryable();
  }

  public T Add(T entity)
  {
    _items.Add(entity);
    return entity;
  }

  public T Attach(T entity)
  {
    _items.Add(entity);
    return entity;
  }

  public TDerivedEntity Create<TDerivedEntity>()
    where TDerivedEntity : class, T
  {
    return Activator.CreateInstance<TDerivedEntity>();
  }

  public T Create()
  {
    return new T();
  }

  public abstract T Find(params object[] keyValues);

  public ObservableCollection<T> Local
  {
    get
    {
      return _items;
    }
  }

  public T Remove(T entity)
  {
    _items.Remove(entity);
    return entity;
  }

  public IEnumerator<T> GetEnumerator()
  {
    return _items.GetEnumerator();
  }
```

```
IEnumerator IEnumerable.GetEnumerator()
{
  return _items.GetEnumerator();
}

public Type ElementType
{
  get { return _query.ElementType; }
}

public Expression Expression
{
  get { return _query.Expression; }
}

public IQueryProvider Provider
{
  get { return _query.Provider; }
}
  }
 }
}
```

 When calling DbSet.Attach, Entity Framework will throw an exception if the object you are attaching is already being tracked by the context. If this is important behavior for your FakeDbSet, you could implement some logic to emulate that behavior.

There are a number of notable points to make about this implementation.

The first is that FakeDbSet is an **abstract** class. That is due to another notable point, which is that there is an abstract method: Find. As we don't anticipate having a DbCon text to interact with, it will be too difficult to arrive at a generic way of handling IDbSet.Find for any entity. For example, the Trip type has a key named Identifier. So Find will need to build a query using Identifier, whereas for other types it might need to build a query around Id.

 Find is a member of the IDbSet interface. The Include, AsNoTracking, and Load methods, which you used earlier in this book, are extension methods on IQueryable. When using FakeDbSet or other IDbSet implementations, those methods will be run without throwing exceptions. But they won't have any impact on your fake set or context. For example, a method that uses Include won't emulate Include logic in your fake queries unless you implement special Include logic in your fake DbSets.

FakeDbSet contains two local fields: an ObservableCollection named _items and an IQueryable called _query. The _items is used to manage the data so that we can respond to the IDbSet methods such as Add and Remove as well as enumeration supplied by IEnumerable. We're using ObservableCollection to make it easy to implement the

Local property. The _query field is to support members of IQueryable: Expression and Provider.

Also notable are the implementations of Create. The Create methods are needed to create new entity instances when your entity types are using dynamic proxies. This allows the context to be aware of the instance. You learned about working with dynamic proxies in Chapter 3.

> While acting as a technical reviewer for this book, Mikael Eliasson took this implementation a step further to enable the generic FakeDbSet to be aware of the key property so that you're not required to override the class simply to expand upon the Find method. See his solution at *https://gist.github.com/783ddf75f06be5a29a9d*.

Abstracting BreakAwayContext for Tests

There's one more function to plan for, which is that the repository class currently expects a BreakAwayContext to be used to perform the query. The current BreakAwayContext brings with it the concrete DbSets and therefore the database. We'll abstract the BreakAwayContext class by creating an interface that matches the contract (or expectation) of what should be in a BreakAwayContext class. Then we can tell the repository to expect anything that implements the interface, not just the concrete one it's using now:

```
public interface IBreakAwayContext
{
  IDbSet<Destination> Destinations { get; }
  IDbSet<Lodging> Lodgings { get;}
  IDbSet<Trip> Trips { get; }
  IDbSet<Person> People { get; }
  IDbSet<Reservation> Reservations { get; }
  IDbSet<Payment> Payments { get; }
  IDbSet<Activity> Activities { get; }

  int SaveChanges();
}
```

> This interface is only demonstrating what's needed to satisfy the repository method and to make sure existing BreakAwayContext examples from this chapter continue to function. As you build out an application and repositories, you'll need more features, whether they are built into this particular interface or other interfaces and classes.

Notice that the interface returns IDbSet properties instead of concrete classes. This is how it will be possible to create a context that explicitly builds and returns FakeDbSets.

Now you can modify the repository class so that it expects an IBreakAwayContext instead of the BreakAwayContext class. Example 8-10 shows the revised first eight lines of the TripRepository class. The _context will now be an IBreakAwayContext.

Example 8-10. Beginning of revised TripRepository class

```
public class TripRepository
{
  IBreakAwayContext _context;

  public TripRepository(IBreakAwayContext context)
  {
    _context = context;
  }
}
```

If you want to use BreakAwayContext here, it will now need to implement the interface. First, you need to add the interface implementation into the class declaration. And because BreakAwayContext is now implementing the interface, it needs to match the interface. Destinations now must return an IDbSet<Destination> and so forth. You can see the relevant portion of the revised BreakAwayContext class in Example 8-11.

Example 8-11. BreakAwayContext revised to implement IBreakAwayContext

```
public class BreakAwayContext : DbContext, IBreakAwayContext
{
  public IDbSet<Destination> Destinations { get; set; }
  public IDbSet<Lodging> Lodgings { get; set; }
  public IDbSet<Trip> Trips { get; set; }
  public IDbSet<Person> People { get; set; }
  public IDbSet<Reservation> Reservations { get; set; }
  public IDbSet<Payment> Payments { get; set; }
  public IDbSet<Activity> Activities { get; set; }
```

If you were to rerun the GetCustomersOnFutureTripReturnsListOfPeople and GetCusto mersOnPastTripReturnsNull tests, they will still pass. The repository is happy to have the BreakAwayContext instantiated in the tests because that class implements IBreakA wayContext. And the DbContext that BreakAwayContext derives from will ensure that the IDbSet properties return DbSet types so that you continue to interact with the database.

Now it's time to focus on creating a context that you can use for testing that won't hit the database. When you create a new context class that implements IBreakAwayCon text, you'll get all of the IDbSet properties. Since our repository method doesn't need access to all of the IDbSet's, the code in Example 8-12 only initializes the one that we'll be working with—Reservations.

Example 8-12. FakeBreakAwayContext class

```
using System.Data.Entity;
using DataAccess;
using Model;

namespace Testing
```

```
{
  public class FakeBreakAwayContext : IBreakAwayContext
  {
    public FakeBreakAwayContext()
    {
      Reservations = new ReservationDbSet();
    }

    public IDbSet<Destination> Destinations { get; private set; }
    public IDbSet<Lodging> Lodgings { get; private set; }
    public IDbSet<Trip> Trips { get; private set; }
    public IDbSet<Person> People { get; private set; }
    public IDbSet<Reservation> Reservations { get; private set; }
    public IDbSet<Payment> Payments { get; private set; }
    public IDbSet<Activity> Activities { get; private set; }

    public int SaveChanges()
    {
      return 0;
    }
  }
}
```

What you don't see yet in the listing is how the fake sets are populated; we'll leave it up to the automated tests to provide relevant data where necessary. The tests we're currently focused on won't even require any seed data.

And now for the derived FakeDbSet classes, which are key to the FakeBreakAwayCon text class. Each has its own way to implement Find based on knowledge of its key field. Example 8-13 shows the ReservationDbSet class needed for this example. You can use this as a basis for the others. Just be sure to use the key properties in the Find method (for example, DestinationId in DestinationDbSet). You are not required to implement the other fake sets to follow along with the rest of this chapter.

Example 8-13. ReservationDbSet deriving from and overriding FakeDbSet

```
using System;
using System.Linq;
using Model;

namespace Testing
{
  public class ReservationDbSet : FakeDbSet<Reservation>
  {
    public override Reservation Find(params object[] keyValues)
    {
      var keyValue = (int)keyValues.FirstOrDefault();
      return this.SingleOrDefault(r => r.ReservationId == keyValue);
    }
  }
}
```

This is one approach to abstracting the DbSets. Another idea is presented in the sidebar.

FakeDbSets for Similar Types

It is more likely that you have a common pattern to key names and may not need explicit Find methods for each type. In that case you might have a single derived class that knows how to query on a single key name. Here's an example of a derived class designed for types whose key properties follow the pattern type name + "Id", such as Destina tionId, ReservationId, and others:

```
internal class TypesWithIdDbSet<T> : FakeDbSet<T>
where T : class
{
  public override T Find(params object[] keyValues)
  {
    var keyValue = (int)keyValues.FirstOrDefault();
    return this.SingleOrDefault(t => (int)(t.GetType()
      .GetProperty(t.GetType().Name + "Id")
      .GetValue(t,null)) == keyValue);

  }
}
```

To see this in action, you'll need to modify the tests so that they use the FakeBreakAwayContext instead of the BreakAwayContext. The updated listing is shown in Example 8-14.

Example 8-14. Automated test that uses the fake context, fake sets, and fake data

```
[TestMethod]
public void FakeGetCustomersOnPastTripReturnsNull()
{
  var trip = new Trip { StartDate = DateTime.Today.AddDays(-1) };
  var context = new FakeBreakAwayContext();
  var rep = new TripRepository(context);
  Assert.IsNull(rep.GetTravelersOnFutureTrip(trip));
}

[TestMethod]
public void FakeGetCustomersOnFutureTripDoesNotReturnNull()
{
  var trip = new Trip { StartDate = DateTime.Today.AddDays(1) };
  var context = new FakeBreakAwayContext();
  var rep = new TripRepository(context);
  Assert.IsNotNull(rep.GetTravelersOnFutureTrip(trip));
}
```

Now you can rerun the tests. You can debug them to verify that the tests are indeed using the FakeBreakAwayContext.

Now it's possible to verify that the GetCustomersOnFutureTrip method in the TripRepo sitory functions properly without involving the database.

Reviewing the Implementation

We covered a lot of ground in this section, so let's catch our breath and make sure you haven't lost sight of the big picture. When writing automated tests, it's not uncommon to test logic in a method that, in addition to the logic your test is concerned with, also happens to interact with the database. In order to avoid this, we created a way to fake the database interaction leveraging the IDbSet interface that's provided in the DbContext API. We created a concrete implementation of IDbSet called FakeDbSet, which is generic so that we can create FakeDbSets of any of our model types. In order to use non-database-oriented implementations of IDbSet, we also abstracted the BreakAwayContext into its own interface that returns IDbSet for querying then implemented FakeDbContext from there.

Figure 8-1 shows how the FakeBreakAwayContext context and the BreakAwayContext both implement the IBreakAwayContext interface. BreakAwayContext uses DbSet properties for direct interaction with the database, while FakeBreakAwayContext works with FakeDbSets populated with objects created in memory.

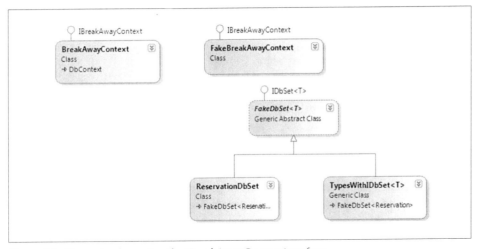

Figure 8-1. Classes implementing the IBreakAwayContext interface

With these abstractions in place, TripRepository will work with any implementation of IBreakAwayContext. For the sake of the AutomatedTripTests, the test methods use the FakeBreakAwayContext and avoid database interaction while the application uses instances of BreakAwayContext to pass into the repository.

Supplying Data to a FakeDbSet

These test methods did not need any data available to do their jobs, but you may have tests that do require some fake data. Example 8-15 shows a new method that returns the count of Reservations for a single Trip.

Example 8-15. Repository method to retrieve a reservation count

```
public int ReservationCountForTrip(Trip trip)
{
  return _context.Reservations
    .Where(r => r.Trip.Identifier == trip.Identifier)
    .Count();
}
```

In order to test this method, the fake context will need to contain data. You can supply that data as part of a test. Example 8-16 demonstrates one such test, ReservationCount ForTripReturnsCorrectNumber.

Example 8-16. Testing the ReservationCountForTrip method

```
[TestMethod]
public void ReservationCountForTripReturnsCorrectNumber()
{
  var context = new FakeBreakAwayContext();

  var tripOne = new Trip { Identifier = Guid.NewGuid() };
  var tripTwo = new Trip { Identifier = Guid.NewGuid() };

  context.Reservations.Add(new Reservation { Trip = tripOne });
  context.Reservations.Add(new Reservation { Trip = tripOne });
  context.Reservations.Add(new Reservation { Trip = tripTwo });

  var rep = new TripRepository(context);
  Assert.AreEqual(2, rep.ReservationCountForTrip(tripOne));
}
```

The context will need to contain some Reservation data in order to return a count. While you might consider adding a number of Reservation instances that are fully described with Payments, a Traveler, and a Trip, you can see in the example that only the most minimal information is required to perform the test accurately. Three new Reservations are added to the context but each Reservation contains no more information than its Trip property. Notice also that we created two Reservations with the Trip we are searching for and one Reservation assigned to another Trip. Once the context is seeded, we can use the assertion to verify that the query is properly filtering, not simply returning all of the Reservations that we created.

Depending on the logic you are testing, you can build up more complex fake data in your test.

Accessing the Database Directly from DbContext

DbContext communicates with the database any time you execute a query or call Save Changes. You can take advantage of DbContext's access to the database through its Database property. With DbContext.Database, you can communicate directly with the database if your application calls for such interaction.

You may not have realized that Code First leverages the `Database` property for the database initialization tasks. It uses the `Database.Exists` property to check for the database. `Database` has a `Delete` method and a `Create` method and even one called `CreateIfNotExists`. All four of these members are public, so you could use them directly if you want to. In fact, early technical previews of Code First required developers to use those properties and methods to perform database initialization manually. It wasn't until later that the `SetInitializer` classes were introduced which encapsulated the most common initialization workflows.

Once your `DbContext` is instantiated, it will be aware of the connection string it will use to work with the database, even if you haven't yet performed any tasks that would initiate the connection. You can use the `DbContext.Database` property to interact with the connection or the database itself.

Not all of the `Database` members require direct interaction with the database. For example, here is some code that writes the connection string of the `Database` associated with that context to a console window using the `Database.Connection` property, which returns a `System.Data.Common.DbDataConnection`:

```
using (var context=new BreakAwayContext())
{
  Console.WriteLine(context.Database.Connection.ConnectionString);
}
```

A more common use of the `Database` property is to execute raw queries and commands directly on the database for those odd occasions when you need to perform a query that's not supported by your model or by Entity Framework.

Executing Queries with Database.SqlQuery and DbSet.SqlQuery

`DbContext.Database.SqlQuery` lets you execute a query on the database and return any type that you specify. It will use the connection from the context that you are calling `Database.SqlQuery` from. For example, the database might have a view named `DestinationSummaryView`. Even if there is no `DestinationSummary` model type, you can declare the class and then query the view using `SqlQuery`. As long as the results of the `SqlQuery` match the type that you want it to populate, Entity Framework will be happy.

The `DestinationSummary` class might look something like Example 8-17.

Example 8-17. DestinationSummary class

```
public class DestinationSummary
{
  public int DestinationId { get; set; }
  public string Name { get; set; }
  public int LodgingCount { get; set; }
  public int ResortCount { get; set; }
}
```

Then you can call the `Database.SqlQuery` from an instance of `DbContext` as follows:

```
var summary = context.Database.SqlQuery<DestinationSummary>(
  "SELECT * FROM dbo.DestinationSummaryView");
```

SqlQuery returns an SqlDbQuery. You'll have to execute the SqlQuery with a LINQ method such as ToList to execute the query.

What About the Database Class in a Fake Context?

If you make calls to DbContext.Database in your application and want to build tests around that logic, you'll want your fake contexts to be able to handle that logic. For example, you may have raw SqlQuery statements in methods for which you want to write automated tests using the fake context and fake sets you learned about earlier. One approach to covering this feature in your tests would be to encapsulate the raw SqlQuery code into methods that are part of IBreakAwayContext. Then you can implement those methods as desired in BreakAwayContext and any other classes that also implement the interface.

For example, you could add this method to IBreakAwayContext:

```
List<DestinationSummary> GetDestinationSummary();
```

In BreakAwayContext you could implement it as follows:

```
public List<DestinationSummary> GetDestinationSummary()
{
  return this.Database.SqlQuery<DestinationSummary>(
    "SELECT * FROM dbo.DestinationSummaryView").ToList();
}
```

And in the FakeBreakAwayContext, you could initially implement the method like this:

```
public List<DestinationSummary> GetDestinationSummary()
{
  throw new NotImplementedException();
}
```

When the time comes that you want data to be returned by FakeBreakAwayContext.Get DestinationSummary, you could add in logic to create and return one or more Destina tionSummary instances in the list.

Now rather than calling DbContext.Database.SqlQuery directly in your code to get the DestinationSummary, you can call the GetDestinationSummary method that is supported by the interface.

If your query is returning types that are exposed in the context through DbSet properties, you can use the DbSet.SqlQuery method instead. This version of SqlQuery does not require you to supply the return type as a parameter, since the DbSet knows the type. Example 8-18 shows DbSet.SqlQuery, which demonstrates how explicit you need to be when constructing the query. The Destination maps to the baga.Locations table and that table's field names don't match the Destination property names. SqlQuery expects the results to match the type exactly, including matching the names and types correctly. The order of the columns in the result set is not critical.

Example 8-18. Executing a query with SqlQuery

```
var dests = context.Database.SqlQuery<Destination>
    (@"SELECT LocationId as DestinationId, LocationName as Name,
        Description, Country, Photo
        FROM baga.locations where country={0}","Australia");
 var results = dests.ToList();
```

The resulting dests will be a List of Destination types. Because of the string Format syntax (that is, {0}), Entity Framework will execute this in the database as a parameterized query.

 SqlQuery is not supported for types that contain complex type properties. Therefore you cannot return a Person type from a SqlQuery because it has a PersonalInfo field and an Address field that are both complex types.

If you need to build dynamic queries, we recommend that you be conscientious of the possibility of SQL injection or other security attacks. You should build parameterized queries as you did in Example 8-18, rather than concatenate values directly into the SQL. Alternatively, you can use an overload of SqlQuery that accepts SqlParameters. Example 8-19 shows how you would use parameters with SqlQuery. The particular query could be performed very easily with LINQ to Entities and is only used here for demonstration purposes.

Example 8-19. Executing a query with SqlQuery

```
var destSql = @"SELECT LocationId as DestinationId,
                    LocationName as Name, Description,
                    Country,Photo
                    FROM baga.locations
                    WHERE country=@country";
var dests = context.Database.SqlQuery<Destination>
  (destSql, new SqlParameter("@country", "Australia"))
  .ToList();
```

Earlier in this chapter, we modified BreakAwayContext to use IDbSet properties instead of concrete DbSet properties. SqlQuery is a method of DbSet. If you are using IDbSet, you'll first need to cast it to DbSet in order to use DbSet.SqlQuery. That means that for methods that include SqlQuery, you'll be limited with respect to what types of automated tests you can perform.

Here is the SqlQuery statement from Example 8-19 revised to work with an IDbSet that needs to be cast to DbSet:

```
    var dests = ((DbSet<Destination>)context.Destinations)
            .SqlQuery(destSql, new SqlParameter("@country", "Brazil"))
            .ToList();
```

Tracking Results of SqlQuery

When you execute a SqlQuery from Database, the results are never tracked by the context, even if the query returns types that are in the model and known by the context. If you do not want the results to be change-tracked, use DbContext.Database.SqlQuery.

Results of a DbSet.SqlQuery will be tracked by the context. Ensuring that results are change-tracked is the primary reason you would choose to use DbSet.SqlQuery over Database.SqlQuery.

Executing Commands from the Database Class

DbContext.Database also lets you execute commands, not just queries, on the database directly if you encounter an odd function you want to perform in the database. You can do this with the ExecuteSqlCommand method. ExecuteSqlCommand takes two parameters: a SQL string expression and an array of SqlParameters. Although as you saw with the SqlQuery, you might prefer using the cleaner-looking string Format syntax to achieve parameterized commands. ExecuteSqlCommand returns an int representing the number of rows affected in the database.

Like SqlQuery, ExecuteSqlCommand will use the connection of the context from which you are calling the command. Depending on the permissions granted for the active context instance, you could execute Insert, Update, and Delete commands or even commands that affect the database schema.

ExecuteSqlCommand is designed to handle special scenarios and isn't meant as a replacement for Entity Framework's main mechanisms for persisting data in the database.

If you have read *Programming Entity Framework: Code First*, you may recall how ExecuteSqlCommand was used to enhance seeding a database during initialization. See the sidebar.

Using ExecuteSqlCommand to Enhance Database Seeding

The following is extracted from Chapter 6 of *Programming Entity Framework: Code First*.

In addition to seeding a database when Code First creates it, you may want to affect the database in ways that can't be done with configurations or data seeding. For example, you may want to create an Index on the Name field of the Lodgings table to speed up searches by name.

You can achieve this by calling the DbContext.Database.ExecuteSqlCommand method along with the SQL to create the index inside the Seed method. Here is an example of a Seed method that forces this Index to be created before the data is inserted:

```
protected override void Seed(BreakAwayContext context)
{
    context.Database.ExecuteSqlCommand
      ("CREATE INDEX IX_Lodgings_Name ON Lodgings (Name)");
```

> Code First Migrations, available in Entity Framework 4.3, includes native support for creating indexes in your database without dropping down to `ExecuteSqlCommand`.

Providing Multiple Targeted Contexts in Your Application

So far in this book we've used a single context class, `BreakAwayContext`, to represent our model and expose all of our domain classes for a solution's data access needs. In a large solution, it is likely that you have different areas of your application that address a specific business process and will only require interaction with a subset of your domain classes. If you have a lot of domain classes, there are a number of benefits to creating `DbContexts` that are targeted to these various processes rather than one all-purpose context. Most important is maintainability. As your application grows, so will the `DbContext` class. It can become unwieldy if it's responsible for many `DbSet` properties and fluent configurations for many classes. Adding and modifying existing logic will get more difficult. If you have multiple contexts, each responsible for a certain function of your application, they will each contain a smaller set of properties and configurations. It will be much easier to maintain each context as well as locate the logic you need within it.

Performance is another consideration. When Entity Framework creates an in-memory model of the context, the larger the context is the more resources are expended to generate and maintain that in-memory model.

Reusing Classes, Configurations, and Validation Across Multiple Contexts

Throughout this book you've seen us attempt to organize and refactor code as our application grew. From the beginning, we've kept the domain classes in their own project. If you have read *Programming Entity Framework: Code First*, you saw that when we used the Fluent API to configure our entities, we created separate classes to contain the Fluent configuration logic for each type. In the validation chapters, you saw that we encapsulated logic from the `ValidateEntity` method so that the method wouldn't get loaded down with details of each custom validation being performed. Organizing logic in this way makes it easier to reuse that logic and lets us share classes and logic across our multiple contexts.

 These smaller contexts follow a pattern critical to Domain Driven Design called *Bounded Contexts*. I like to think of the technique of aligning the design of each individual small `DbContext` class with its related Domain *Context* as *Bounded DbContexts*.

Using the BreakAway domain, let's look at a concrete example.

Let's say that the Sales department is responsible for selling reservations. They would need to add reservations and payments. Sales does not design trips or create relationships with lodgings. Sales would need to perform a bit of customer service as well. If the person purchasing the reservation is a new customer, Sales would need to add the customer. Sales would need to look up trips and destinations but only as a lookup list. They wouldn't need to work with `Trip` and `Destination` entities in a way that would enable change-tracking and modification.

In a simple scenario, this means Sales would need access to

- Person (Lookup, Add, Edit)
- Address (View from Person, Add, Edit)
- Reservations (Lookup, Add, Edit)
- Payments (View from Reservation, Add)
- Read-Only Lists: Trip Dates, Destination Name, Activities

What about the Trip Planning department? They need access to

- Trip (Lookup, Add, Edit)
- Destination (Lookup, Add, Edit)
- Activity (Lookup, Add, Edit)
- Lodging (Lookup, Add, Edit)
- Person (Lookup, Add, Edit)

What might the contexts for these two application scenarios look like?

`SalesContext` could have `DbSet` properties for `People`, `Reservations`, and `Trips`. This would allow sales to look up or add `People` and their `Addresses`; look up and add `Reservations` and their properties; and search for `Trips` along with their `Destination`, `Lodging`, and `Activity` details. `SalesContext` can draw from the pool of available classes in the `Model` project. Example 8-20 shows a minimal `SalesContext` class.

Example 8-20. SalesContext class

```
public class SalesContext:DbContext
{
  public DbSet<Person> People { get; set; }
  public DbSet<Reservation> Reservations { get; set; }
  public DbSet<Trip> Trips { get; set; }
}
```

Let's see what Code First draws into the model based on these three `DbSets`.

Here's a small console method that instantiates the context, and then drills down to the `ObjectContext` to query for `EntityTypes` from conceptual model (CSDL) using the MetadataWorkspace API. `MetadataWorkspace` reads the in-memory metadata of the model and then lists them in the console window. You'll need a using for the `System.Data.Metadata.Edm` namespace to use the `EntityType` class.

Example 8-21. Forcing model creation and listing types

```
private static void ForceContextModelCreation()
{
  using (var context = new SalesContext())
  {
    var entityTypes = ((IObjectContextAdapter)context).ObjectContext
      .MetadataWorkspace.GetItems<EntityType>(DataSpace.CSpace);

    foreach (var entityType in entityTypes)
    {
      Console.WriteLine(entityType.Name);
    }
  }
}
```

Below are the SalesContext model types as they are listed in the console window:

```
Person
Lodging
Destination
InternetSpecial
Resort
Hostel
PersonPhoto
Reservation
Trip
Activity
Payment
```

Not only do you see the three types returned by the DbSets (Person, Reservation, and Trip), but all related types as well. When building a model, Code First will pull in all types that are reachable by types in the model. For example, Trip has a relationship to Destination, so Destination class was pulled into the model as well. The complex types, Address and PersonInfo, are in the model but not represented in the screenshot. You can see them by requesting GetItems<ComplexType>(DataSpace.CSpace) from the Metada taWorkspace.

Code First used its convention to decide what types needed to be in the model. In this case, all of the types that it included make sense for this model. But the context is still simpler to work with, since it doesn't have explicit DbSets for all of those types.

 If you are using the Fluent API to configure the model, be sure that mappings necessary for all of the classes in your model are included in your configurations, not just mappings for types represented by DbSets.

By default Code First did us a favor. It created a new SalesContext database. That's not the desired effect. What we'll want is to have the complete BreakAwayContext database available to us. Let's set this problem aside for later in this chapter and instead, look at our other targeted context, TripPlanning:

```
public class TripPlanningContext : DbContext
{
  public DbSet<Trip> Trips { get; set; }
  public DbSet<Destination> Destinations { get; set; }
  public DbSet<Lodging> Lodgings { get; set; }
  public DbSet<Activity> Activities { get; set; }
  public DbSet<Person> People { get; set; }
}
```

 We're using common types in both the SalesContext and TripPlanning Context. What about sharing entity instances across instances of these contexts? Read the sidebar at the end of the chapter ("Sharing Types Across Multiple DbContexts" on page 233) for some insight into this scenario.

Modify the ForceContextModelCreation method from Example 8-21 to instantiate the context variable as a TripPlanningContext rather than a SalesContext. The output of the modified method, showing the types in the TripPlanningContext model is as follows:

```
Trip
Destination
Lodging
InternetSpecial
Person
PersonPhoto
Reservation
Payment
Resort
Hostel
Activity
```

Code First pulled more entities into the model than we will need. We'll want Person Photo for creating any new Person types. But there's no need for Reservation and Pay ment types in the model.

In rare cases, it will be safe to use the Fluent API's Ignore method to trim back entities that you don't want in the model. But doing so could easily lead you to breaking relationship constraints and losing access to foreign key properties in a model.

 It is not recommended to remove entities from a model that were pulled in by Code First because they are reachable by another entity. There's a good chance that you will create problems with relationship constraints and foreign keys, which may or may not be caught by exceptions. This could lead to invalid data in your database.

It won't always be possible to ignore a class that you don't need in the model. For example, if you decided to remove Person from TripPlanningContext, an exception will be thrown when Code First attempts to create the model. The reason is that there are configurations in the Lodging class that depend on the Person class. The DbModel Builder will try to work that out but will fail because there's no Person in the model.

Ensuring That All DbContexts Use a Single Database

Now let's see how to use these small contexts against a single database.

By convention, the context will force Code First to look for a database with the same name as the context. That's not what we want. We want them all to use the BreakAwayContext database. We could use a connection string in the config file to point to the correct database. But there's another wrinkle. The context will look for a connection string that matches its name. We'd have to have a SalesContext connection, a Trip PlanningContext connection, and additional connections specified in the config file for every context. That's not very maintainable.

Another tool we have at our disposal is an overload of the context constructor. We can pass in a database name. That solves the problem; however, it means that every time we instantiate a new SalesContext or any other context in our solution, we'd have to pass in a string or a variable representing "BreakAwayContext". That's also undesirable. Not only is it unnecessarily repetitive, you have to worry about someone forgetting to use the overload. However, you could lean on a base class to apply the connection string for you each time.

Example 8-22 shows a handy generic base class pattern suggested by Arthur Vickers from the Entity Framework team. Not only will this base class ensure that the any context that inherits from it uses the appropriate connection, but by setting the initializer on the given context to null, it ensures that Code First won't attempt to initialize a database for the context. Because the constructor is telling DbContext to look for a connection in the configuration file, you would need to add a connection string named "breakaway" to your *app.config* or *web.config* file.

Example 8-22. BaseContext to set connection string and disable database initialization

```
public class BaseContext<TContext> : DbContext
where TContext : DbContext
{
  static BaseContext()
  {
    Database.SetInitializer<TContext>(null);
  }

  protected BaseContext()
    : base("name=breakaway")
  {
  }
}
```

Note that the `BaseContext` constructor is static. That ensures that the initializer setting is set per application instance of the given constructor, not per context instance. Initializer settings should be application-wide, so this is desirable.

You can then modify the context classes to inherit from `BaseContext` instead of inheriting from `DbContext` directly.

Here are the revised declarations for `TripPlanningContext` and `SalesContext`:

```
public class TripPlanningContext : BaseContext<TripPlanningContext>

public class SalesContext : BaseContext<SalesContext>
```

Validating Relationship Constraints and Other Validations with Multiple Contexts

Each context will be responsible for its own validations. The context will check to make sure relationship constraints between classes are satisfied. If you have required relationships between classes, if one of those classes is in a model, the other needs to be as well. You should take advantage of automated testing to make sure that your small models don't break relationships.

If you have custom logic that needs to be triggered in `ValidateEntity`, be sure to put it in a project that is accessible by your different contexts. In Chapter 7, for example, Example 7-5 demonstrated calling out to a custom method, `ValidateLodging` from `ValidateEntity`. In any context class where you anticipate using `Lodging` types, you'll probably want to call that `ValidateLodging` method. So rather than declare `Validate Lodging` a `private` method inside of the `BreakAwayContext` class file, you could make it public and put it into a separate project where it can be called from other context classes.

Getting Code First to Create Full BreakAwayContext Database

You still may want to leverage Code First's database initialization while developing this application. Even though you don't want the `SalesContext` or `TripPlanningContext` classes to be involved with database initialization, you could create a `DbContext` class just for the sake of database initialization. It might even involve Code First Migrations or a custom initializer with a `Seed` method. All you should need to do is create one context class that will involve all of the classes. You can ensure all of the classes are pulled into the model by creating `DbSets` for each of the entities rather than hoping that relationships and hierarchies between your domain classes will create all of the relevant tables in the database. If you are using fluent configurations, you'll need to add all of them to the `modelBuilder.Configurations` to be sure that all of the mappings are created properly. In our test classes we have one test, which then recreates the database for us as needed:

```
private static void ForceBreakAwayDatabaseCreation()
{
  Database.SetInitializer(new InitializeBagaDatabaseWithSeedData());
  using (var context = new BreakAwayContext())
  {
    context.Database.Initialize(force: false);
  }
}
```

 Remember that the InitializeBagaDatabaseWithSeedData class currently derives from DropCreateDatabaseAlways.

Sharing Types Across Multiple DbContexts

When creating multiple smaller bounded DbContexts, you are able to reuse types and configurations. For example both the SalesContext and the TripPlanningContext encapsulate Trip types, Person types, and more.

Developers often ask about sharing instances between multiple contexts. Before doing so, the first question you should ask yourself is if you have defined your contexts well for your domain if you find a need to share instances of your types. If you are satisfied that moving instances between contexts is truly what you want to do, there are a few rules you should be considerate of.

- An entity can only be attached to one context at a time. This architecture works best with short-lived contexts where the instance to be shared will be completely disassociated from one context before it is attached to another.
- Entities that are attached to different contexts cannot be attached to one another.

Here's some code that demonstrates moving an entity from one context to another. The code instantiates a SalesContext and uses that to retrieve a Person instance. Then we detach that person from the context by setting its Entry.State to Detached. Now the person is free to be attached to a TripPlanningContext. Once attached, the code loads all of the lodgings for which that person is a primary contact:

```
Person person;
using (var sC = new SalesContext())
{
  person = sC.People.FirstOrDefault(p => p.FirstName == "Dave");
}
using (var tC = new TripPlanningContext())
{
  tC.People.Attach(person);
  tC.Entry(person).Collection(p => p.PrimaryContactFor).Load();
}
```

You should be careful about (or just avoid) moving Added, Modified, or Deleted entities from one context to another. You can benefit from many of the lessons you learned about working with disconnected entities and graphs in Chapter 4 of this book when moving entities between contexts.

CHAPTER 9

What's Coming Next for Entity Framework

So far, this book has walked through all the DbContext API functionality that was available at the time of writing. The companion to this book, *Programming Entity Framework: Code First*, covers the remainder of the functionality that was available in the EntityFramework NuGet package at the time of writing. However, there are some notable features that will soon be available for preview.

The Entity Framework team has indicated that they are about to release Entity Framework 5.0 (EF 5.0), which will include some long-awaited features, including support for enum properties and spatial data.

Understanding Entity Framework's Version Numbers

Historically, Entity Framework releases have been strongly tied to .NET Framework releases. The first version of Entity Framework shipped with .NET 3.5 SP1. The second release was included in .NET 4 and was named Entity Framework 4 (EF 4), to align with the .NET version. The DbContext API and Code First were released out-of-band of the .NET Framework as EF 4.1. This number was chosen to indicate that it was a small update that built on the functionality in .NET 4.

When the time came to ship bug fixes for EF 4.1, the team released EF 4.1 Update 1. This release, and some other releases from Microsoft, caused some confusion in the community about how releases are versioned. Based on this feedback, the Entity Framework team has now adopted *semantic versioning* for its releases. You can read more about semantic versioning at *http://semver.org*.

After adopting semantic versioning, the Entity Framework team released EF 4.2, which included some bug fixes. They then released EF 4.3, which included the new Code First Migrations feature, along with a handful of high-priority bug fixes.

Entity Framework 5.0

EF 5.0 introduces a set of long-awaited features and makes use of some work the Entity Framework team has done in the next version of the .NET Framework (.NET 4.5). Entity Framework 5.0 will become available as an update to the EntityFramework NuGet package. At the time of writing, a prerelease version of EF 5.0 was not yet available. The Entity Framework team has indicated they will be making the first preview of EF 5.0 available shortly after the next preview of .NET 4.5 is released. The rest of this section provides a brief overview of the major features that the Entity Framework team has indicated will be in the EF 5.0 release.

Entity Framework 5.0 is dependent on .NET 4.5 because a number of the new features required changes to the core Entity Framework components. These core components, including ObjectContext and other related types, are still part of the .NET Framework. For example, adding enum support to the DbContext API and Code First required adding enum support to ObjectContext. The Entity Framework team is working to move more of these core components out of the .NET Framework in the future. This would enable more features to be added without updates to the .NET Framework.

Enums

Developers have been asking for support for enum properties in Entity Framework since it was first released. This feature will allow you to define a property on a domain class that is an enum type and map it to a database column of an integer type. Entity Framework will then convert the database value to and from the relevant enum as it queries and saves data.

Spatial Data

SQL Server 2008 introduced support for geometry and geography data types. A set of operators is also included to allow queries to analyze spatial data. For example, a query can filter based on the distance between two geographic locations. EF 5.0 will allow new spatial data types to be exposed as properties on your classes and map them to spatial columns in your database. You will also be able to write LINQ queries that make use of the spatial operators to filter, sort, and group based on spatial calculations performed in the database.

Performance Improvements

EF 5.0 will include some updates and a new feature to enhance performance. The most notable new feature is *automatic caching of compiled LINQ queries*. When Entity Framework runs a LINQ query, it goes through a process of converting your LINQ query into SQL to be executed in the database. This process is known as *query compilation* and is an expensive operation, especially for complex queries. In the past you could use compiled queries to make Entity Framework cache the compiled query and reuse it, potentially with different parameters. In EF 5.0 the compiled query will be automatically cached and reused if you run the same query again, even if you have different parameter values in the query.

For example, if you run a LINQ query for all Locations where the DestinationId is equal to a value stored in an integer variable, Entity Framework will cache the translation that knows how to select a set of Locations filtered by DestinationId. If you later run another query for all Locations where the DestinationId is equal to a value stored in a different integer variable, Entity Framework will reuse the cached translation, even if the value stored in the variable is different than the first query.

EF 5.0 will also include improvements to the SQL it generates. The SQL will be simpler to read and will result in performance gains. In particular, there are improvements to make querying faster when working with an inheritance hierarchy that is mapped using the table-per-type (TPT) strategy.

Multiple Result Sets from Stored Procedures

Entity Framework allows you to use stored procedures to query for data and to insert, update, and delete data. Previously, when selecting data, the stored procedure could only return a single result set. EF 5.0 will allow you to use a stored procedure that returns multiple result sets. The different result sets can represent data for different entity types or projections.

 While Entity Framework supports mapping to stored procedures, this functionality is not supported in Code First. The Entity Framework team is not planning to add stored procedure support to Code First in EF 5.0. They have indicated that there are no definite plans around when this will be added.

Table Value Functions

Table Value Functions (TVFs) are functions in the database that return a well-known result set. TVFs are composable and can therefore be included in a query in much the same way a table can. EF 5.0 allows you to include TVFs in your model and define a function on your context that represents the TVF. This function can then be used in a LINQ query in the same way you would use a DbSet. TVFs will not be supported in Code First in EF 5.0.

Following the Entity Framework Team

There are a number of ways you can keep up to date on new features that the Entity Framework team is developing—and even influence what features they work on next. The ADO.NET Team Blog (*http://blogs.msdn.com/adonet*) is used by the EF team to share announcements about new and upcoming releases. The EF team also has an EF Design Blog (*http://blogs.msdn.com/efdesign*), where they share early thinking about features they are about to start working on. This allows you to have input into the design of features before they are implemented and end up in a preview. Finally, the EF team has a user voice site (*http://ef.mswish.net*) where you can add and vote on feature requests.

About the Authors

Julia Lerman is the leading independent authority on the Entity Framework and has been using and teaching the technology since its 2006 inception. She is well known in the .NET community as a Microsoft MVP, ASPInsider, and INETA Speaker. Julia is a frequent presenter at technical conferences around the world and writes articles for many well-known technical publications, including the "Data Points" column in *MSDN Magazine*. Julia lives in Vermont with her husband, Rich, and gigantic dog, Sampson, where she runs the Vermont.NET User Group. You can read her blog at *www.thedatafarm.com/blog* and follow her on Twitter at @julielerman.

Rowan Miller works as a program manager for the ADO.NET Entity Framework team at Microsoft. He speaks at technical conferences and blogs at *http://romiller.com*. Rowan lives in Seattle, Washington, with his wife, Athalie. Prior to moving to the US, he resided in the small state of Tasmania in Australia. Outside of technologym Rowan's passions include snowboarding, mountain biking, horse riding, rock climbing, and pretty much anything else that involves being active. The primary focus of his life, however, is to follow Jesus.

Get even more for your money.

Join the O'Reilly Community, and register the O'Reilly books you own. It's free, and you'll get:

- $4.99 ebook upgrade offer
- 40% upgrade offer on O'Reilly print books
- Membership discounts on books and events
- Free lifetime updates to ebooks and videos
- Multiple ebook formats, DRM FREE
- Participation in the O'Reilly community
- Newsletters
- Account management
- 100% Satisfaction Guarantee

Signing up is easy:

1. **Go to: oreilly.com/go/register**
2. **Create an O'Reilly login.**
3. **Provide your address.**
4. **Register your books.**

Note: English-language books only

To order books online:
oreilly.com/store

For questions about products or an order:
orders@oreilly.com

To sign up to get topic-specific email announcements and/or news about upcoming books, conferences, special offers, and new technologies:
elists@oreilly.com

For technical questions about book content:
booktech@oreilly.com

To submit new book proposals to our editors:
proposals@oreilly.com

O'Reilly books are available in multiple DRM-free ebook formats. For more information:
oreilly.com/ebooks

Spreading the knowledge of innovators   oreilly.com

Have it your way.

O'Reilly eBooks

- Lifetime access to the book when you buy through oreilly.com
- Provided in up to four DRM-free file formats, for use on the devices of your choice: PDF, .epub, Kindle-compatible .mobi, and Android .apk
- Fully searchable, with copy-and-paste and print functionality
- Alerts when files are updated with corrections and additions

oreilly.com/ebooks/

Safari Books Online

- Access the contents and quickly search over 7000 books on technology, business, and certification guides
- Learn from expert video tutorials, and explore thousands of hours of video on technology and design topics
- Download whole books or chapters in PDF format, at no extra cost, to print or read on the go
- Get early access to books as they're being written
- Interact directly with authors of upcoming books
- Save up to 35% on O'Reilly print books

See the complete Safari Library at safari.oreilly.com

O'REILLY®

CPSIA information can be obtained at www.ICGtesting.com
Printed in the USA
BVOW031002290212

284100BV00001B/1/P